The Campus History Series

THE LINSLY SCHOOL

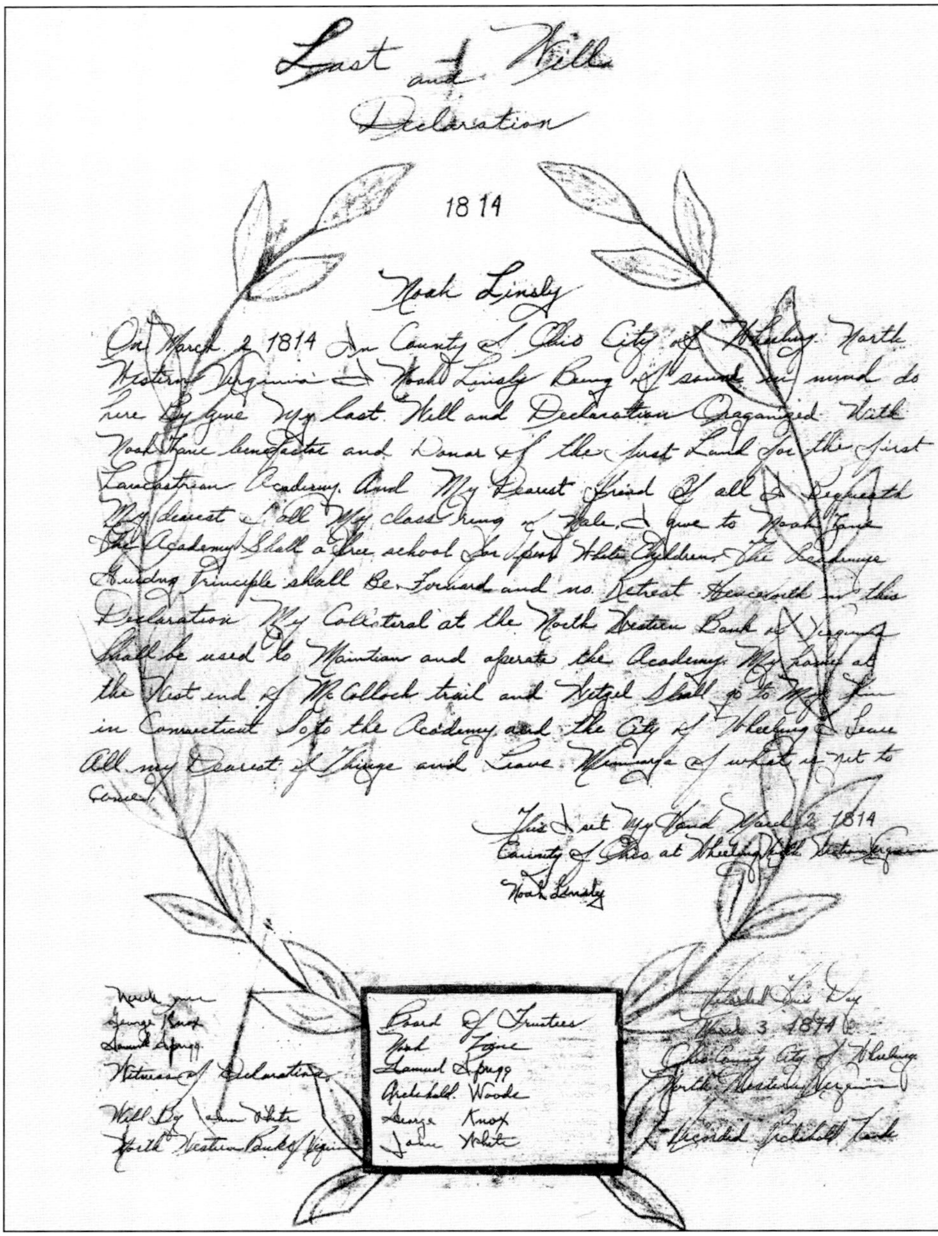
Last and Will Declaration

1814

Noah Linsly

On March 2 1814 In County of Ohio City of Wheeling North Western Virginia I Noah Linsly Being of sound in mind do here By give My last Will and Declaration Oraganized With Noah Zane benefactor and Donar of the first Land for the first Lancastrian Academy. And My Dearest friend of all I Bequeath My dearest of all My class ring of Yale. I give to Noah Zane The Academy Shall a free school for poor White Children. The Academys Guiding Principle shall Be Forward and no Retreat. Henceforth in this Declaration My Collateral at the North Western Bank of Virginia Shall be used to Maintian and operate the Academy. My house at the West end of McColloch trail and Wetzel Shall go to My Kin in Connecticut So to the Academy and the City of Wheeling I Leave All my Dearest of Things and Leave Memorys of what is not yet to Come

This I set My Hand March 2 1814
County of Ohio at Wheeling North Western Virginia
Noah Linsly

Noah Zane
George Knox
Samuel Sprigg
Witness of Declaration
Will By John White
North Western Bank of Virginia

Board of Trustees
Noah Zane
Samuel Sprigg
Archibald Woods
George Knox
John White

Recorded This Day
March 3 1814
Ohio County City of Wheeling
North Western Virginia
Recorded Archibald Tank

Noah Linsly's Will, Dated March 2, 1814. Last Will and Declaration 1814 Noah Linsly. On March 2, 1814 In County of Ohio City of Wheeling North Western Virginia I Noah Linsly Being of sound in mind do here By give My last Will and Declaration Oraganized (sic) with Noah Zane benefactor and Donar(sic) of the first Land for the first Lancastrian Academy. And My Dearest friend of all I Bequeath My dearest of all My class ring of Yale. I give to Noah Zane the Academy Shall a free school for poor White Children. The Academys Guiding Principle shall be, Forward and no Retreat. Henceforth in this Declaration My Collateral at the North Western Bank of Virginia Shall be used to Maintian (sic) and operate the Academy. My house at the West end of McColloch trail and Wetzel Shall go to My Kin in Connecticut So to the Academy and the City of Wheeling I Leave all my Dearest of Things and leave memorys (sic) of what is not yet to Come. This I set My Hand March 2, 1814 County of Ohio at Wheeling, North Western Virginia.

The Campus History Series

The Linsly School

Robert W. Schramm

ARCADIA
PUBLISHING

ISBN 978-0-7385-1531-1

Published by Arcadia Publishing
Charleston, South Carolina

Printed in the United States of America

Library of Congress Catalog Card Number: 2003103940

For all general information contact Arcadia Publishing at:
Telephone 843-853-2070
Fax 843-853-0044
E-mail sales@arcadiapublishing.com
For customer service and orders:
Toll-Free 1-888-313-2665

Visit us on the Internet at www.arcadiapublishing.com

To the memory of Henry C. Brown and H. Douglas Haigwood, with admiration and respect.

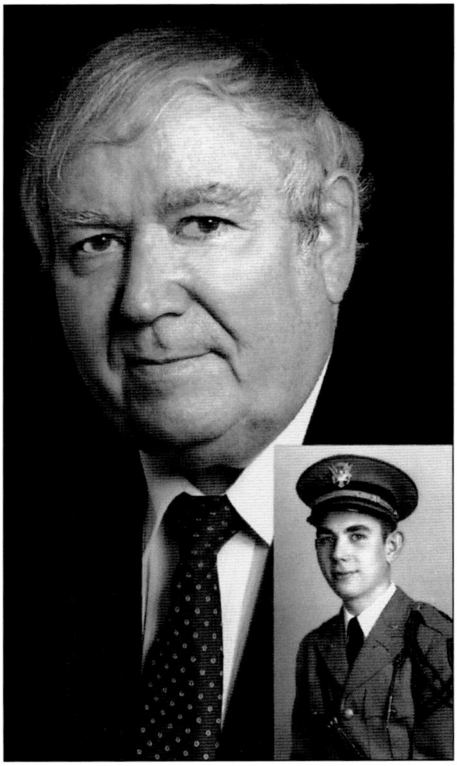

Author's Notes

In writing this history of my old school I am reminded of the fact that history is not necessarily what happened but what was recorded; thus, one can only hope that the records are accurate. For anything that happened after about 1840, we may be fortunate to have photographs. But for anything that happened before then we must rely on verbal descriptions, documents, and artists' renderings. In preparing this history I have made every attempt to be as accurate as possible and, at the same time, present the history of the school in such a way that the reader will get a feeling for what life was like for the students of each time period. The fact that Linsly has managed to survive almost two centuries is a tribute to the many individuals in the past who have provided inspired guidance and leadership when it was needed. I will be describing these people in the following pages—how they influenced the school's development and held true to Noah Linsly's directive of "Forward and no retreat!"

Robert W. Schramm
Professor Emeritus, West Liberty State College
Linsly, Class of 1952

CONTENTS

Acknowledgments

Once again I thank my beloved wife Jeanne for her assistance with editing, her opinions on what should and should not be included in this manuscript, and her support in general.

I also wish to thank Dr. Alan Fawcett for his enthusiastic encouragement and aid in preparing this book, without which it would not have come to fruition. John Hershey has also been a continual source of help in preparing this manuscript. I am grateful to Jim Hawkins for providing historical information as well as some of the photographs. His memory of the history of Linsly is awesome.

Additional thanks to the following Linsly personnel: Reno F. DiOrio, James D. Buchwach, William L. Brubaker, David Coutts, Terry Depew, Jimmie McCamic, and to Michael Chokel for his expert photography.

Invaluable help was provided by the following persons and organizations: Professor John Cuthbert, West Virginia Regional History Collection, West Virginia University; Travis Zeik, curator, Oglebay Institute Mansion Museum; Robin Rhodes, Kirk's Photo-Art Store; David B. McKinley, McKinley and Associates, Inc.; Sister Joanne Gonter, historian and archivist, Mount de Chantal Visitation Academy; Jeanne Cobb, archivist, Phillips Library, Bethany College; Margaret Brennan, historian, Wheeling; Mrs. T. Stewart Hopkins, Michael Rempe, William Victorson, Susan Lockhart Stobbs, and the staff at the Ohio County Public Library.

Introduction

The year was 1769. A young, 22-year-old frontiersman named Ebenezer Zane came to a place on the banks of the Ohio River, liked what he saw, proceeded to build a small cabin, and cleared an area of about 10 acres of fertile bottom land. The following year he brought his wife, Elizabeth McColloch Zane, his children, and some friends to settle there, and the settlement became the frontier town of Wheeling, Virginia. The original cleared area is today that portion of Wheeling from about Eleventh Street to Tenth Street.

A frontier fort was later constructed near Zane's cabin on the river bank. Fort Henry, as it came to be called, was where the Zane family and other settlers helped fight the last battle of the American Revolutionary War in 1782. It was during this battle that Zane's younger sister Betty saved the fort by running through a hailstorm of bullets to carry gunpowder from the blockhouse to the fort when the supply was running critically low.

In 1778, a son was born to the Zanes who would be named Noah. He was their first son to survive infancy. Twenty-one years later, in 1799, another "Noah," Noah Linsly, came to Wheeling from Morgantown, Virginia, in order to establish a law practice. The two Noahs were fated to become close friends, and their friendship would result in the establishment of an institution that has survived almost two centuries.

Noah Linsly was born in Branford, Connecticut, on February 9, 1772. He was the third son of Josiah Linsly and Rachel Fowler. He attended Dr. Todd's School in East Gifford, Connecticut and was admitted to Yale College in 1789. He graduated with a B.A. degree in 1791. After graduation he became an instructor at Williams Academy (now Williams College) and later at Yale. In 1795, he received an M.A. degree from both Yale and Williams Academy. Linsly moved to Morgantown in 1797 to practice law but his practice did not flourish, hence his move to Wheeling two years later.

In 1804, Linsly was appointed Commonwealth Attorney. He then became a member of the town council and, from March 1810 to March 1814, he served as the fourth mayor of Wheeling, which, at the time, consisted of about 300 houses and a population of around 1,200. Linsly lived on Main Street about 15 houses north of Tenth Street. His friend Noah Zane lived in a house built by his father on the corner of Eleventh and Main.

Noah Linsly, who never married, has been described by his peers as a tall man, six feet in height, with a florid complexion and auburn hair, which he wore in a queue. He was known to be extremely particular in his dress and very dignified in his manner. No valid likeness of him is known to exist.

Unfortunately, he was in ill health, and on March 25, 1814, he died from a lung hemorrhage at the young age of 42. Possibly he was suffering from tuberculosis but, in the winter of 1813–1814, a mysterious illness known as the "cold plague" swept eastward from Ohio. Its symptoms were sudden chills and great pulmonary congestion. In Wheeling Linsly's popularity was so great that all business in the city was suspended during his funeral.

Noah Linsly must have known his days were numbered. His will is dated March 2, 1814, less than a month before his death, and in it he mentions certain arrangements that he must have discussed with his good friend and the executor of his estate, Noah Zane. It is with this last will and declaration that the story of The Linsly School begins. In it, Linsly directs Noah Zane to use the bulk of his estate to create a "Lancastrian Academy." Curiously, he also directs that the "guiding principle of the school shall be forward and no retreat." As it turned out, this statement was prophetic indeed for it has been ever present throughout the 189 years of the school's existence. Today this idea is reflected in the school's current theme, "Never, never, never quit!" and the "no quit" policy. Finally, Noah Linsly left to the Academy and to the City of Wheeling "memorys (sic) of what is not yet to come."

What follows is an attempt to record those "memories" to which Noah Linsly was referring. These memories are not just of The Linsly School but also those of the city of Wheeling, its citizens, and its institutions. In order to tell the story of The Linsly School it is necessary to include some of the history of Wheeling and its people as well.

A Note on the Name of the School

Like many institutions, Linsly has gone through a number of name changes. In Linsly's case these name changes are confusing because some of them were formal and some informal. In addition, some writers in the 1800s chose to change the spelling of "Linsly" to "Linsley" or "Lindsley" depending on the writer.

The school has had three different official names. The first, the *Lancastrian Academy*, was in Noah Linsly's will and in the original charter in 1814. The second, *Linsly Institute*, was in the second charter dated 1942. The third, *The Linsly School*, is a result of an action by the Board of Directors in October of 1983.

Through the years there have been a variety of unofficial names. By about 1822, the *Lancastrian Academy* was referred to as "Linsly Academy" and then a few years later as "Linsly Institute." The title "Linsly Military Institute" was in common usage starting in 1941 (although it may have been used prior to this time) and lasting until the military program was discontinued in 1979. At that time the School reverted to the title, "Linsly Institute." Four years later the name which is used today, *The Linsly School*, was adopted.

One

The Lancastrian Academy

Although Noah Linsly provided the funds and the idea of an Academy in Wheeling, it was his close friend Noah Zane who brought the Academy into existence. One of his first acts was to obtain a charter from the Virginia legislature. This charter, dated November 29, 1814, placed the management of the school in the hands of a board of trustees. At the board's first meeting, in May, 1815, Noah Zane was elected president. Zane donated two lots on the corner of Monroe and Fourth Streets (now Thirteenth and Chapline Streets) in Wheeling where the board had the first building constructed. It was completed in 1820.

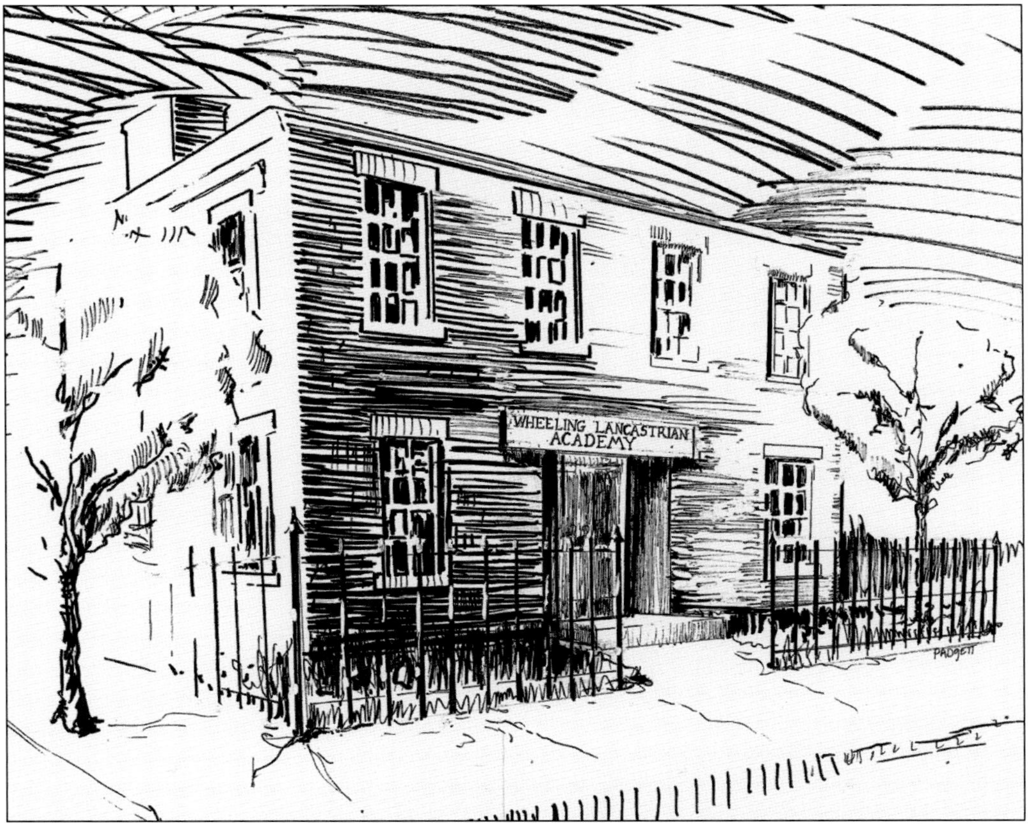

The Lancastrian Academy Building, Artist's Rendering by Paul Padgett. Linsly's first building was a two-story brick building. One large room on the ground floor served as the first classroom.

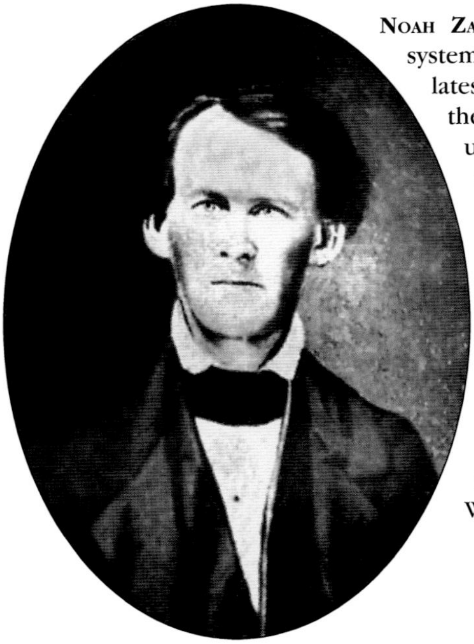

Noah Zane, Daguerreotype of a Painting. The Lancastrian system of education had its origin in England and was the latest concept in teaching. It was based on two ideas: the utilization of play in the learning process and the use of older students as tutors, or "monitors," for the younger students. This is similar to the methods used in modern Montessori schools and not unlike the prefect system, which is in use at Linsly today. The school was coeducational and the schoolyard was divided into girls' and boys' playgrounds by means of a fence. Samuel Sprigg, one of the original trustees, had three daughters who attended the Lancastrian Academy. By 1821, a more classic approach to education was also adopted and the Lancastrian system began fading in popularity. At this time, George Washington's nephew, Lawrence Washington, was a member of the board.

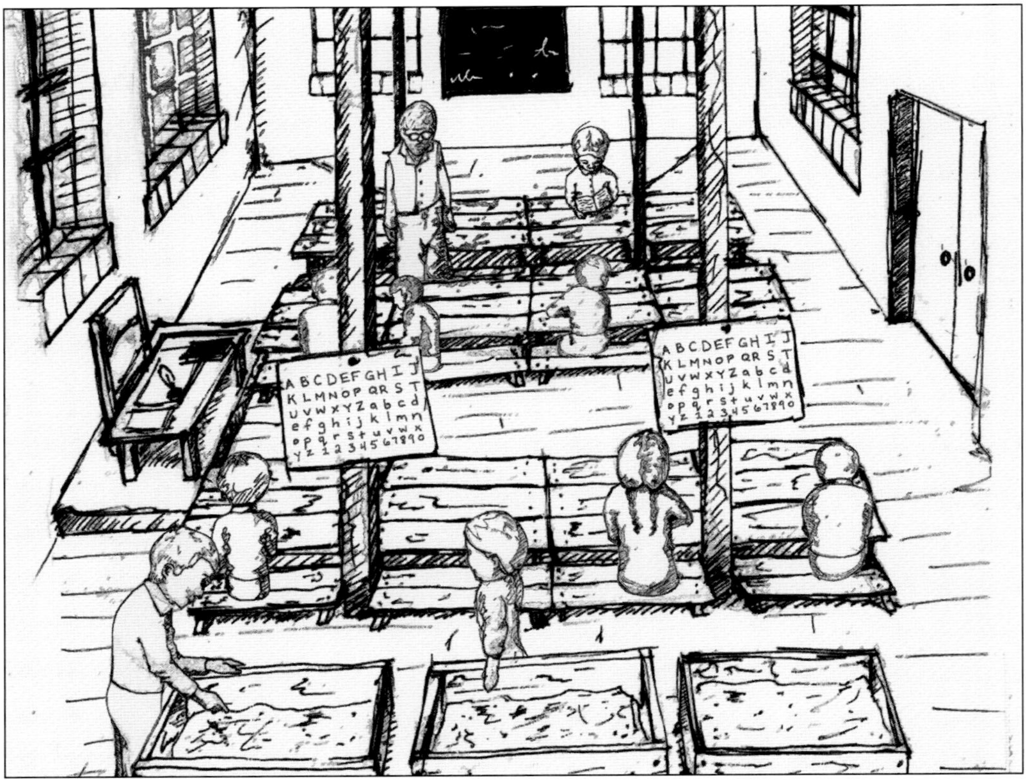

Lancastrian Academy Classroom, 1820, Artist's Rendering by Nicholas Rohrbaugh. The room was large, light, and airy. The master teacher sat on a platform on the western side. In front of this platform was an aisle extending to the front entrance. At the end of the room were sand boxes. Boards supported on posts were painted with the alphabet and numerals, which the "beginners" copied by making characters in the sand with their fingers.

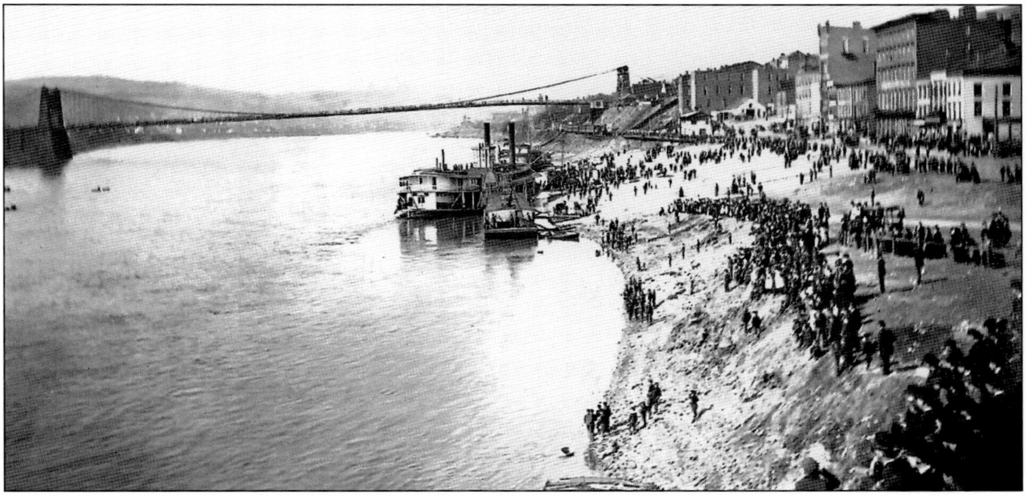

WHEELING'S WATERFRONT, *c.* 1860. A great deal of excitement was generated when General Lafayette visited Wheeling on May 24, 1825. He arrived at 11:30 a.m. on the steamboat *Herald* and was greeted at the landing by crowds of citizens, the "Independent Blues" under the command of Capt. William McConnell, and the arrangements committee, which included Academy trustees Woods, Sprigg, and Chapline. After addressing the crowd, General Lafayette and Noah Zane climbed into a barouche and rode up Main Street to Mr. Simm's Hotel, accompanied by the crowd and escorted by the "Independent Blues." In June of 1825, General Lafayette wrote to Noah Zane, "I shall never forget to be escorted up your Main Street with you Noah under military escort from the Lancastrian Academy." Evidently the General thought that the "Independent Blues" were made up of Academy students, but the Academy had no military program at that time. The letter was signed, "General Marquis de Lafayette,Yorktown, Virginia."

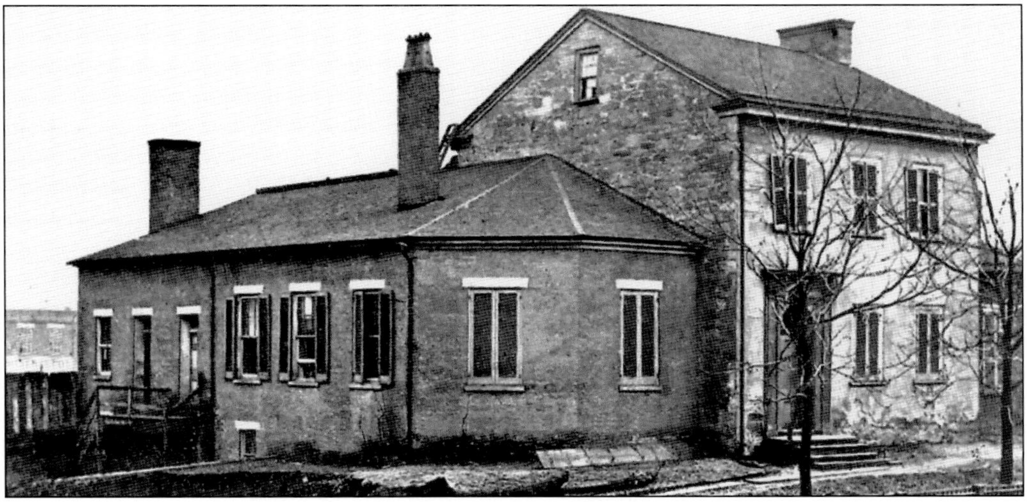

NOAH ZANE'S HOME AT ELEVENTH AND MAIN STREET. In April 1828, Linsly's first instructor, John F. Truax, was succeeded by Daniel Deady, who, after a term of a year or two, gave way to Alexander Magee. Perhaps this was because, in addition to his teaching, Deady was required to keep the school building in repair, clean the rooms, and whitewash the walls. He was a combined teacher, janitor, and maintenance man. The completion of the Cumberland Road (National Road) from Cumberland, Maryland, to Wheeling, Virginia in 1818 had attracted immigrants and speculators in land and mineral resources. A stagecoach line was established in 1830 and the population of Wheeling had increased to 5,221. Enrollment at the Academy had likewise risen.

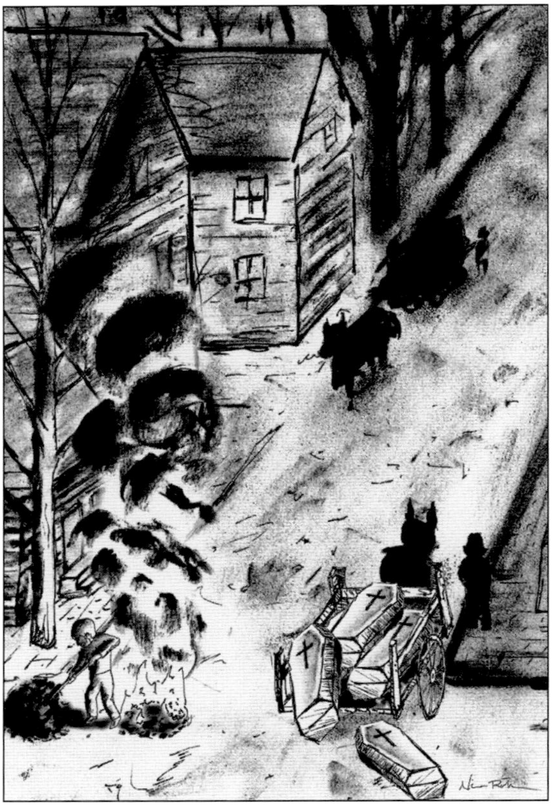

The Streets of Wheeling, Summer 1833, Artist's Rendering by Nicholas Rohrbaugh. In the summer of 1833, a deadly Asiatic cholera epidemic struck the city of Wheeling. It was thought to have been brought up the Ohio River by steamboat. Stores were closed, trade and business were suspended, and those who could left the city. The city health officer ordered that the streets be cleaned, the litter treated with lime and sulphate of iron, and the cellars of the houses be limed. The sale of fruits and vegetables was prohibited. Coal fires were burned on every street corner in hopes that the sulfur would kill the cholera germs. The mortality in Wheeling was "50–60%." Coffins were stacked up awaiting burial at Greenwood Cemetery and the local physicians worked "until exhausted." Sadly, one of the victims was Noah Zane. Although no records exist, the epidemic must have claimed the lives of some Academy students as well. The epidemic ended by 1834 but the city suffered a business depression three years later.

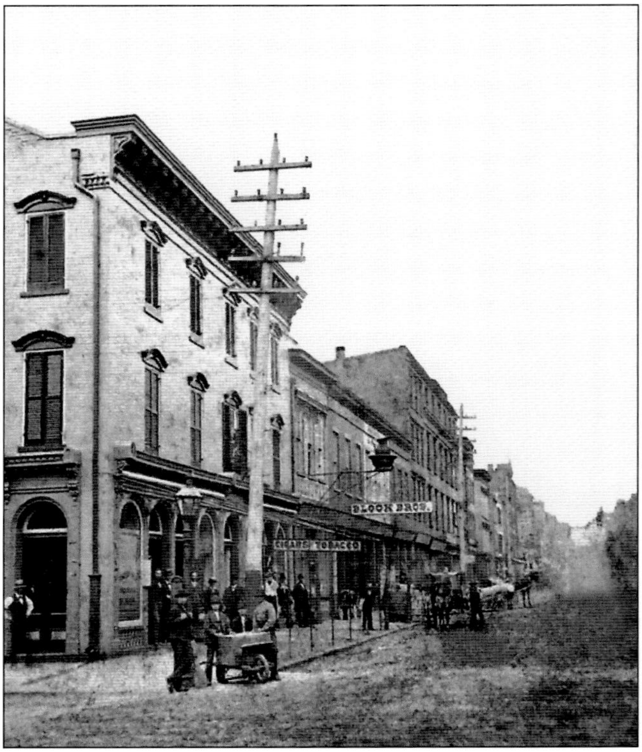

Main and Fourteenth Streets, 1849. The poles are for telegraph wires. The first line was completed in 1847. Block Brothers began selling the famous Wheeling "stogie" in 1840. In 1833, free area public schools were established. These competed with the Academy for pupils, and the board of trustees resisted proposals on three separate occasions to integrate the Academy into the new public school system. Possibly because a number of members had passed away or resigned, the board did little (including not keeping any records) from about 1835 until they were reorganized in 1845 with John McLure as president. The first principal under the new board was James McBurnie under whose leadership the Academy prospered and grew.

Wheeling Female Academy, c. 1852. After repeated requests by Bishop Richard V. Whelan, to whose diocese the city of Wheeling belonged, a group of sisters from the Visitation Order in Baltimore came to Wheeling in 1848 to establish an academy and parochial school for girls. This academy, which was located next to Saint James's Church at Fifth and Quincy Streets (now Eoff and Fourteenth Streets), was incorporated in 1852 as the Wheeling Female Academy. By 1865, it was in need of newer and larger quarters. The sisters left the Eoff Street location and moved to the present facility on Washington Avenue known today as Mount de Chantal.

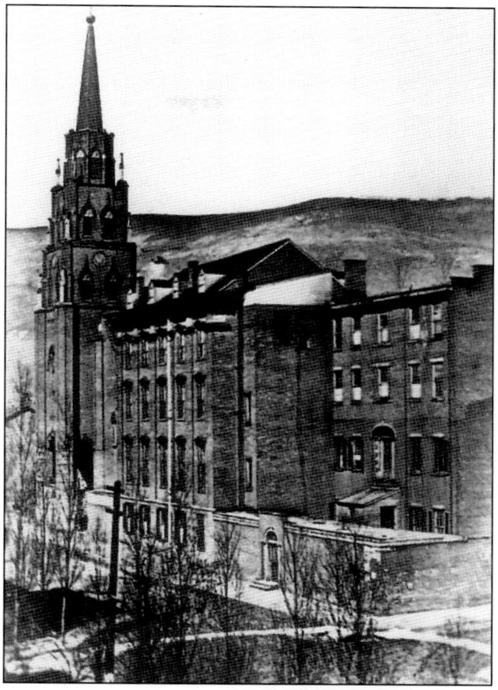

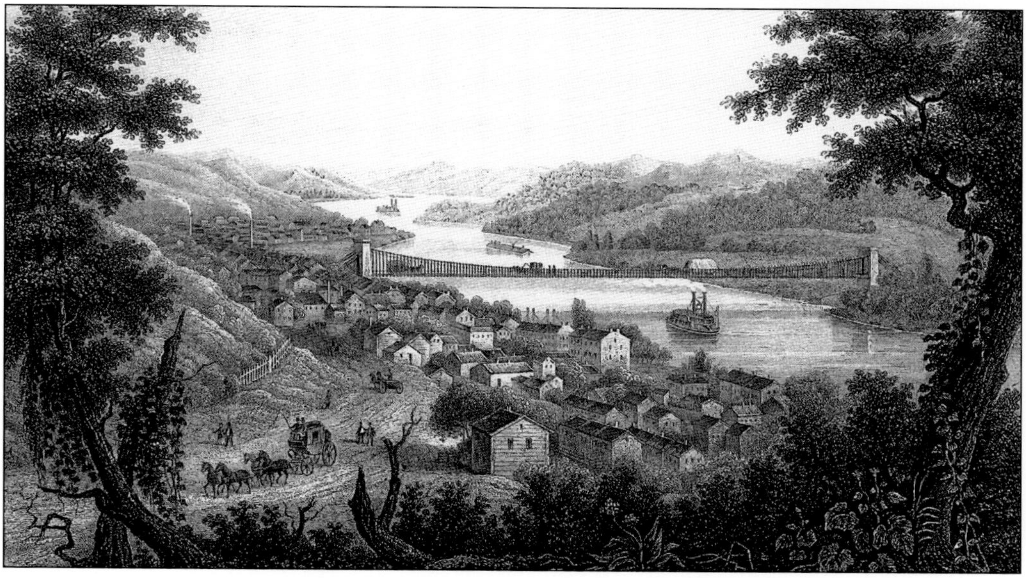

View from Wheeling Hill, 1850. As enrollment at the Female Academy grew, the number of girls attending Linsly declined. The free public schools also contributed to the declining enrollment. This was likely one of several factors that caused the board to decide, about the time of the beginning of the Civil War (1861), that Linsly would become an all-boys school. John W. Scott, later president of Washington and Jefferson College and then vice-president of West Virginia University, headed Linsly's instructional program from 1847 until 1852. During that period the Academy's enrollment increased. Probably this was partly due to the fact that the population of Wheeling, by 1850, had swelled to 13,000. Likely, the completion of the Suspension Bridge in 1849 was a contributing factor because it brought more people to the Wheeling area via the National Road. By this time Wheeling was known as the "gateway to west."

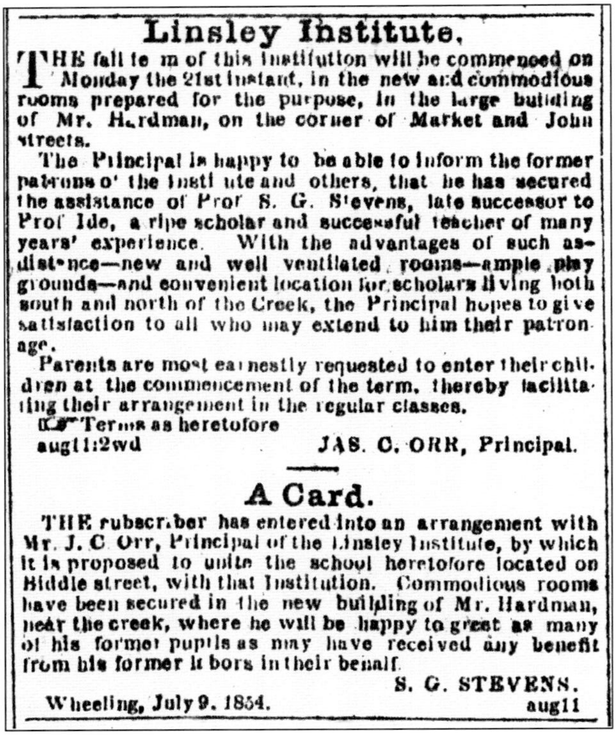

Linsley Institute.

THE fall term of this institution will be commenced on Monday the 21st instant, in the new and commodious rooms prepared for the purpose, in the large building of Mr. Hardman, on the corner of Market and John streets.

The Principal is happy to be able to inform the former patrons of the institute and others, that he has secured the assistance of Prof S. G. Stevens, late successor to Prof Ide, a ripe scholar and successful teacher of many years' experience. With the advantages of such assistence—new and well ventilated rooms—ample play grounds—and convenient location for scholars living both south and north of the Creek, the Principal hopes to give satisfaction to all who may extend to him their patronage.

Parents are most earnestly requested to enter their children at the commencement of the term, thereby facilitating their arrangement in the regular classes.

☞Terms as heretofore

aug11:2wd JAS. C. ORR, Principal.

A Card.

THE subscriber has entered into an arrangement with Mr. J. C. Orr, Principal of the Linsley Institute, by which it is proposed to unite the school heretofore located on Biddle street, with that Institution. Commodious rooms have been secured in the new building of Mr. Hardman, near the creek, where he will be happy to greet as many of his former pupils as may have received any benefit from his former labors in their behalf.

S. G. STEVENS.

Wheeling, July 9, 1854. aug11

ADVERTISEMENT IN THE *WHEELING INTELLIGENCER*, 1854. The old Academy building had deteriorated to the point where repairs were no longer feasible. In an article appearing in the *Wheeling Intelligencer* dated August 11, 1854, an announcement was made that "the buildings of the Linsley (sic) Institute on Fourth Street, will be torn down, and a new and improved one erected . . . . In the meantime, the institution will be conducted in rooms of Hardman's fine building, corner of Market and John [Sixteenth] Streets." Noah Linsly's body had been disinterred, probably from the Thirteenth Street location, and moved to Mount Wood Cemetery in 1851.

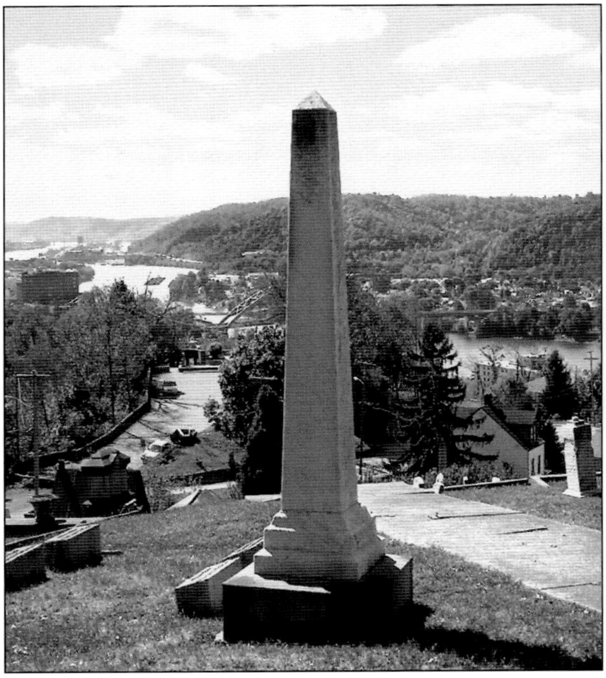

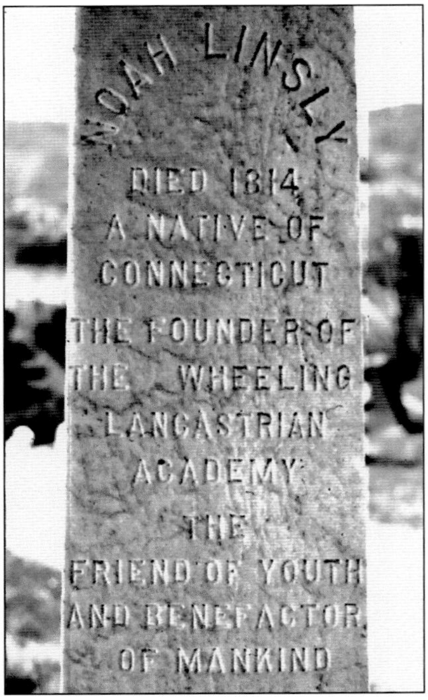

NOAH LINSLY'S GRAVE OVERLOOKING WHEELING, 2003. At a meeting of the board in December 1856, funds were appropriated to erect a monument on the grave of Noah Linsly. and provisions were made for the sale of lot number four on Fourth Street (Chapline) and the purchase of two lots on Fifth and Centre Streets (Eoff and Fifteenth Streets). The board also entered into a contract for the erection of a new school building.

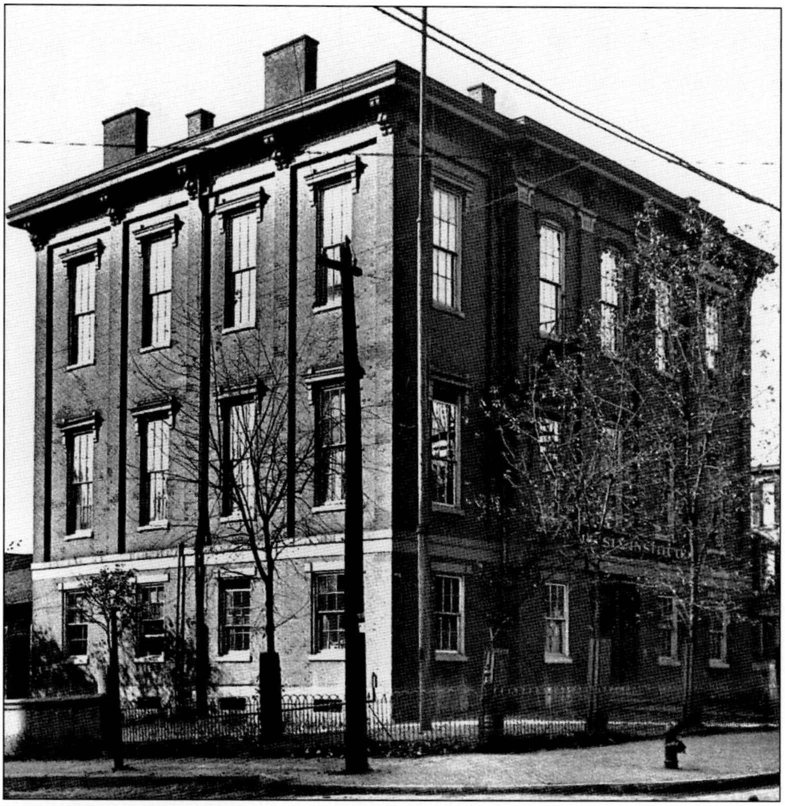

Linsly's Second Building, 1859. Construction began on Linsly's second building in 1858 at the corner of Fifth and Centre Streets (Eoff and Fifteenth Streets), and was completed in the same year. This three-story brick building was, at the time, considered to be one of the finest buildings in the city of Wheeling. The academy opened in this building on September 1, 1859.

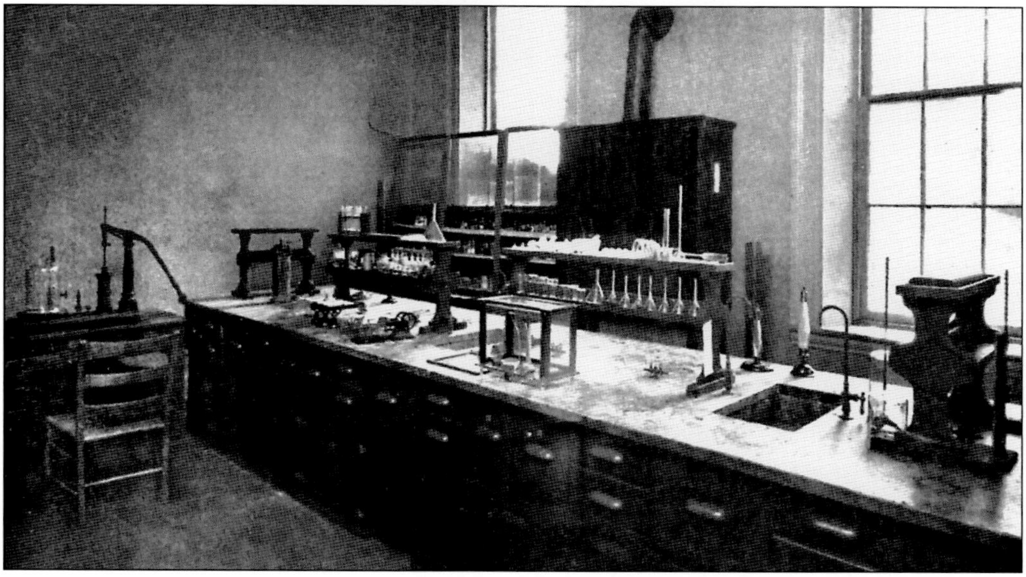

Science Laboratory, 1918. Linsly was able to use its new building for less than 10 years. In 1863, the new State of West Virginia was formed in Wheeling, and Linsly's board of trustees leased the building to the newly formed government of the State of West Virginia to be used as its first Capitol. Inauguration of the first state government took place on the lawn in front of the building. The assembly room on the third floor became the delegates' chamber while the junior room on the second floor became the senate chamber.

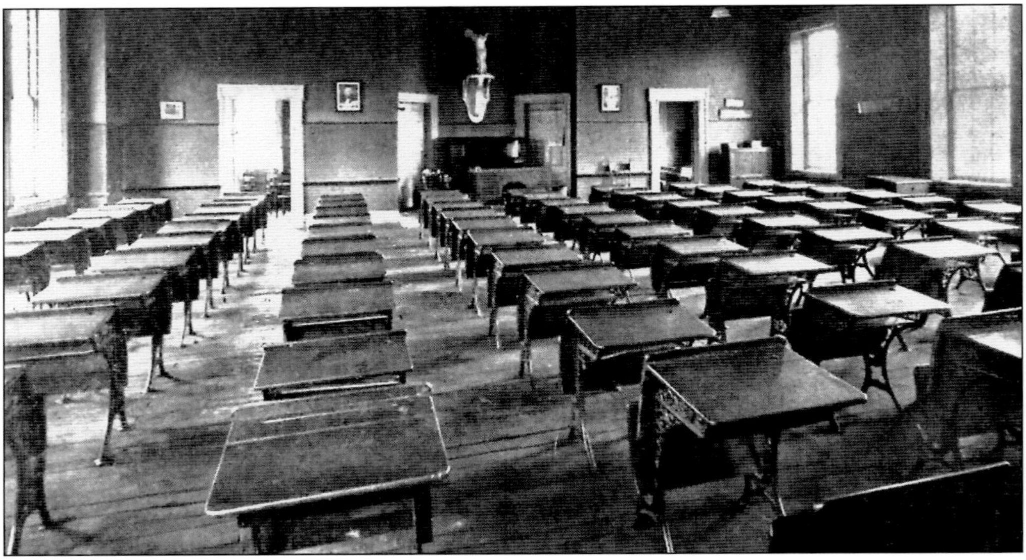

Assembly Hall, 1918. The state occupied the Linsly Institute building from 1863 until 1870. The Academy's classes were held in rented quarters nearby, first in the Odd Fellows Hall, which was at the corner of Twelfth and Chapline Streets, and then, later, in what was known as the Fruit Building. The state government moved to Charleston in 1870 and the Academy regained the use of its building. But during the Reconstruction period the school's fortunes did not improve, and the Panic of 1873 made economic conditions in Wheeling even worse.

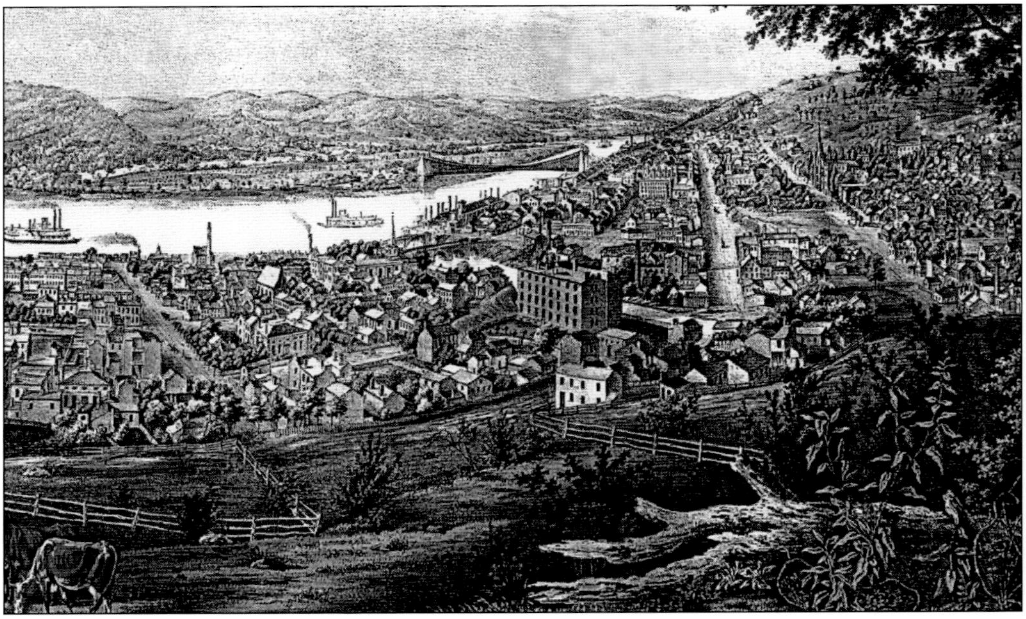

Drawing of Wheeling Showing the Fifteenth and Eoff Street Area, 1853. There is an empty lot in the location where Linsly's second building was to be constructed. The board of trustees seemed to take little interest in the school during the postwar era but, in 1873, they decided to begin making much-needed repairs to the school property and, in 1874, I.F. Jones, who was principal during and after the Civil War years, was replaced by John Michael Birch. Birch proved to be the catalyst for Linsly's rebirth. The changes he introduced altered the nature of the school and set in motion principles that molded the Academy into the institution we know today.

Two

The Military School and The Prep School

John M. Birch immediately began making changes by, first, actively integrating the school into the community. In 1877, he formed the Linsly Literary Society for "the improvement of its members, in declamations, discussions, original essays, orations and debates." The society met every Friday afternoon for readings, debates, recitations, and extemporaneous speaking to which the public was invited. The Literary Society also occasionally performed at community functions. Birch also encouraged students to begin publishing The Lindsley *(sic)* Bulletin, *the first school newspaper (Vol. 1, No. 1 November, 1877). It contained mostly descriptions of the Literary Society's activities but also news of the Female Academy (today, Mount de Chantal).*

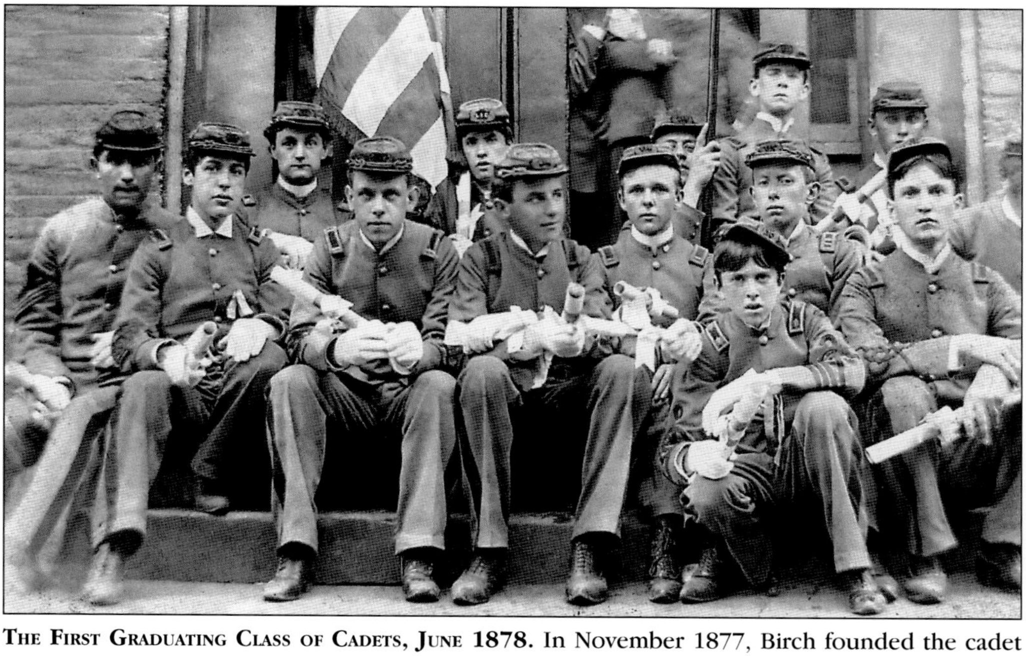

The First Graduating Class of Cadets, June 1878. In November 1877, Birch founded the cadet battalion. It had its first "turnout" on Washington's birthday (February 22) and participated in a sham battle on May 30th. Linsly was to be characterized as a military school for the next 102 years, until the military program was discontinued in 1979 to the disfavor of many of the school's alumni. Although participation was voluntary at first, it later became a requirement.

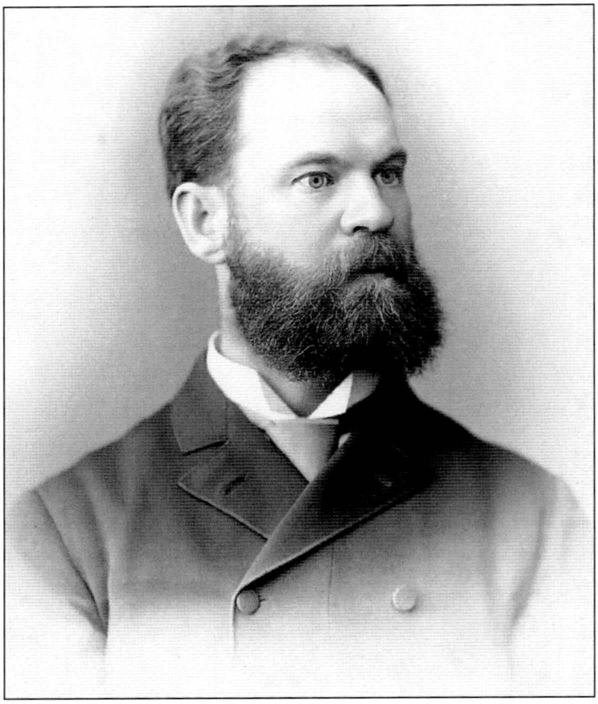

John Michael Birch, 1885. John Michael Birch was a native of Claysville, Pennsylvania. He was born on July 7, 1854 and graduated from Washington and Jefferson College in 1872. Birch served three terms as Linsly's headmaster—from 1874 to 1881, again from 1889 to1890, and from 1910 to 1911. He served as superintendent of the Wheeling Public Schools in 1881 and was United States Diplomat to Japan during President Cleveland's second term from 1881 to 1889.

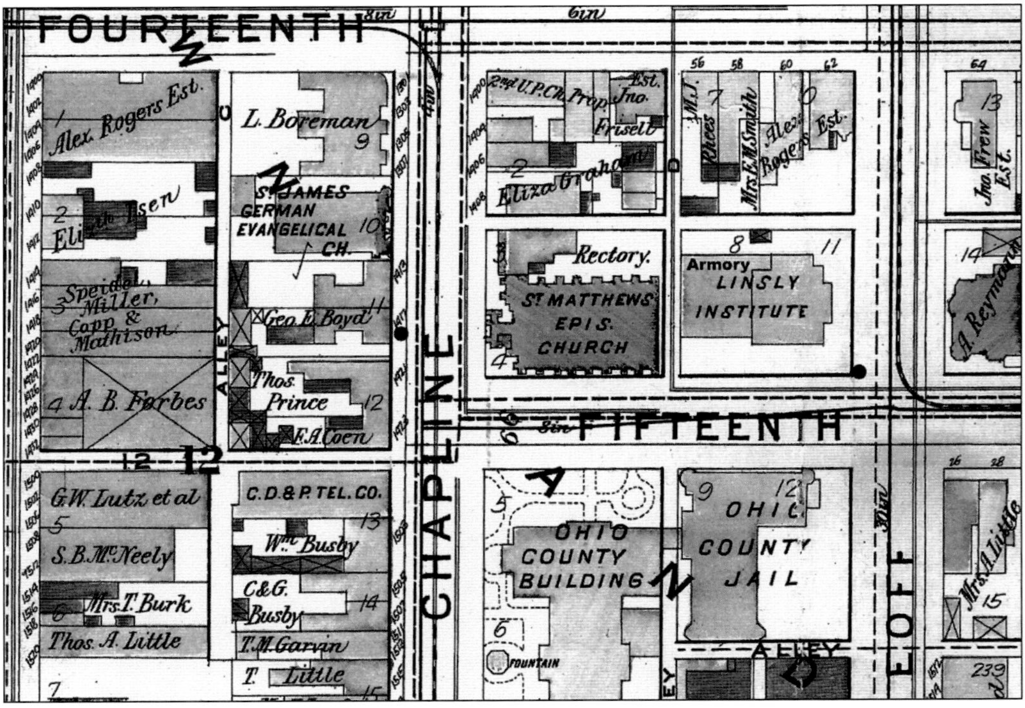

Map of Wheeling Showing the Armory, 1900. By 1889, the military program was officially recognized by the War Department, which established a one-story armory for indoor drill practice in inclement weather and to store Springfield Rifles for the Cadet Corps. The armory was located in the rear of the main building. It was 65 square feet and eventually contained a locker room and shower room.

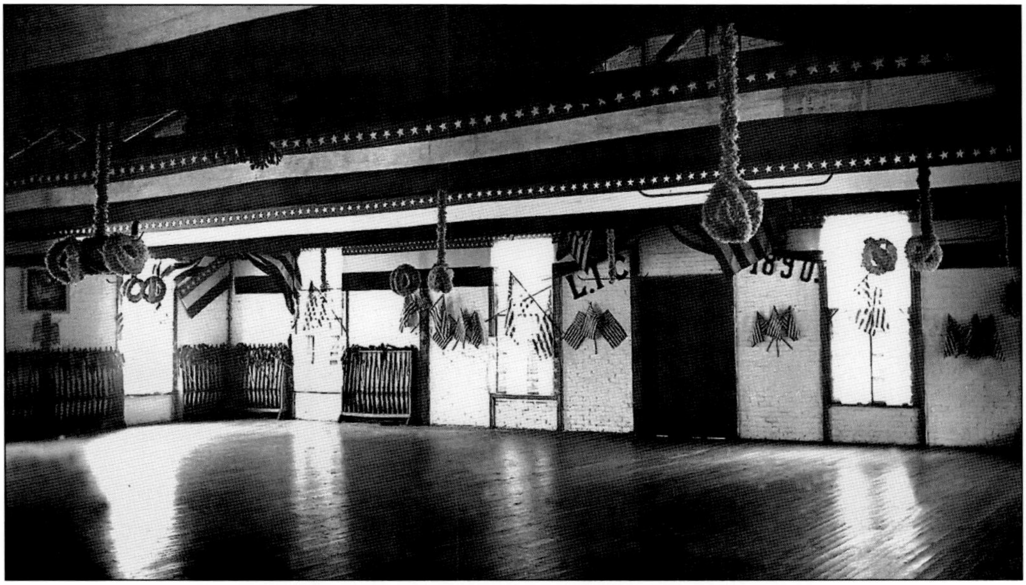

Interior of the Armory, 1890. Notice the racks of rifles on the left. A special act of Congress detailed Lt. William Braunensreuther to serve as Linsly's first Commandant of the Corps and military instructor. Military instruction included bayonet exercises, skirmish drill, inspection, dress parades, and reviews. The cadets marched in parades and participated in sham battles on Wheeling Island. The Academy received Springfield Rifles from the State of West Virginia and purchased bayonets, belts, and cartridge boxes for all the cadets.

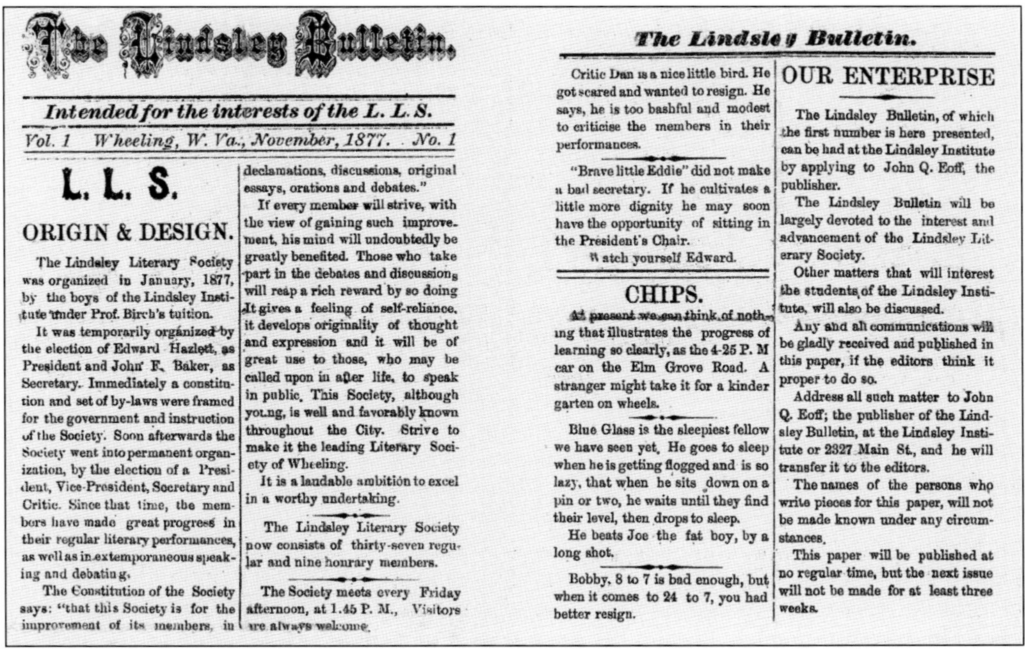

The Lindsley Bulletin.

Intended for the interests of the L. L. S.

Vol. 1 Wheeling, W. Va., November, 1877. No. 1

L. L. S.

ORIGIN & DESIGN.

The Lindsley Literary Society was organized in January, 1877, by the boys of the Lindsley Institute under Prof. Birch's tuition.

It was temporarily organized by the election of Edward Hazlett, as President and John F. Baker, as Secretary. Immediately a constitution and set of by-laws were framed for the government and instruction of the Society. Soon afterwards the Society went into permanent organization, by the election of a President, Vice-President, Secretary and Critic. Since that time, the members have made great progress in their regular literary performances, as well as in extemporaneous speaking and debating.

The Constitution of the Society says: "that this Society is for the improvement of its members, in declamations, discussions, original essays, orations and debates."

If every member will strive, with the view of gaining such improvement, his mind will undoubtedly be greatly benefited. Those who take part in the debates and discussions will reap a rich reward by so doing It gives a feeling of self-reliance, it develops originality of thought and expression and it will be of great use to those, who may be called upon in after life, to speak in public. This Society, although young, is well and favorably known throughout the City. Strive to make it the leading Literary Society of Wheeling.

It is a laudable ambition to excel in a worthy undertaking.

The Lindsley Literary Society now consists of thirty-seven regular and nine honrary members.

The Society meets every Friday afternoon, at 1.45 P. M., Visitors are always welcome.

The Lindsley Bulletin.

Critic Dan is a nice little bird. He got scared and wanted to resign. He says, he is too bashful and modest to criticise the members in their performances.

"Brave little Eddie" did not make a bad secretary. If he cultivates a little more dignity he may soon have the opportunity of sitting in the President's Chair.

Watch yourself Edward.

CHIPS.

At present we can think of nothing that illustrates the progress of learning so clearly, as the 4-25 P. M car on the Elm Grove Road. A stranger might take it for a kinder garten on wheels.

Blue Glass is the sleepiest fellow we have seen yet, He goes to sleep when he is getting flogged and is so lazy, that when he sits down on a pin or two, he waits until they find their level, then drops to sleep.

He beats Joe the fat boy, by a long shot.

Bobby, 8 to 7 is bad enough, but when it comes to 24 to 7, you had better resign.

OUR ENTERPRISE

The Lindsley Bulletin, of which the first number is here presented, can be had at the Lindsley Institute by applying to John Q. Eoff, the publisher.

The Lindsley Bulletin will be largely devoted to the interest and advancement of the Lindsley Literary Society.

Other matters that will interest the students of the Lindsley Institute, will also be discussed.

Any and all communications will be gladly received and published in this paper, if the editors think it proper to do so.

Address all such matter to John Q. Eoff; the publisher of the Lindsley Bulletin, at the Lindsley Institute or 2327 Main St., and he will transfer it to the editors.

The names of the persons who write pieces for this paper, will not be made known under any circumstances.

This paper will be published at no regular time, but the next issue will not be made for at least three weeks.

First Issue of *The Lindsley* (sic) *Bulletin*, November, 1877. Birch transformed the instructional program from one that provided only the rudiments of basic education into a demanding college preparatory program to build the student's character, as well as his academic skills. Thus, students graduating from Linsly were accepted at leading colleges on the basis of their certificate of graduation and the reputation of the school, without the need of an entrance examination.

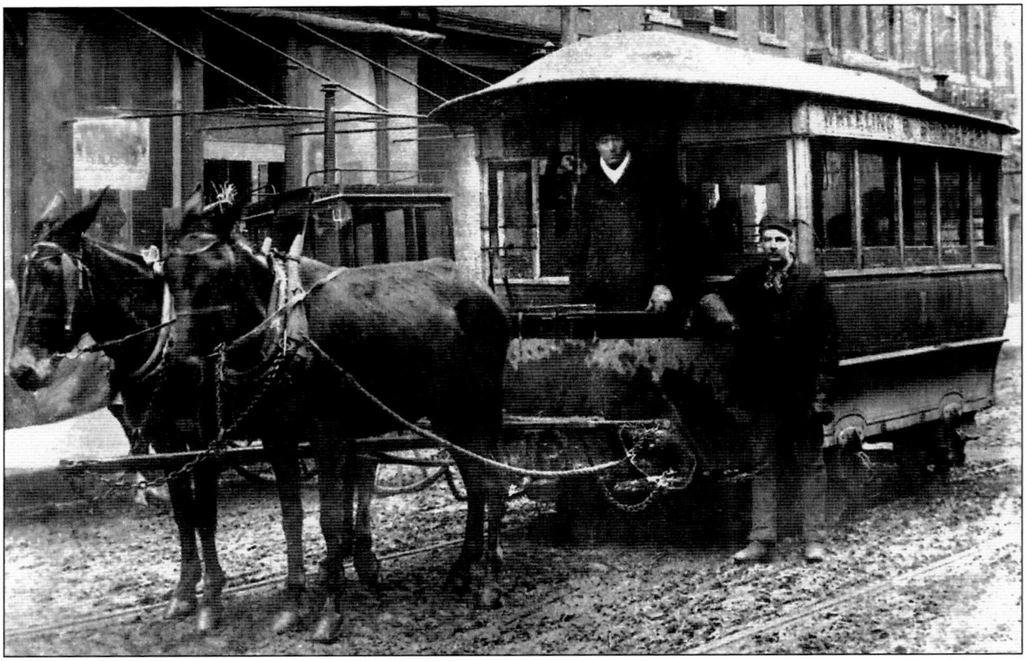

Horse Car on Main Street, 1887. This "horse car" is being pulled by mules. The first streetcars ran in Wheeling in 1876. No doubt the Linsly students rode on them. The first telephone was used in Wheeling in 1879, and A.J. Sweeney and Son introduced electric lighting in 1882. The first electric trolley car ran in 1888.

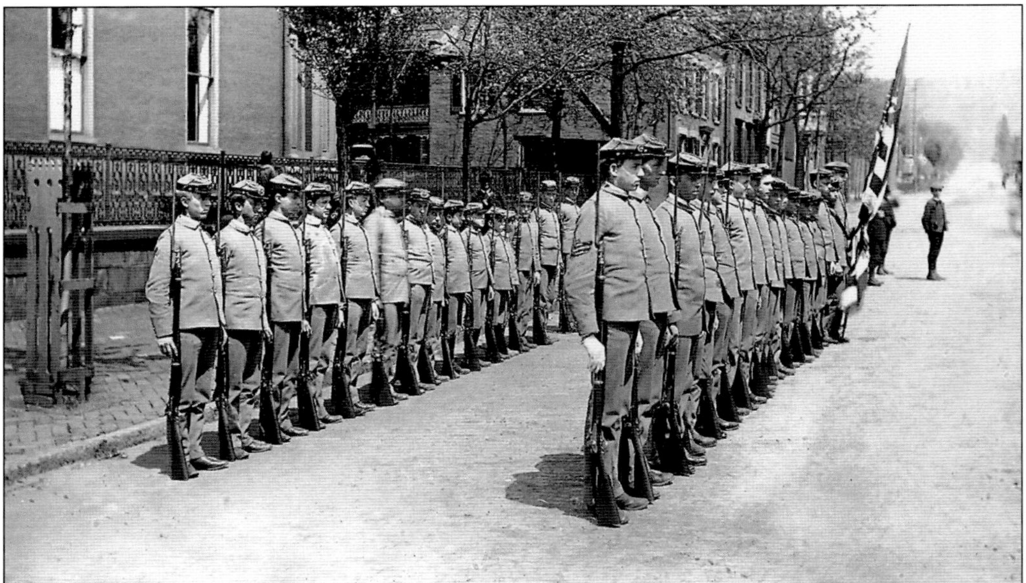

The Cadet Battalion, 1890. During the 1880s the enrollment at the Academy was about 114 students. Their course of study included spelling, reading, writing, arithmetic, algebra, geometry, trigonometry, calculus, English grammar, Latin (Caesar, Virgil, Cicero, Horace), Latin history, Latin composition, Greek (Homer's *Iliad*,) Greek grammar, Greek history, Greek composition, German, French, telegraphy, natural philosophy (physics), zoology, botany, surveying, astronomy, and logic. A chapter of the Bible was read at the daily drill formation.

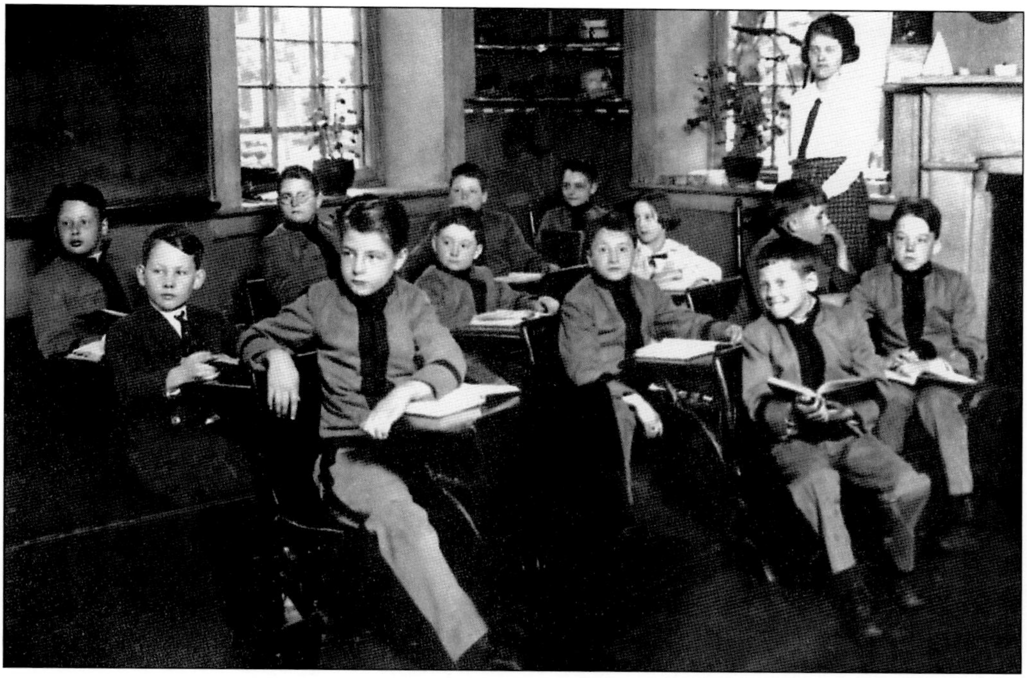

A Grade School Class, 1919. The girl was the daughter of the teacher and was permitted to attend Linsly. In 1892, gymnastic equipment was purchased to be placed in the Armory and in 1899, the board authorized the purchase of physics equipment for the science laboratory.

Cadet Ivan Fawcett, Fifth Grade, 1898. The rifle seems to be almost too big for this grade school student. Note the bayonet in his belt. The uniform is similar to Civil War style. The hat emblem "LIC" stands for "Linsly Institute Corps." The rifle is a former percussion cap and ball firearm that has been modified to accept a metallic cartridge by means of a loading door on the breech. This Springfield rifle was manufactured in 1885 and came to be known as the "trapdoor" Springfield. Note in the photograph of the cadet battalion on page 20 that the cadets have fixed bayonets.

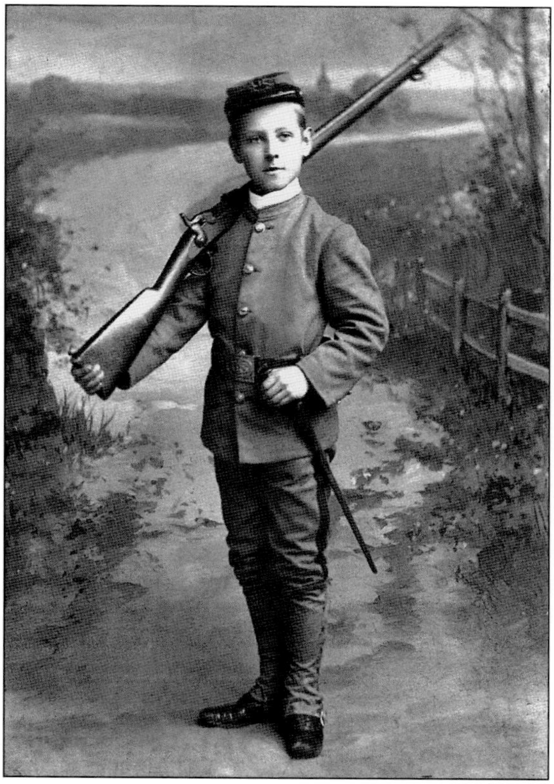

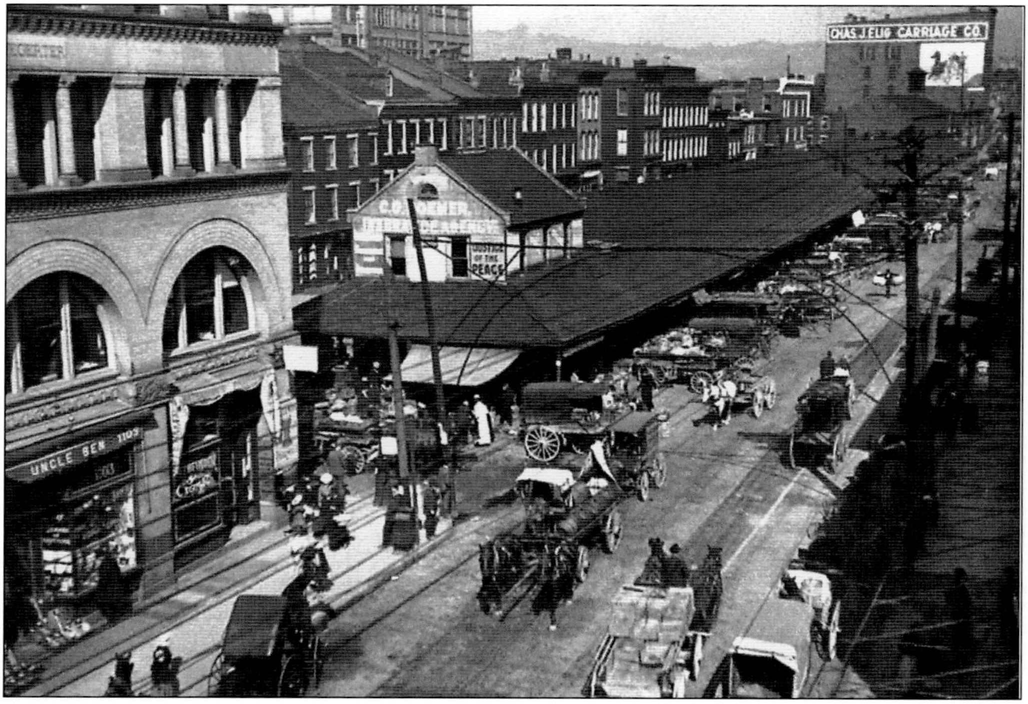

Wheeling Market House, 1901. After the turn of the century, Linsly's fortunes began to decline. Competition from the public schools, plus a lack of interest in military training after the Spanish-American War, led to a drop in enrollment. Only nine students graduated from the Academy in 1906 and the total enrollment in 1910 was less than 60 students.

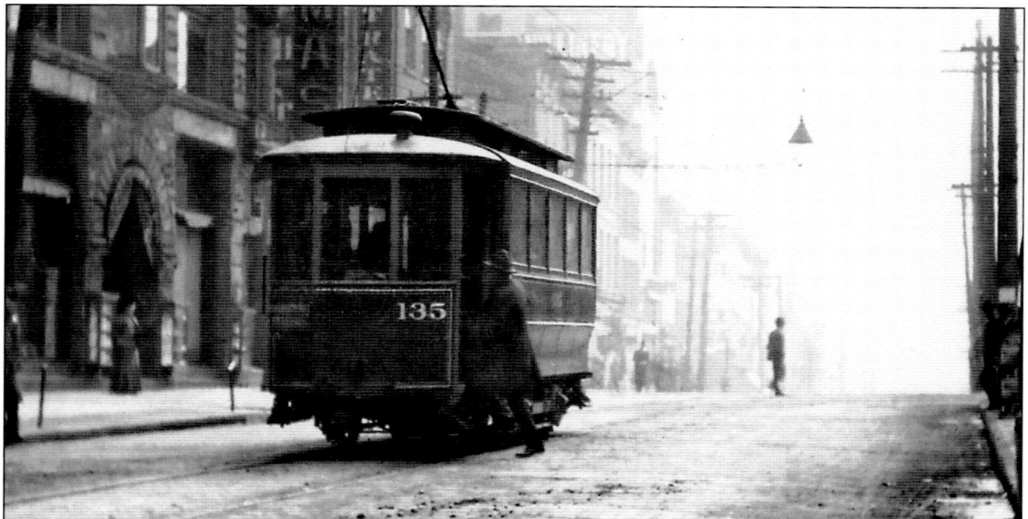

Wheeling Traction Company Car On Main Street Near Eleventh Street, c. 1900. In a March 1907 meeting of the board, a proposal was made to turn the property of the Academy over to the Wheeling Board of Education to be used for a high school called "Linsly High School." The vote was four to four. At the April 1907 meeting of the board, this idea was again proposed. This time the board must have been inspired by the motto, "Forward and no retreat," because there was only one affirmative vote, which was later changed so that the proposal lost unanimously.

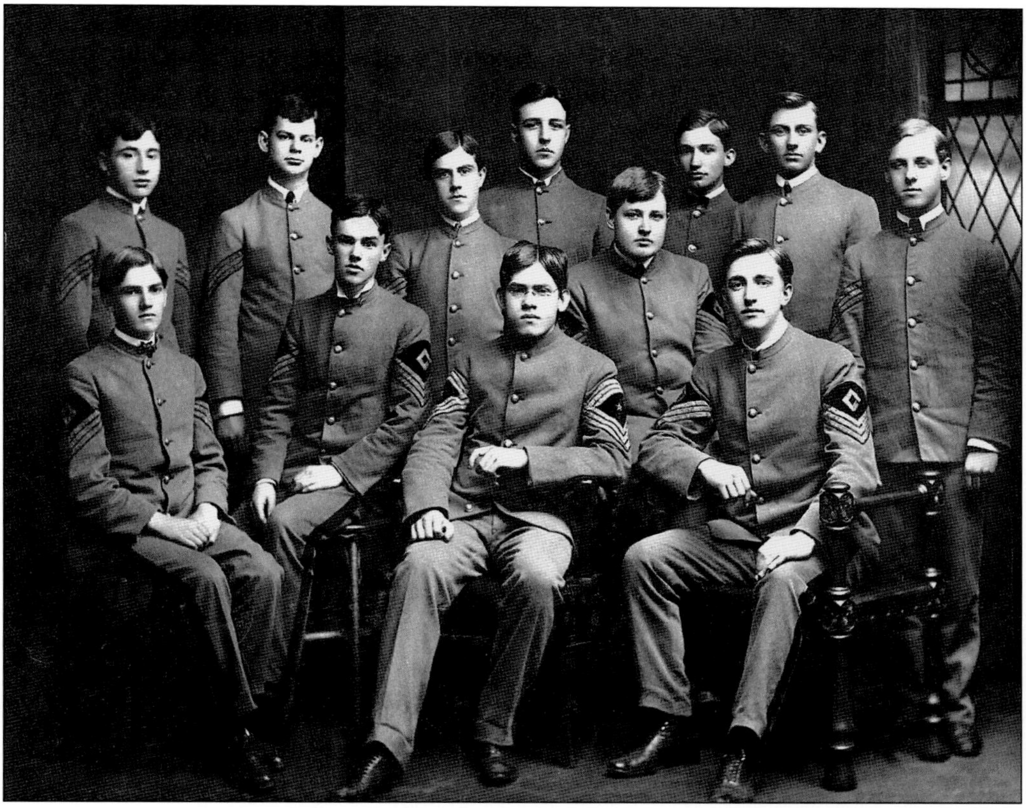

Linsly Class of 1906. The Institute building was falling into disrepair and the lingering business recession of 1907 just made matters worse. The trustees suspended the military program and that infuriated many of the alumni. An alumni association was formed in 1910 and, with the help of a *Wheeling Intelligencer* reporter, the association began publishing the *Linsly Magazine*. This publication included sketches of the school's history and encouraged the alumni to support their alma mater in meaningful ways.

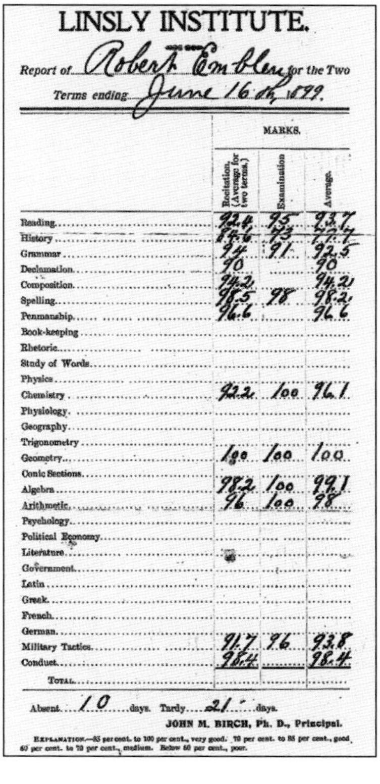

LINSLY INSTITUTE.

Report of Robert Emblem for the Two Terms ending June 16th, 1899.

	MARKS.		
	Recitation. (Average for two terms.)	Examination	Average.
Reading	92.4	95	93.7
History	84.6	73	77.7
Grammar	94	91	92.5
Declamation	90		90
Composition	94.2		94.2
Spelling	98.5	98	98.2
Penmanship	96.6		96.6
Book-keeping			
Rhetoric			
Study of Words			
Physics			
Chemistry	92.2	100	96.1
Physiology			
Geography			
Trigonometry			
Geometry	100	100	100
Conic Sections			
Algebra	98.2	100	99.1
Arithmetic	96	100	98
Psychology			
Political Economy			
Literature			
Government			
Latin			
Greek			
French			
German			
Military Tactics	91.7	96	93.8
Conduct	98.4		98.4
Total			

Absent 10 days. Tardy 21 days.

JOHN M. BIRCH, Ph. D., Principal.

Explanation.—85 per cent. to 100 per cent., very good. 70 per cent. to 85 per cent., good. 60 per cent. to 70 per cent., medium. Below 60 per cent., poor.

Grade Report for Robert Emblem, 1899. John Birch was brought back for a third term in 1910. Optimism ran high that he would put Linsly back on course. Though Birch was to serve only one year (he died in 1911), his leadership boosted everyone's morale and set the stage for the future growth of the school. But it was the prospect of war looming on the horizon that was largely responsible for Linsly's resurgence. The political situation in Europe made military programs legitimate again in the eyes of the public.

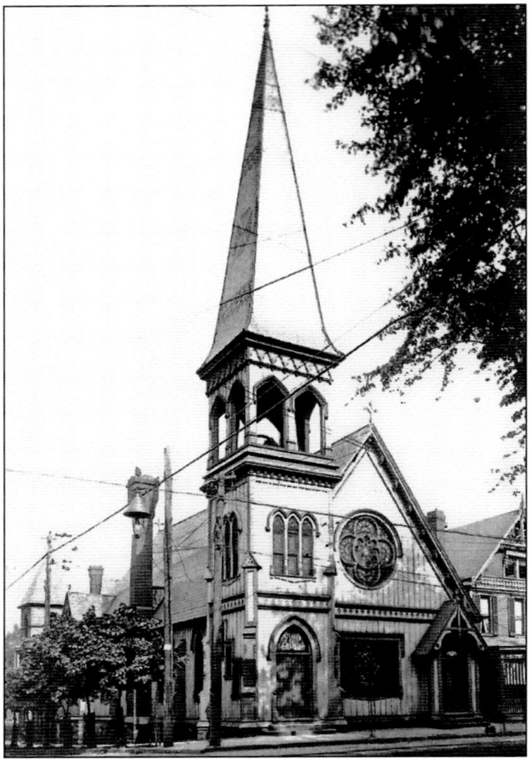

Saint Luke's Church on Wheeling Island, *c.* 1910. In 1914, the school observed its 100th anniversary. On Tuesday, November 29, the cadets assembled and marched across the Suspension Bridge to Saint Luke's Church on Wheeling Island . There they heard Rev. Jacob Brittingham deliver his message, "The righteous shall be held in everlasting remembrance." This address was a fitting reference to Noah Linsly's benevolence. The centennial celebration marked a considerable change in the attitude of the board, which led to an increase in morale on the part of the students, faculty, and administration.

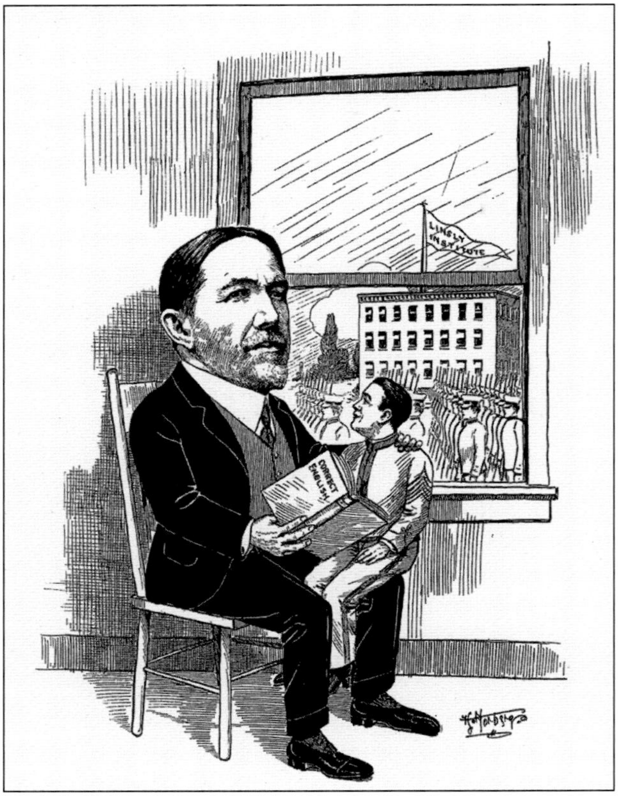

Charles H. Patterson, Headmaster, 1913–1916. The trustees upgraded the school furnishings and modernized the physics and chemistry laboratories. With enrollment now growing, they considered the sale of the building on Fifteenth and Eoff Streets and the purchase of suitable property in the suburbs which would allow for expansion. In 1916, the trustees appointed Guy E. Holden as principal of the Academy. Because of his leadership during the Great Depression, Holden would come to be known as "the man who saved Linsly."

Three

The Man Who Saved Linsly

In May of 1916, H.W. Standerwich and Guy E. Holden, both teachers at the Academy, were appointed co-principals by the board. They served in that capacity until June of 1918 when they were both drafted into the Armed Services. Holden returned in February of 1919, having attained the rank of lieutenant, and restored military exercises to their former popularity. In 1921, he suggested that it would be in the mutual interest of the two institutions to combine West Liberty Normal School with the Academy and move West Liberty's campus to Wheeling. The idea was vigorously debated and seriously considered for a while until several alumni from West Liberty Normal managed to present convincing arguments against such a move.

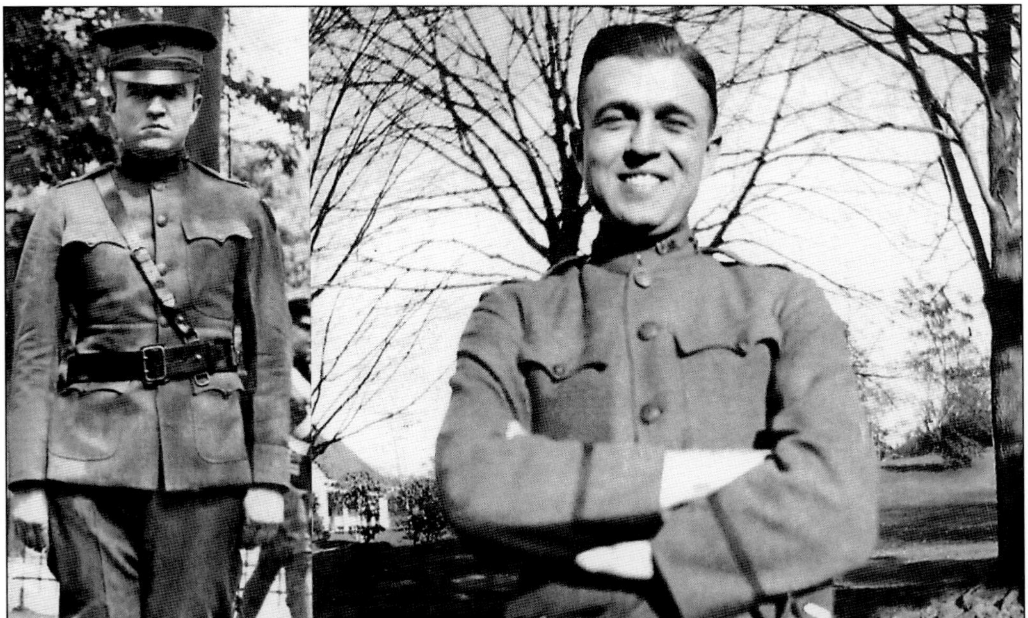

Guy E. Holden Before Going off to War (left) and After Returning (right). Prior to World War I, the enrollment at the Academy had been growing to the point where the Fifteenth and Eoff Street building was no longer adequate. The board was considering constructing a new school building; however, with the onset of the war, enrollment dropped rapidly so these plans were put on hold. At least 116 Linsly students, alumni, and teachers joined the Armed Services. Of these, 61 became officers. The war-induced inflation made it difficult for the Academy to pay its expenses. When Holden returned from the service the deficit was over $3,000 or 14 percent of the entire operating budget. By 1924, the accumulated indebtedness had reached $33,000.

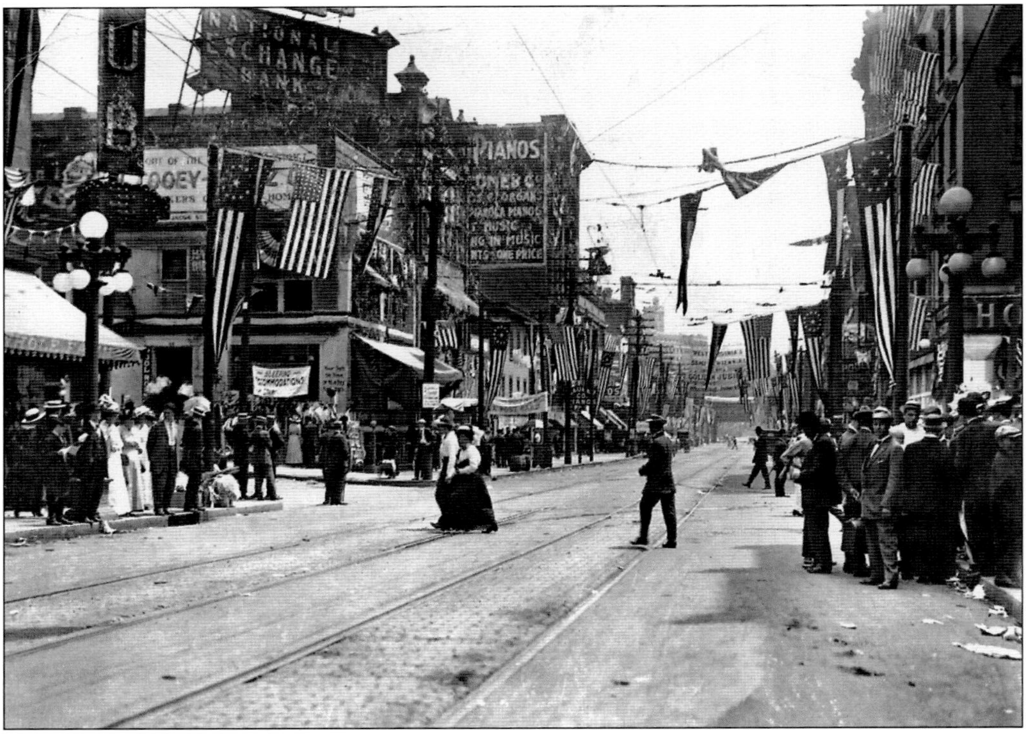

Fourteenth and Market Streets, Looking South, 1913. Wheeling businessman Louis Bertschy made the board an offer to buy the old building and property for $75,000 and allow the Academy to use the building until the school could be relocated. The board accepted and initiated a campaign to raise $400,000. One of the trustees, H.C. Ogden, proposed adding a technical college to the school as a means of encouraging contributions from local industrialists who were in need of technicians. The "Linsly Second Century Fund Drive" was launched early in 1924.

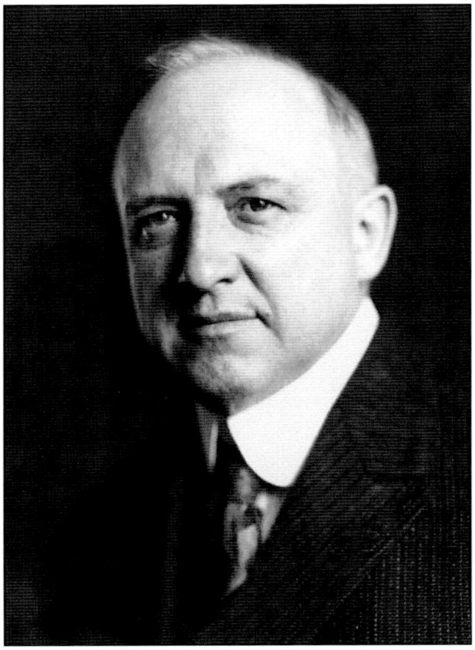

H.C. Ogden. By November, more than the goal of $400,000 had been raised. Over half of that amount was given by 21 donors whose collective contribution was $252,000. The board then began an extensive investigation of possible suburban sites for the new school. Among the sites considered were a hillside site to the east of Warwood, Bridge Park on Wheeling Island, the "poor house" property in Elm Grove, a portion of Greenwood Cemetery, and part of Wheeling Park. All of these were rejected for various reasons, and the board finally settled on a location known as "Thedah Place."

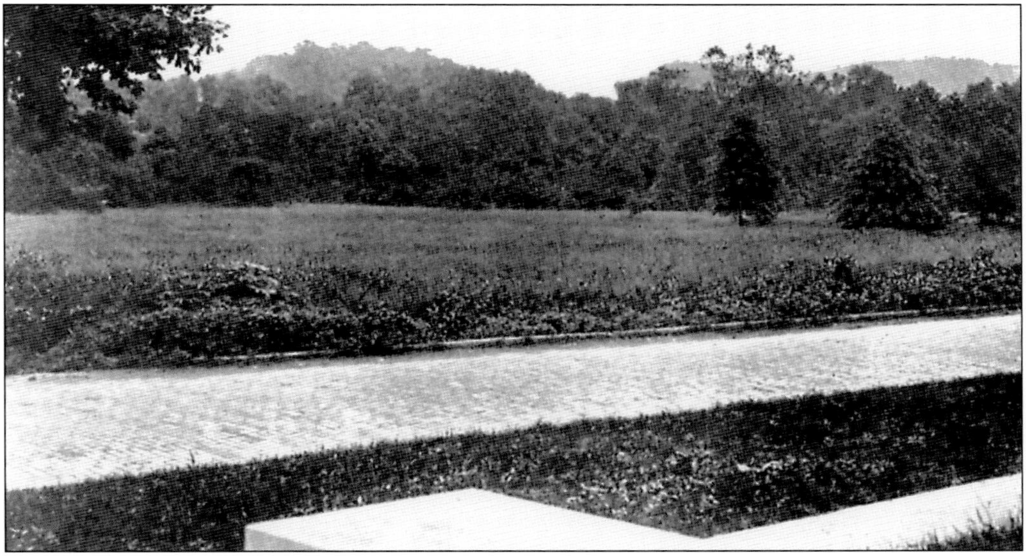

Thedah Place, Pre-1925. Thedah Place was a site originally owned by five families who formed a suburban improvement company to buy land across from their homes in order to prevent factories from being built there. The name is an acronym standing for the last names of the families, namely, Albert **Th**alman, Arthur Greer **H**ubbard, Edwin C. **E**wing, Robert C. **D**alzell and James J. **H**olloway. The "a" was added where a vowel was needed. Though in a suburban location, Thedah Place was 15 minutes by streetcar and 10 minutes by automobile from downtown Wheeling.

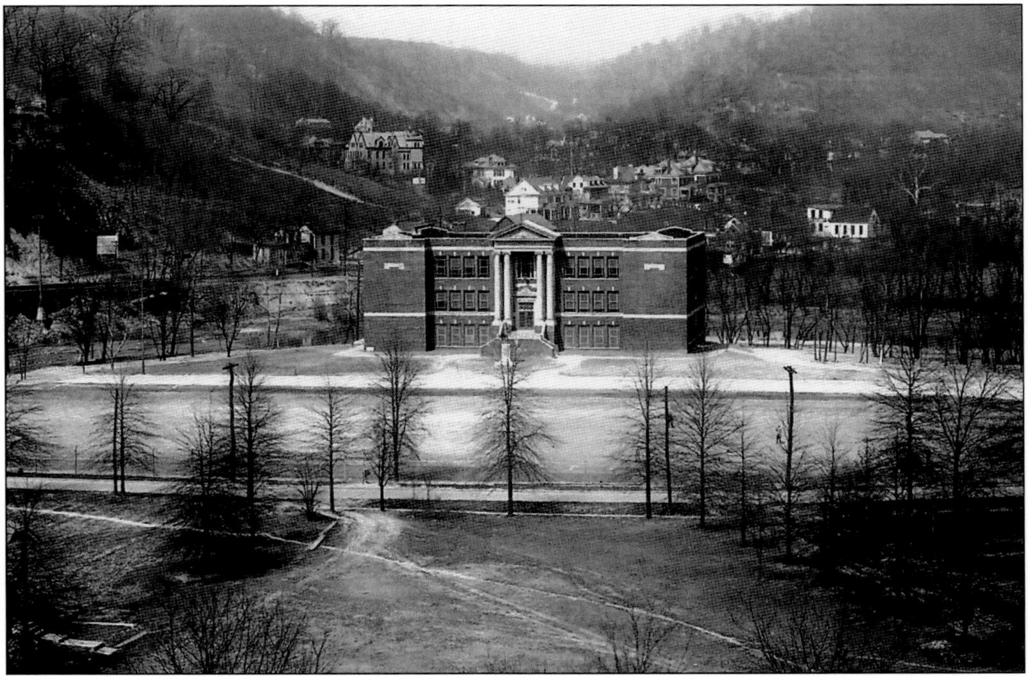

Thedah Place, 1925. In February of 1925, the board awarded R.R. Kitchen the contract to construct the three-story building. The cornerstone was laid on May 10. The building was completed in time for the opening of the 1925–1926 school year. This building later came to be known as "Old Main."

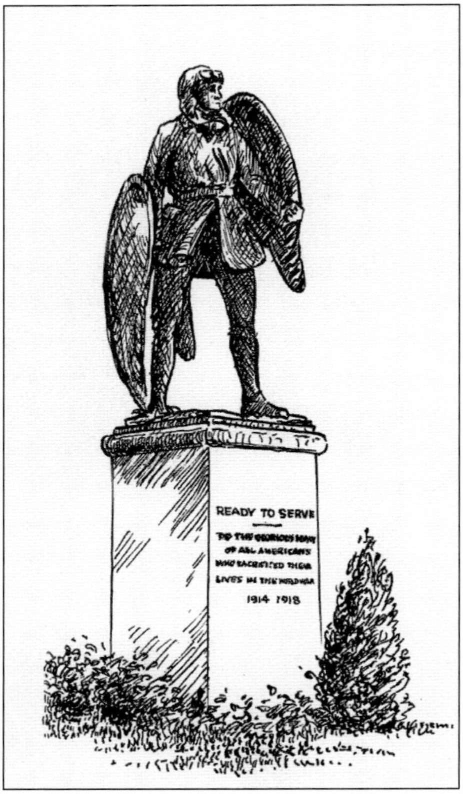

***The Aviator*, Artist's Rendering by Harry Holbert, 1969.** In June, the trustees were offered and accepted a memorial statue to be placed on the campus in memory of Lt. Louis Bennett Jr., of Weston, West Virginia, who was shot down by a German plane while serving with the British in World War I. The base of the bronze monument was inscribed, "Ready to serve; To the glorious memory of all Americans who sacrificed their lives in the World War 1914–1918."

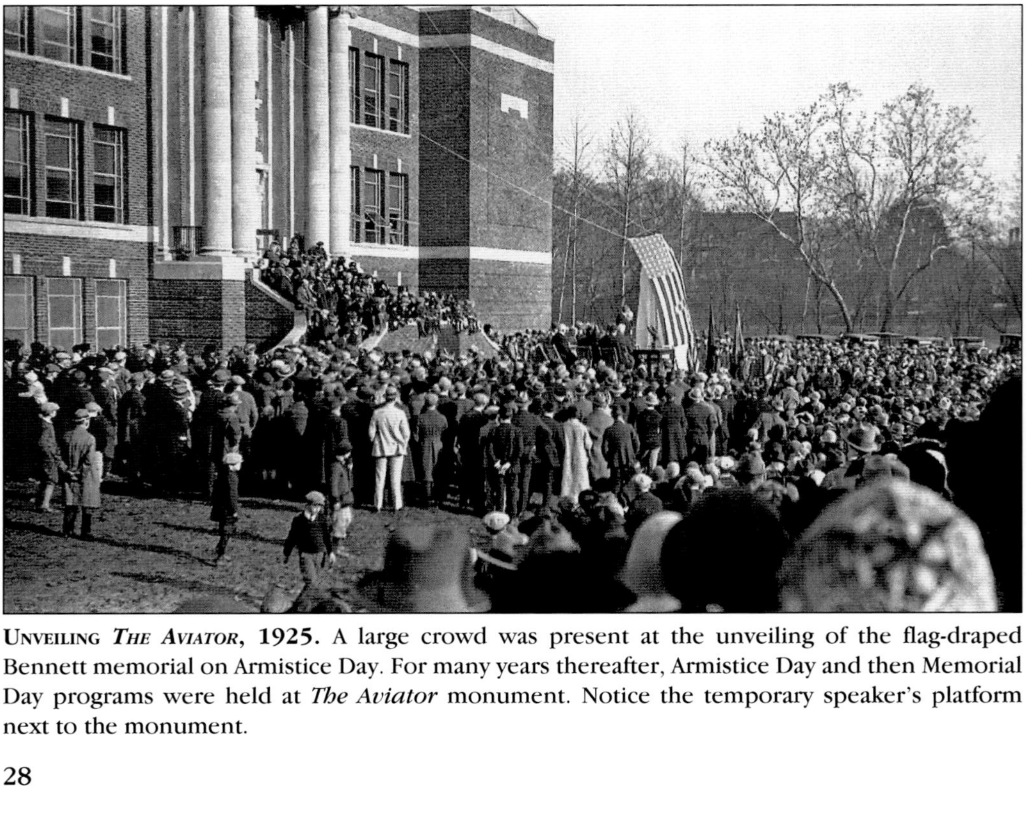

Unveiling *The Aviator*, 1925. A large crowd was present at the unveiling of the flag-draped Bennett memorial on Armistice Day. For many years thereafter, Armistice Day and then Memorial Day programs were held at *The Aviator* monument. Notice the temporary speaker's platform next to the monument.

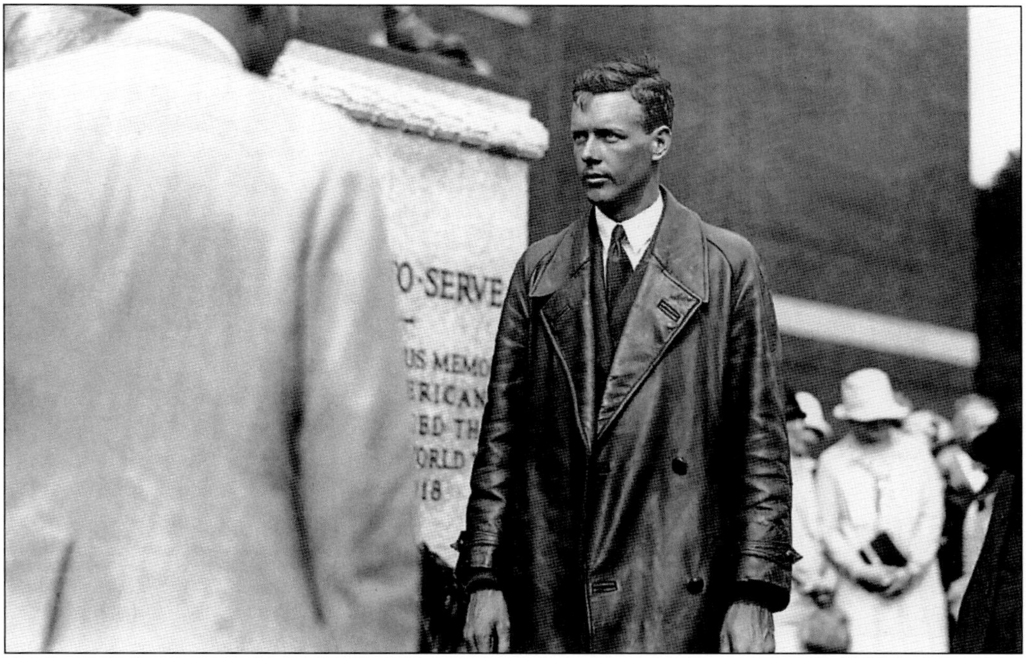

CHARLES LINDBERG AT LINSLY, 1927. When Col. Charles Lindbergh visited the Wheeling area in 1927, he made a special trip to the Linsly Campus where he placed a wreath at the base of the statue in memory of all of the World War I aviators.

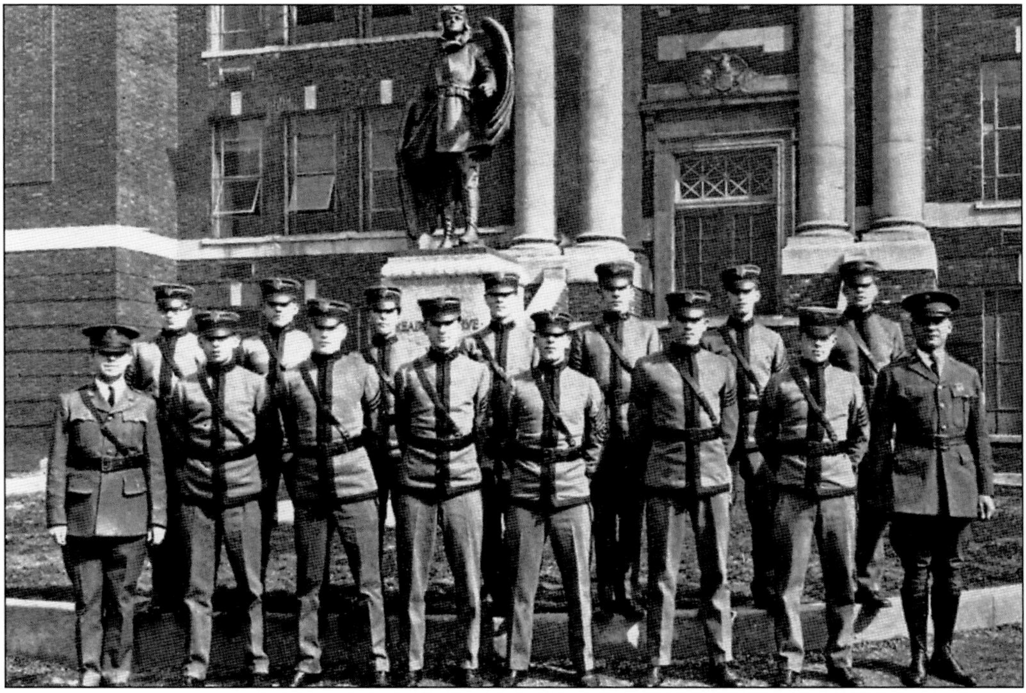

CADET COMMISSIONED OFFICERS IN FRONT OF *THE AVIATOR*, 1927. The following description of the new campus is taken from the 1925–1926 *Linsly Institute Catalog*: "Linsly opens the school year 1925–26 in a splendid new location at Thedah Place, Wheeling, W.Va. The ten acres of school ground lie just south of the National Pike, about fifteen minutes from the center of Wheeling."

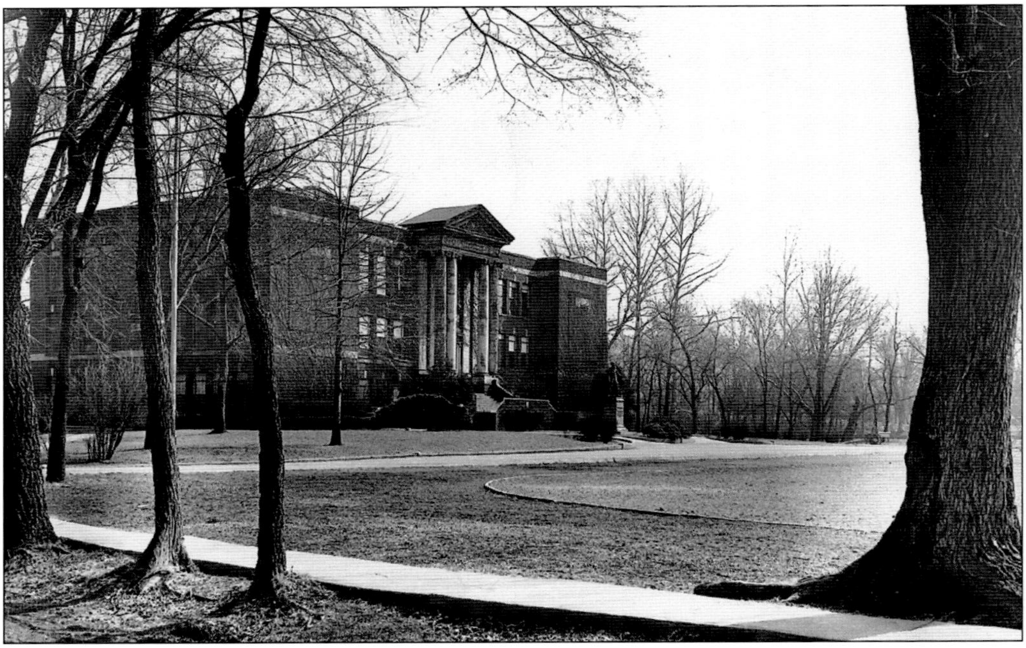

Old Main, 1948. "One of the finest football fields has been provided and other space for outdoor activities is available. The new main building is most modern in every respect, fire proof and arranged to take care of the immediate needs of the school. On the lower floor is the finest gymnasium in the Pan Handle, two locker rooms and showers, a lunch room and boiler room."

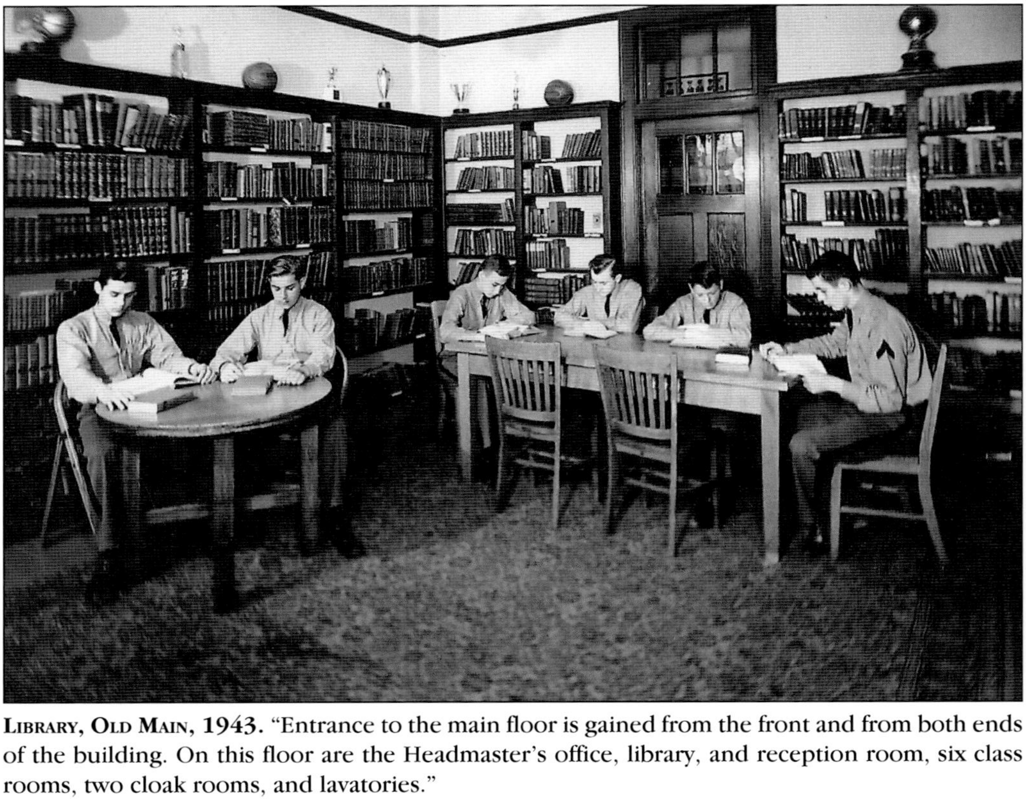

Library, Old Main, 1943. "Entrance to the main floor is gained from the front and from both ends of the building. On this floor are the Headmaster's office, library, and reception room, six class rooms, two cloak rooms, and lavatories."

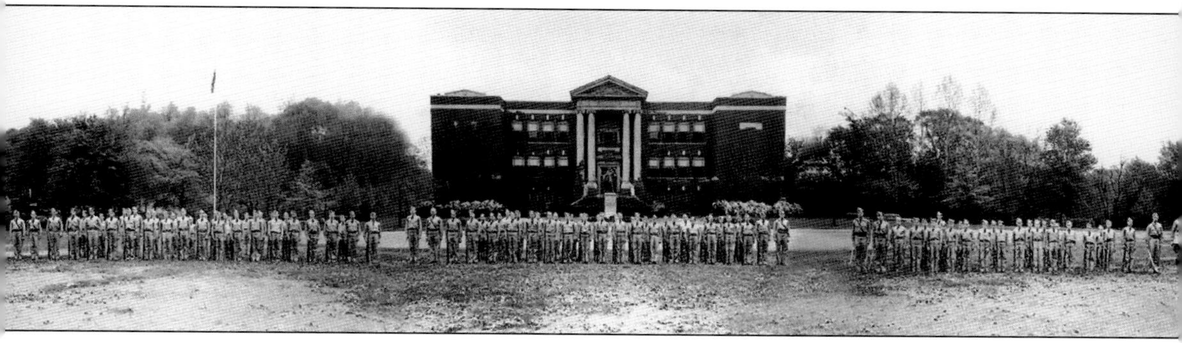

Entire Battalion, 1937. "On the top floor there are four class rooms, a large study hall, general chemistry laboratory, quantitative analysis laboratory, and the Physics and Electrical Laboratories. The building is furnished in the most modern way with special emphasis upon the latest scientific equipment in the laboratories." The new building was designed to accommodate two new junior-college-level programs in industrial chemistry and industrial electricity.

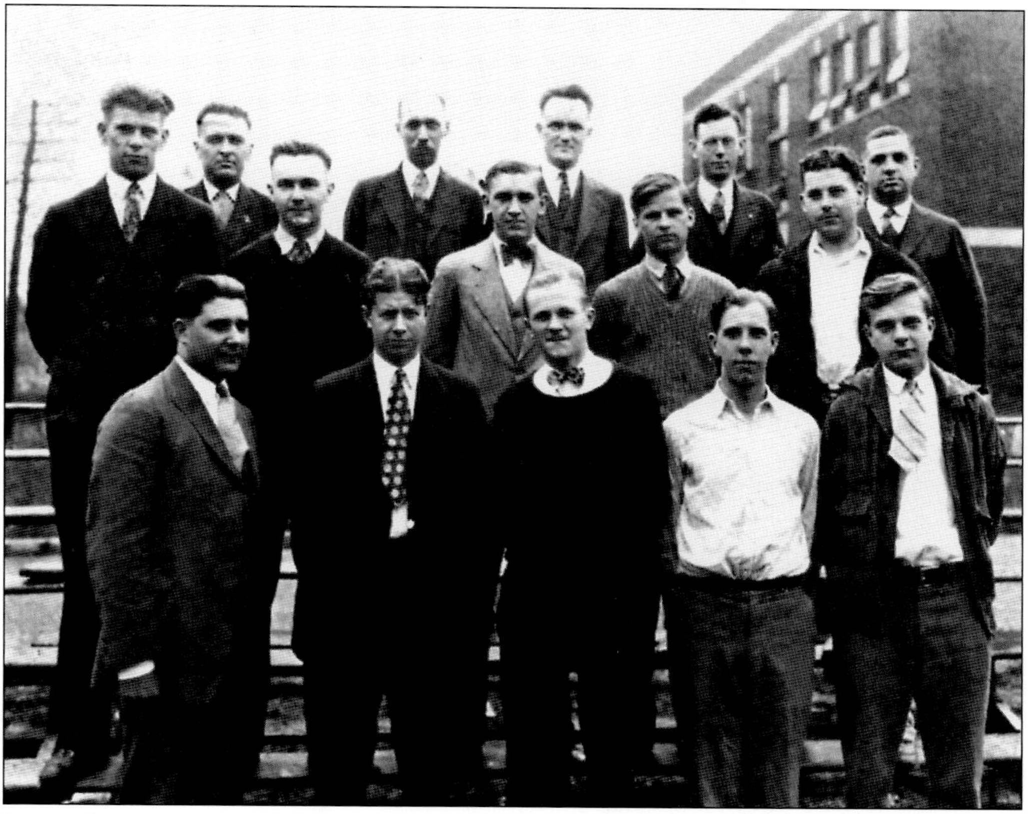

Junior College Students, 1927. The junior-college-level programs provided post-high school training for students not bound for traditional colleges. The high school course was also changed so that it included three paths: college preparatory, scientific, and general. The future seemed wide open for Linsly. Guy Holden and the board had ambitious dreams, but they could not have imagined the difficulties the school would face in just a few years. Linsly's technical junior college was a noble experiment and many fine junior engineers were trained, but the expense of operating this program was substantial. Although the school's enrollment had nearly doubled, by 1929 the operating expenses had doubled as well, and half of these expenses came from the operation of the junior college.

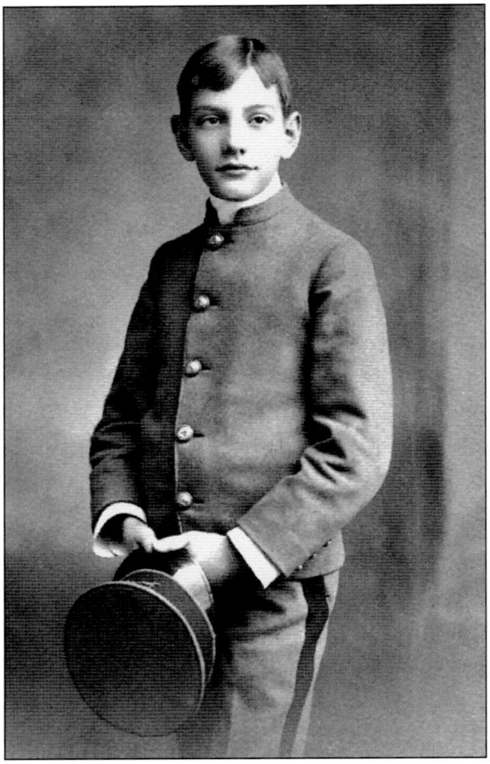

Unidentified Cadet, *c.* 1915. It was at this point that the Great Depression hit. Wheeling was a city that depended on its industry and banking facilities, so it suffered terribly. Linsly was faced with devalued investments and being unable to collect on its pledges. Many parents could no longer afford the luxury of a private education so that enrollment dropped, as did tuition payments. The economy had pretty much reached bottom in 1931 when Holden reported to the board that the school faced a $250,000 shortfall for the following school year and, unless drastic measures were taken, the school would have to close its doors.

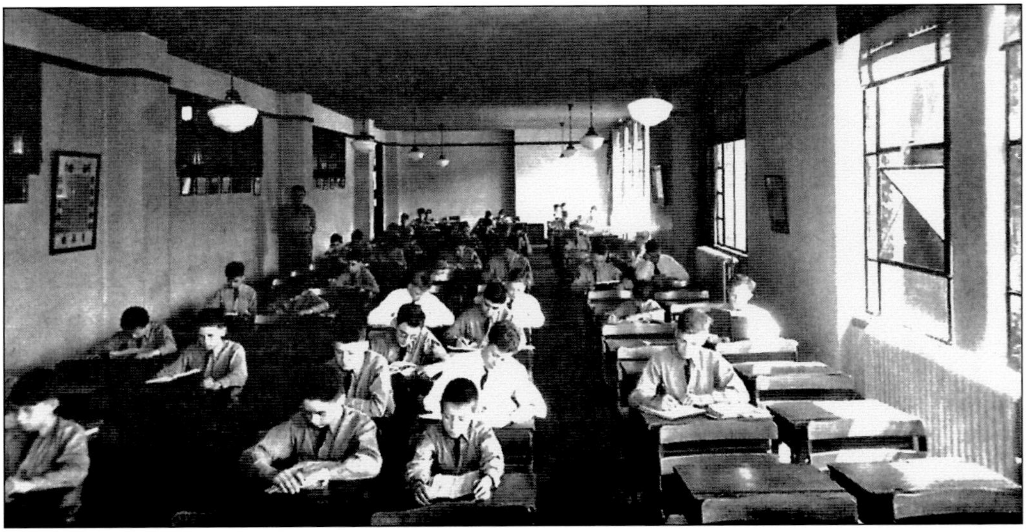

Study Hall, Old Main, 1942. Guy Holden's solution was both drastic and altruistic. Beginning with the 1932–1933 budget, he cut the salaries of all Linsly's instructors, including his own, by nearly 50 percent. A second mortgage and some clever financial maneuvering on the part of the trustees, as well as Holden's extraordinary efforts at canvassing every potential patron and funding source in the area, kept the shortfall to a manageable level.

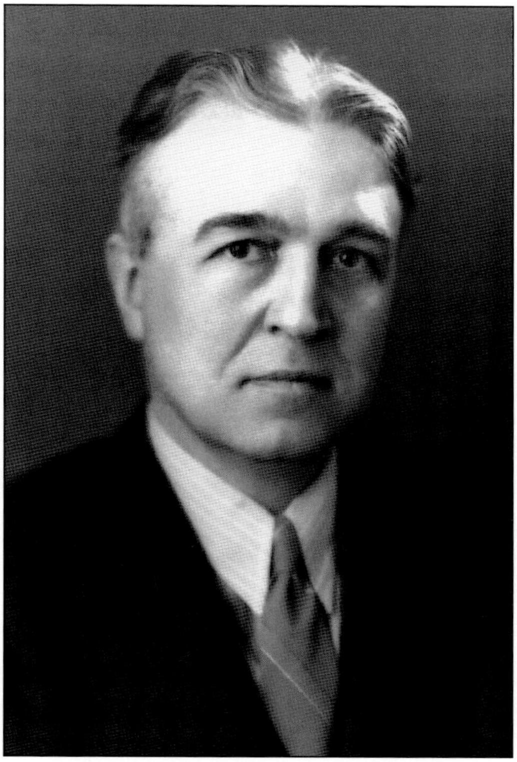

GUY E. HOLDEN. Holden's daughter, Mary Jane Hopkins, recalls, " I remember things were very tough. Every weeknight and many weekends, daddy was out beating the pavement, calling on prospective families, trying to get them to enroll . . . . My parents never went to any social functions, daddy was just gone every night."

CATALOG, LINSLY INSTITUTE OF TECHNOLOGY. By February 1932, the need for additional budget cuts was imperative. At a meeting of trustees and members of the faculty, a plan was presented to expand the college department to three full years, thus creating the "Linsly Institute of Technology." This, it was hoped, would result in a savings of one-half the former operating cost. Also, members of the faculty agreed to additional reductions in salaries. Holden declined his salary altogether and derived his income from the new students' first-year tuitions and the profit from the cafeteria and bookstore.

Linsly Institute of Technology

THEDAH PLACE
WHEELING, WEST VIRGINIA

LANCASTRIAN ACADEMY WHEELING, VA.

COLLEGE OF ENGINEERING
1937 - 1938

SUMMER OFFICE HOURS
Daily (Except Sunday) 2 to 4 p. m.
Telephone: Woodsdale 275

18 LINSLY INSTITUTE

COURSE OF STUDY IN ELECTRICAL ENGINEERING

First Year

First Semester		Second Semester	
Physics A	5	Physics B	5
Chemistry A	5	Chemistry B	5
Algebra A	5	Trigonometry B	5
Drafting A	2	Drafting B	2
English A	3	English B	3
	20		20

Summer School

Surveying S	4
Descriptive Geom. S	3
Mechanics S	3
	10

Second Year

First Semester		Second Semester	
Direct Current C	5	Direct Current Machines D	4
Elect. Meas. C	2	D. C. Gen. and Trans. D	3
Bat. E. M. F., C	1	Alternating Currents D	3
Mag. and E-s Meas. C	1	Calculus-Diff. and Int. D	5
Ind. and Cap. C	1	Drafting D	2
Analytics C	5	Surveying D	3
Drafting C	2		20
Mechanics C	3		
	20		

Third Year

First Semester		Second Semester	
A. C. Circuits E	2	Power Stations F	5
A. C. Machines E	5	Illumination and Ph. F	1
Trans. Systems E	3	Underwriters R. and R., F	1
Thesis E	1	Electrical Design F	3
Calculus E	3	Calculus F	3
Economics E	3	Thesis F	1
Hydraulics E	3	Economics F	3
	20	Mechanics F	3
			20

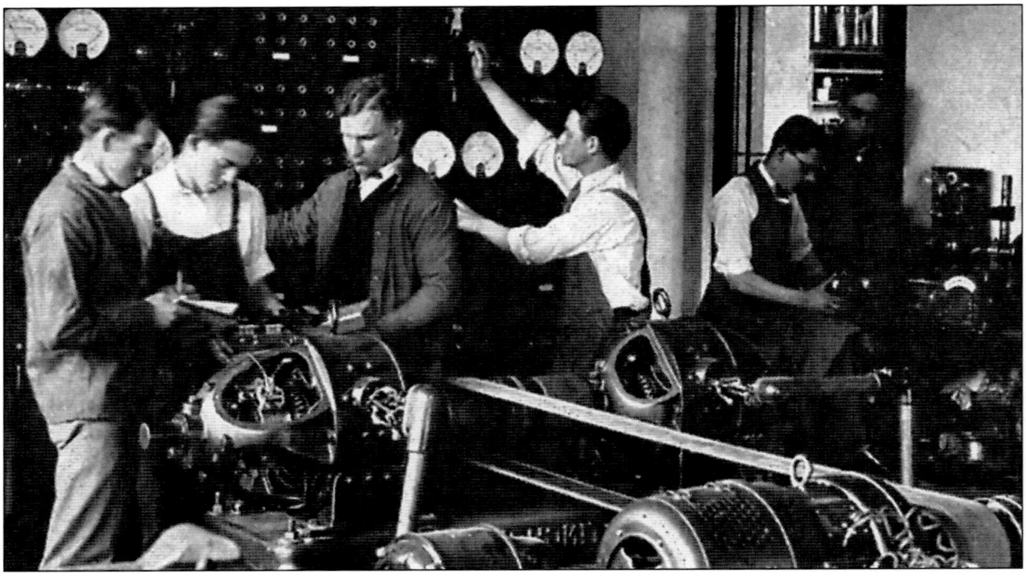

ELECTRICAL ENGINEERING LAB, LINSLY INSTITUTE OF TECHNOLOGY. Linsly's Institute of Technology had a full engineering curriculum offering Bachelor of Science degrees in electrical, chemical, and structural (civil) engineering. The first college degrees to be conferred in Wheeling were awarded by Linsly in 1933. By the late 1930s, the nation and Linsly were cautiously emerging from the Depression. Linsly had survived one of the bleakest periods in its history thanks to the maneuvers of the board and the efforts of Guy Holden. For his service to the Academy he will always be remembered as "the man who saved Linsly."

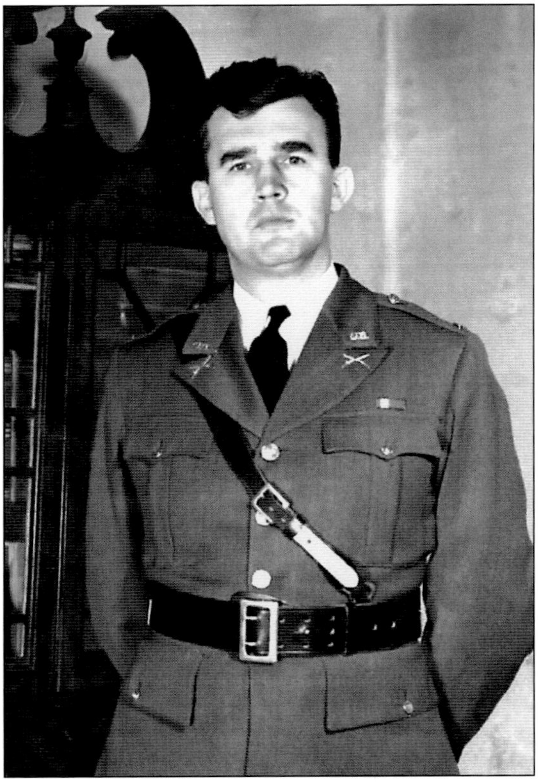

BASIL G. LOCKHART, 1940. In 1940, in what proved to be his last report to the board, Holden wrote, "Linsly is resting on very solid foundations." He also gave some of the credit for this to a young teacher by the name of Basil G. Lockhart, whom he had hired in 1939 to be principal of the cadet department. Holden's health was failing and he died unexpectedly in September of 1940. Because of his youth, the board considered Lockhart too young to assume the heavy burden of headmaster so they appointed him "acting headmaster." He remained acting headmaster for the next 33 years.

Four

The Lockhart Years
The Age of Building

When Basil Lockhart was hired by Holden in 1939 to supervise the cadet department, he began a number of innovations that led to an increased interest in the institution and a raising of the school's morale. He was to prove himself a man of exceptional leadership and administrative skill, as well as a master disciplinarian.

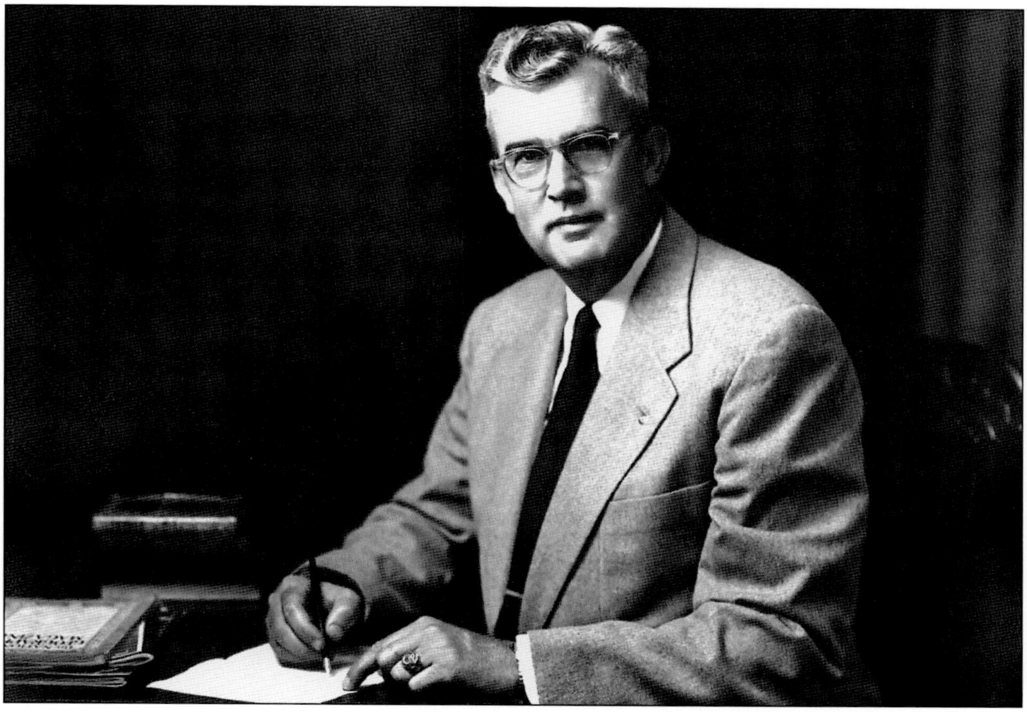

Basil G. Lockhart. On January 13, 1942 Linsly obtained a charter that changed the name from the Lancastrian Academy to Linsly Institute and authorized the trustees "to establish courses of study and give instruction in military science and tactics, in all subjects constituting a technical, scientific, classical or academic education including the right to establish and conduct primary, secondary and collegiate departments and confer degrees." The Linsly Institute of Technology was accredited by the state board of education of West Virginia.

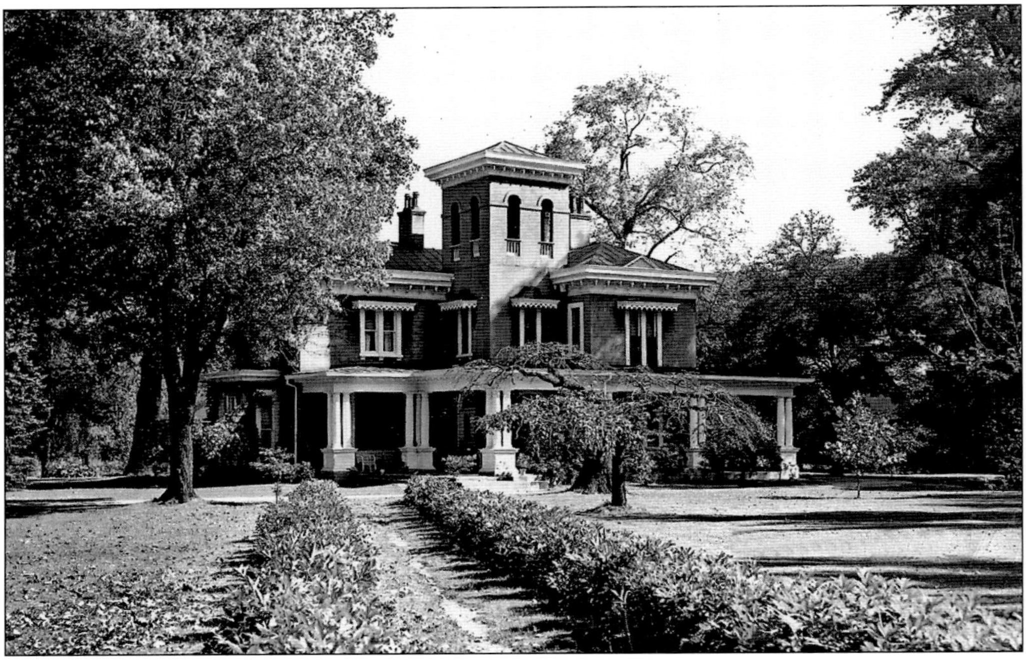

Merriman Hall, 1950. One of Lockhart's first recommendations to the board was the establishment of a boarding department. The school's first acquisition towards that end was the 19-room Tallman mansion in Leatherwood, which was purchased by Mrs. Merriman and endowed to the school in 1941. Merriman Hall became the nucleus of Linsly's boarding department. Since there was increasing interest in private boarding schools at that time, the program was a success.

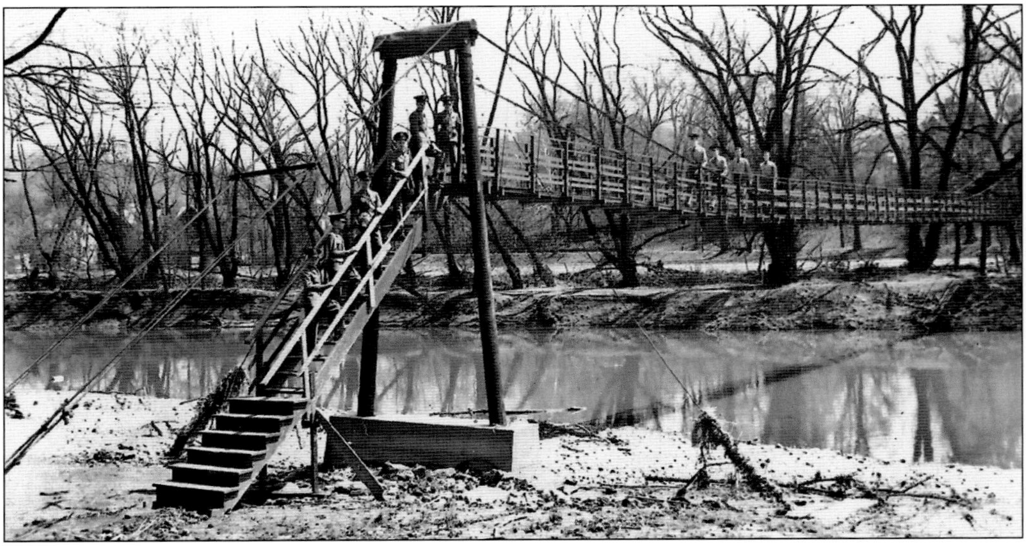

Cadets on the Footbridge after the Flood of 1943. Because Merriman Hall was located on the opposite bank of Wheeling Creek from Main Hall, boarding students needed some way to get to the dormitory without walking a two-mile route along the National Road and down Leatherwood Lane. Consequently, a footbridge was built across the creek. The first bridge was built in the summer of 1942 by a work crew consisting of Peter Stewart, Henry Brown, and Douglas Haigwood.

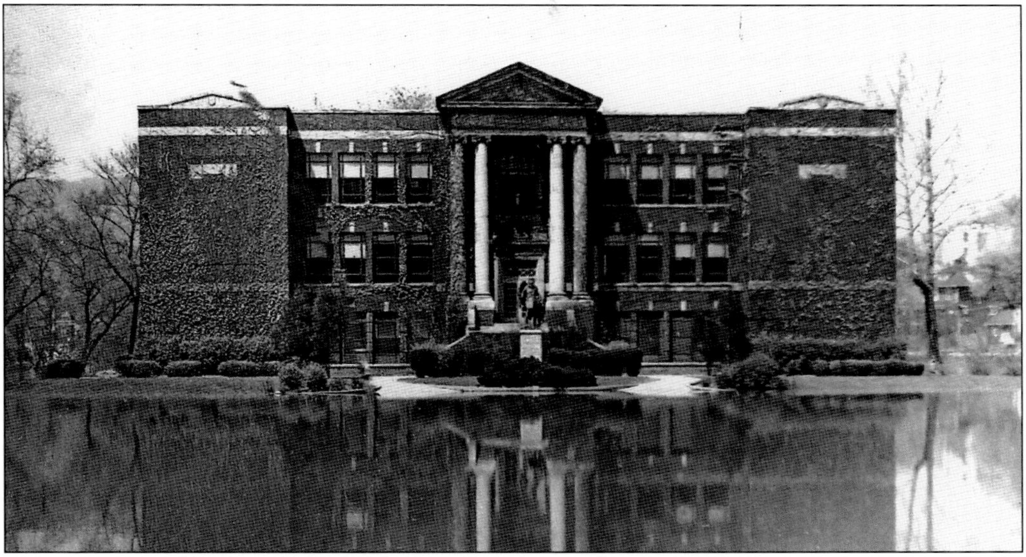

Old Main During the Flood of 1948. The Thedah place location was subject to flooding from Wheeling Creek. When Old Main was first built, the board considered a flood wall but decided it was too expensive. As it turned out, it would have been cheaper in the long run than the expense of the clean-up after the basement of Old Main, which contained the cafeteria and gym, was flooded. In some years the flood waters reached the first floor.

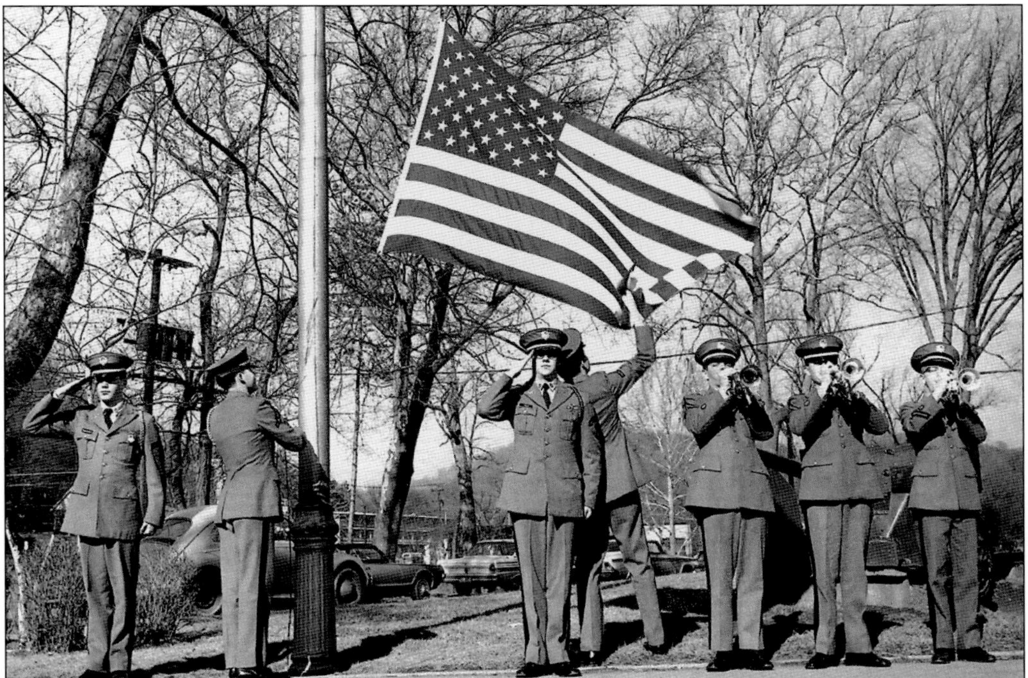

Raising and Lowering the Flag. Every morning the flag was raised and every afternoon it was lowered in a ceremony involving three buglers and a color guard. The nation was once again preparing for war. The economy improved and Linsly, with its military program, was an attractive educational choice once again; however, the students of the college department were among the first to be called into the Armed Services.

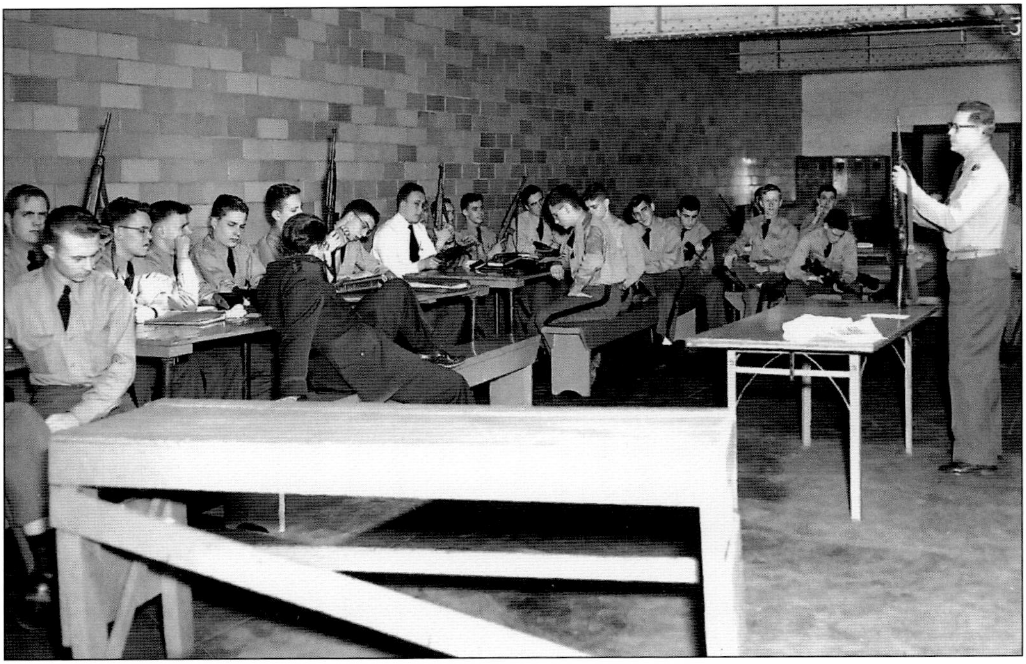

Rifle Range in Old Main. The rifle range was also the lunch room. The target backstop was up against the wall of the kitchen. In 1943, the entire student body of the college left for the service. Thus, on July 1, 1943, the college department ceased to function. With its passing went the dreams and hopes of a number of well-meaning residents of the Wheeling area. The engineering equipment was transferred to Washington and Jefferson College, which had urgent need for it.

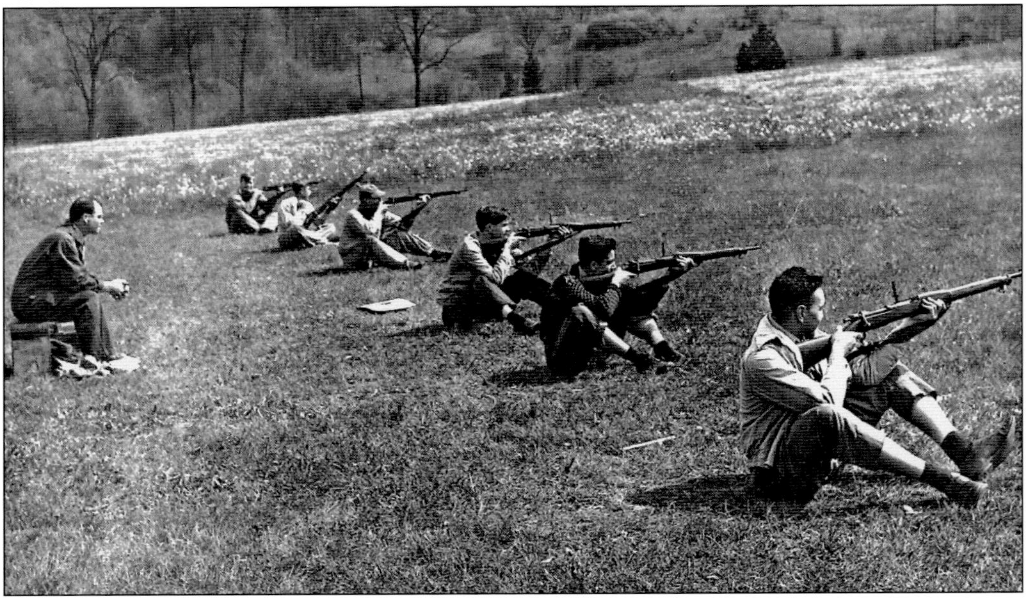

Cadets Firing Springfield 03s, 1948. In 1941, Lockhart brought about the accreditation of Linsly by the North Central Association of Colleges and Secondary Schools. In that year also, Linsly's military training program was recognized by the United States Department of War. The Linsly Corps was under the jurisdiction of the Fifth Corps Area and was given frequent inspections by Army officers. Hence the school came to be known as "Linsly Military Institute."

Cadet Officers Goofing Around with the World War I Cannon. The military program at Linsly was, by this time, well organized, and the school had established a set of rules for dealing with almost any situation. Cadets who were in violation of any number of regulations were assigned punishment duty, which meant that they had to stay after school and march in a repetitive pattern for a specified time depending on the offense. Examples include chewing gum in uniform (two hours), lost rifle (two hours), and failure to salute (one hour).

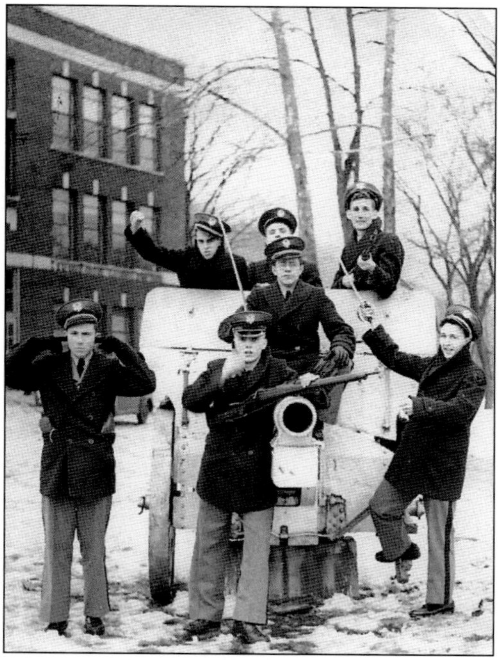

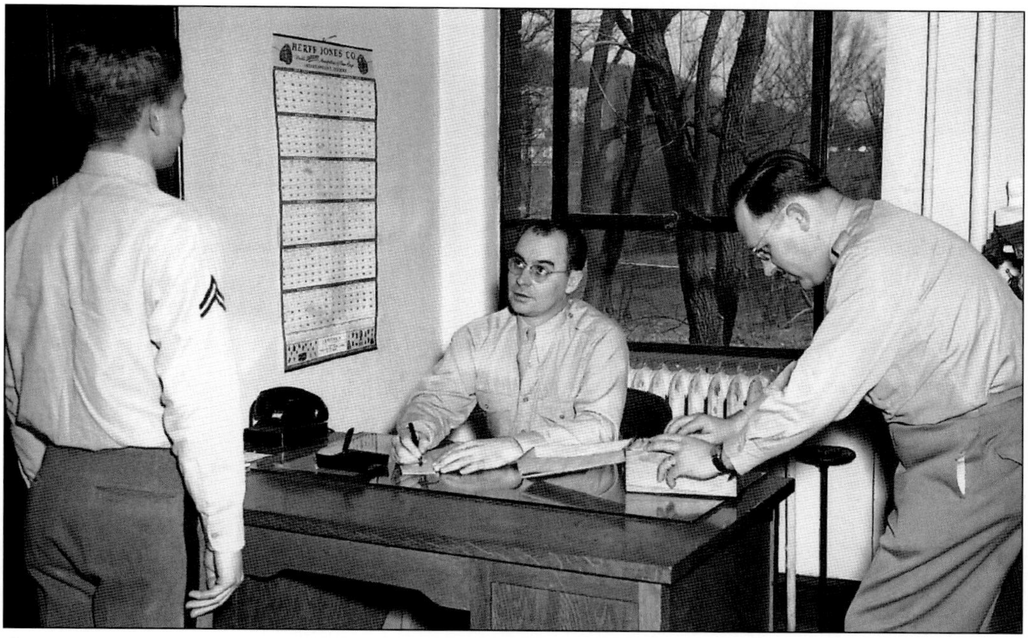

Captain Peters Checks the Records of a Cadet Reporting to Captain Haigwood for Punishment Duty. Insubordination or disloyalty to Linsly resulted in one or more hours of punishment duty or, if severe enough, expulsion. Use of drugs or stealing almost always meant expulsion. Even minor offenses like not having your shoes shined would get a cadet one-half hour of punishment duty. Students were only permitted a maximum number of punishment duty hours in any 30-day period. Cadets who exceeded that number were expelled. Commissioned and non-commissioned officers were permitted only a few hours of punishment duty, and if they exceeded these, they were reduced in rank to private. Linsly did not put up with nonsense. It soon became clear to a new cadet that he was at Linsly to work and learn and not to fool around.

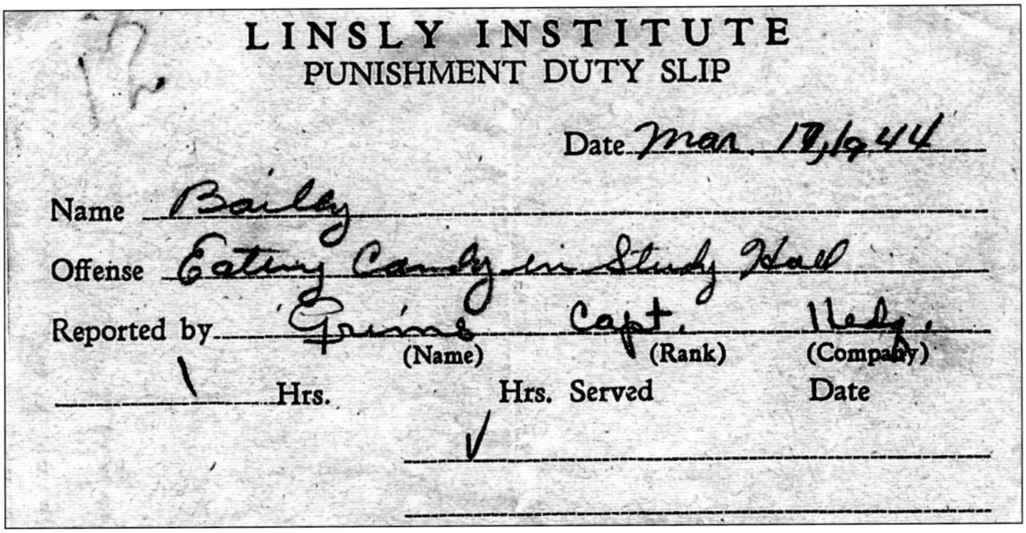
LINSLY INSTITUTE
PUNISHMENT DUTY SLIP

Date Mar. 17, 1944

Name Bailey

Offense Eating Candy in Study Hall

Reported by Grimes Capt. Hdq.
(Name) (Rank) (Company)

1 Hrs. Hrs. Served Date

Punishment Duty Slip, 1944. Cadet Bailey has been issued the dreaded green PD slip by Captain Grimes of Headquarters Co. for eating candy in study hall. Linsly had many rewards for merit, achievement, and leadership, but the greatest competition was for military promotion. The seniors were commissioned officers and the juniors were non-commissioned officers. Promotion was based on a complex point system that began with the cadet's scholastic average for the year squared, plus 100 for each point over 90 percent. Points were awarded for military grades, previous years of work at Linsly, and all sports and extracurricular activities.

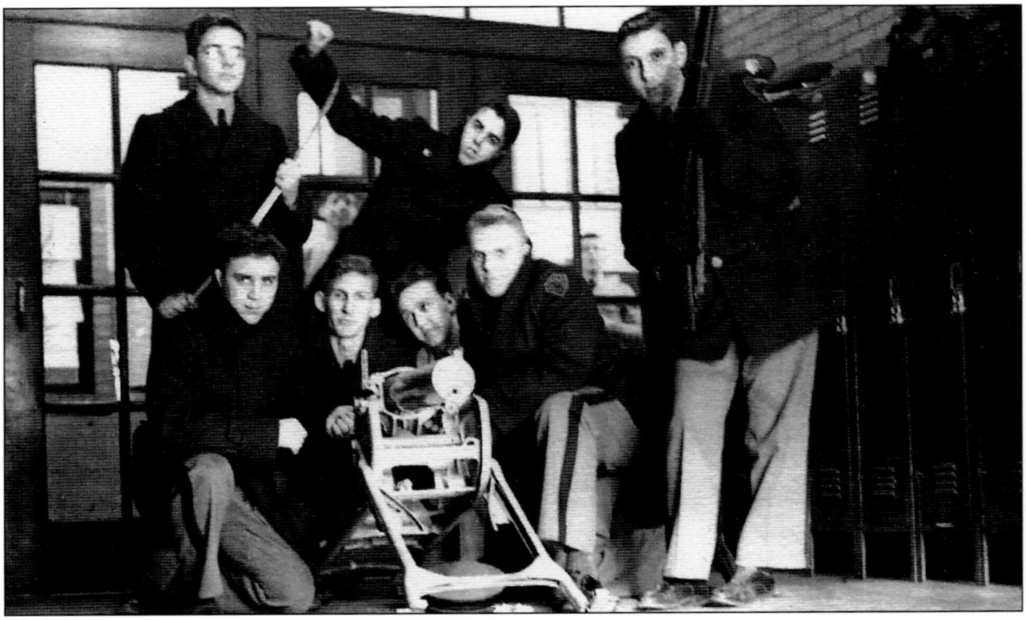

Playing Around with the Machine Gun. A German Maxum 7.92mm water-cooled machine gun was located just inside the main entrance to Old Main. It was a popular place where cadets would pose for a snapshot. Points were deducted for each hour of punishment duty and for a grade of "F" in military classes. The senior with the largest number of points became Cadet Major. Second highest was Captain Adjutant, then there were approximately seven Captains (one for each company) and a number of First and Second Lieutenants. Juniors became First Sargents, Sergeants, and Corporals.

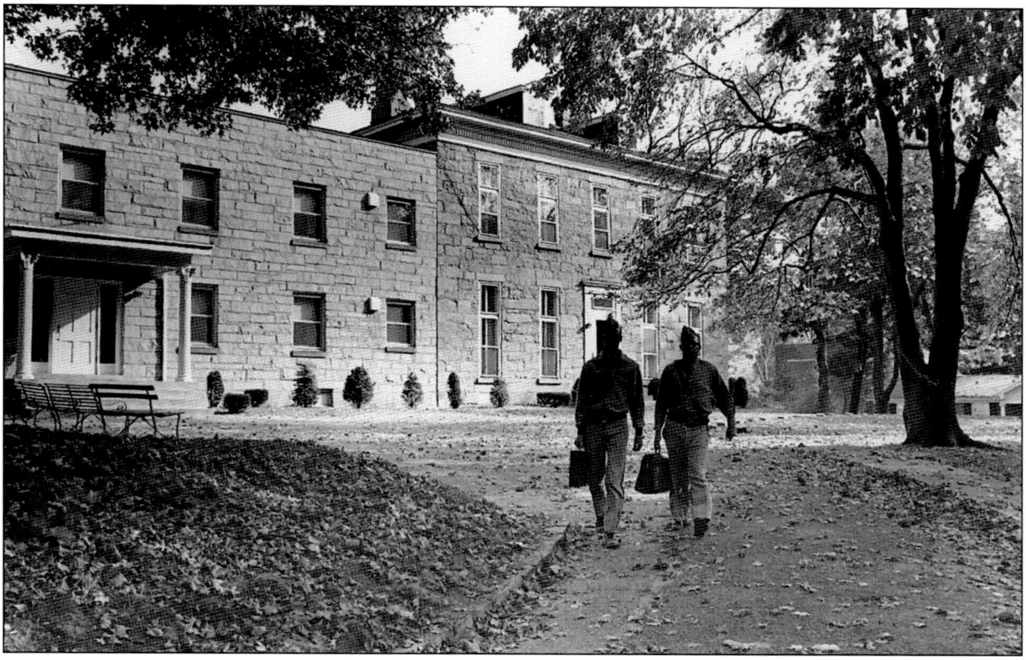

WEISS HALL. In 1943, Mrs. W.E. Weiss gave the Dalzell property to Linsly so that the school acquired its second dormitory (Weiss Hall), thus increasing the space for boarding students. Later the school built an annex, which doubled the dormitory's capacity.

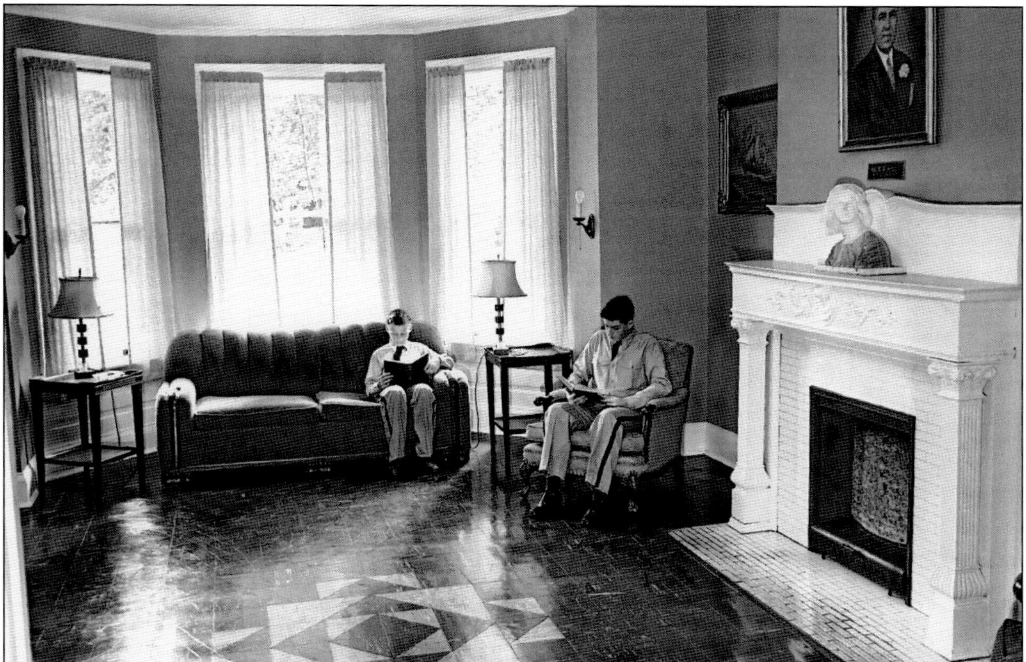

WEISS HALL LIVING ROOM, 1943. Linsly tried to provide a home-like atmosphere in dormitories where cadets could relax and engage in recreational activities and quiet study when they wished to do so. The original dormitories had been private homes; therefore, the surroundings were not the usual sterile decor often found in student accommodations.

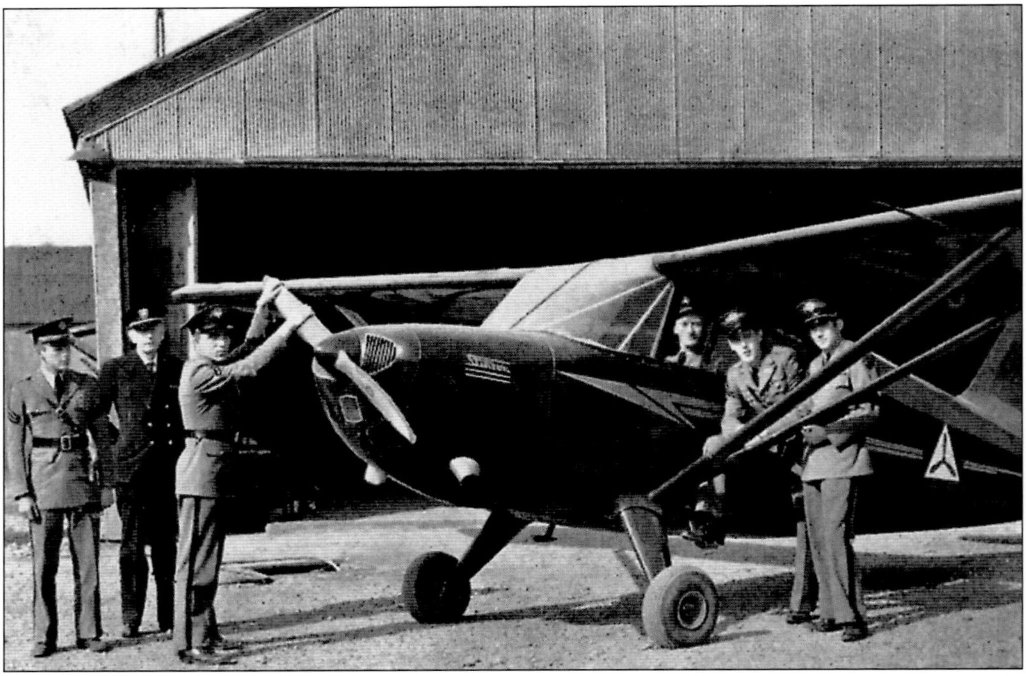

Cadets at Flight School, 1944. At one time Linsly operated a flight school. Cadets could enroll in ground instruction class and flying lessons. Difficulties with obtaining aircraft repair parts and aviation fuel during the war led to abandonment of the program.

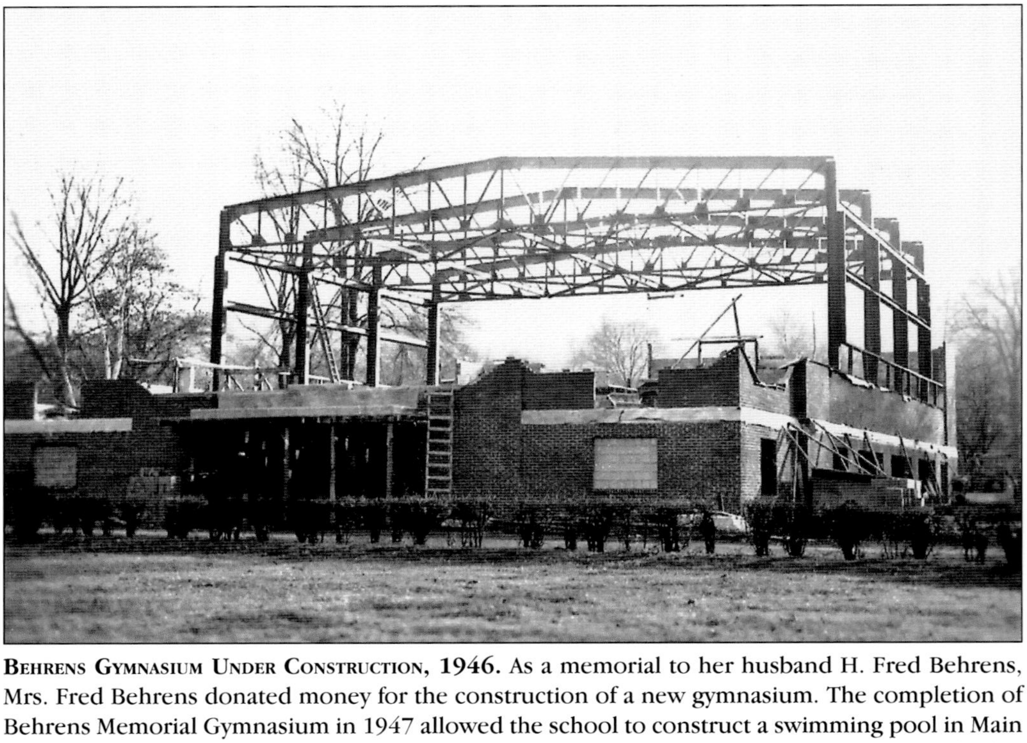

Behrens Gymnasium Under Construction, 1946. As a memorial to her husband H. Fred Behrens, Mrs. Fred Behrens donated money for the construction of a new gymnasium. The completion of Behrens Memorial Gymnasium in 1947 allowed the school to construct a swimming pool in Main Hall where the old gym had been located. It was dedicated to the cadets who served and died in World War II.

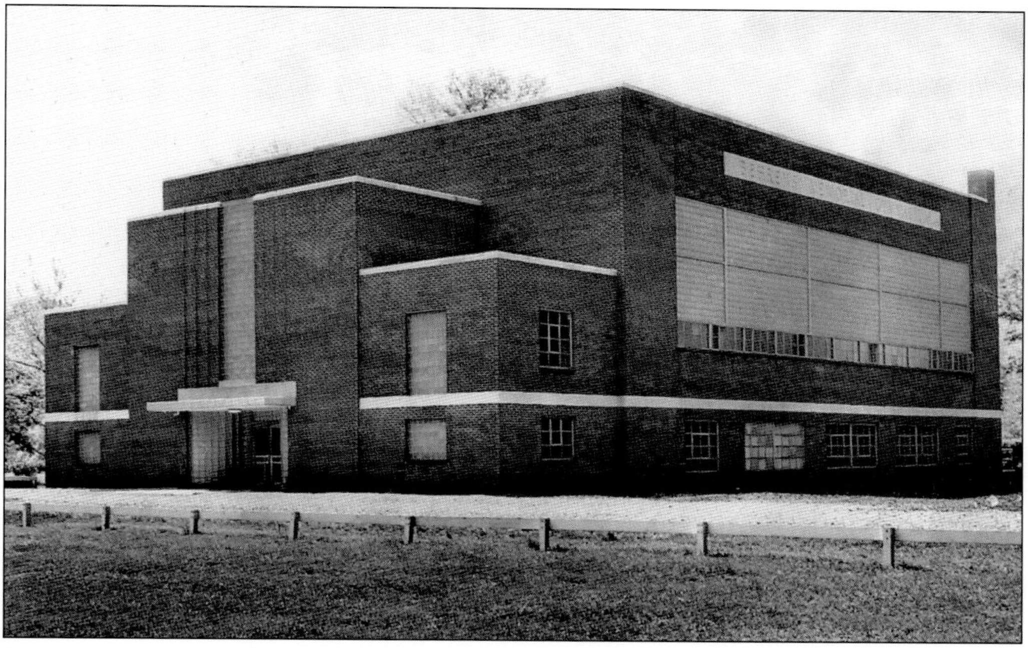

Behrens Gymnasium, 1947. By the mid-1950s the student body had grown to 300 students, 75 of whom were boarding students. This period of sustained growth prompted the addition (annex) to Weiss Hall in 1955 and a rebuilding of the footbridge in 1953, which had become worn as a result of increased traffic.

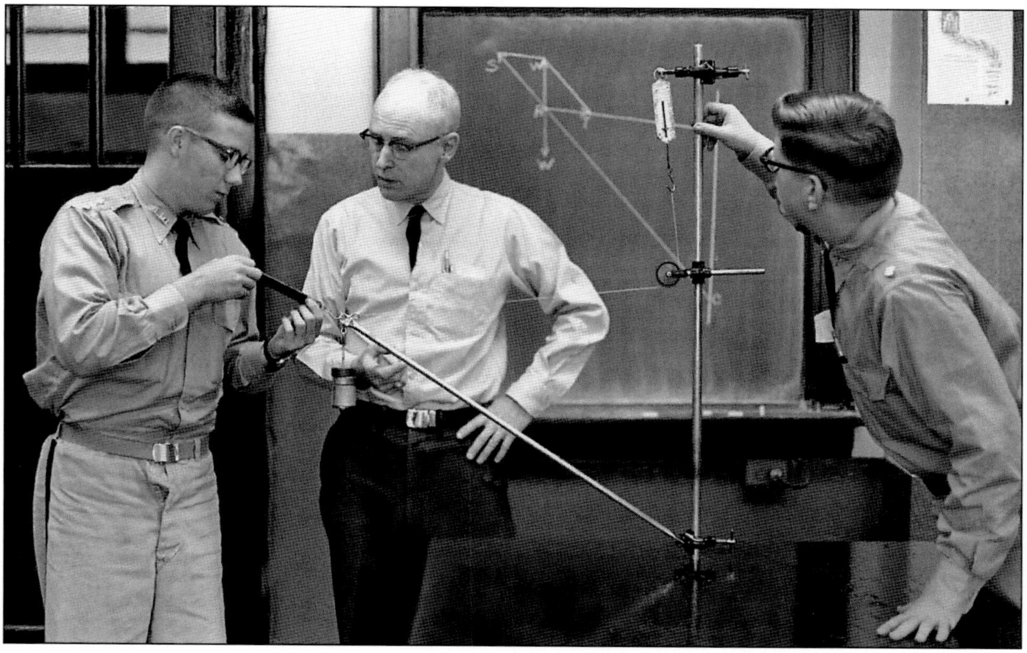

Capt. Henry C. Brown, Instructing Cadets in the Mysteries of Physics. Small classes and individual attention has long been a part of Linsly's instructional program. Many of Linsly's instructors held graduate degrees. Henry Brown had a master's degree in electrical engineering from Carnegie Institute of Technology. He taught physics, chemistry, advanced mathematics, and was the senior class advisor.

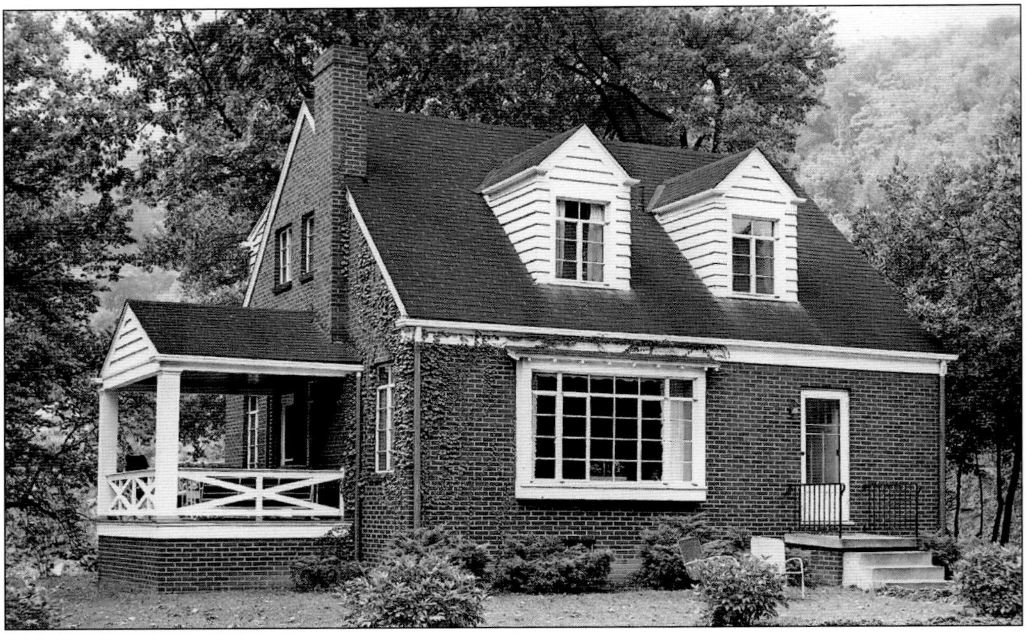

Headmaster's House, 1948. A new home was constructed for Linsly's headmaster and his family in 1948. Basil Lockhart was the first headmaster to occupy it. Later it became a faculty home.

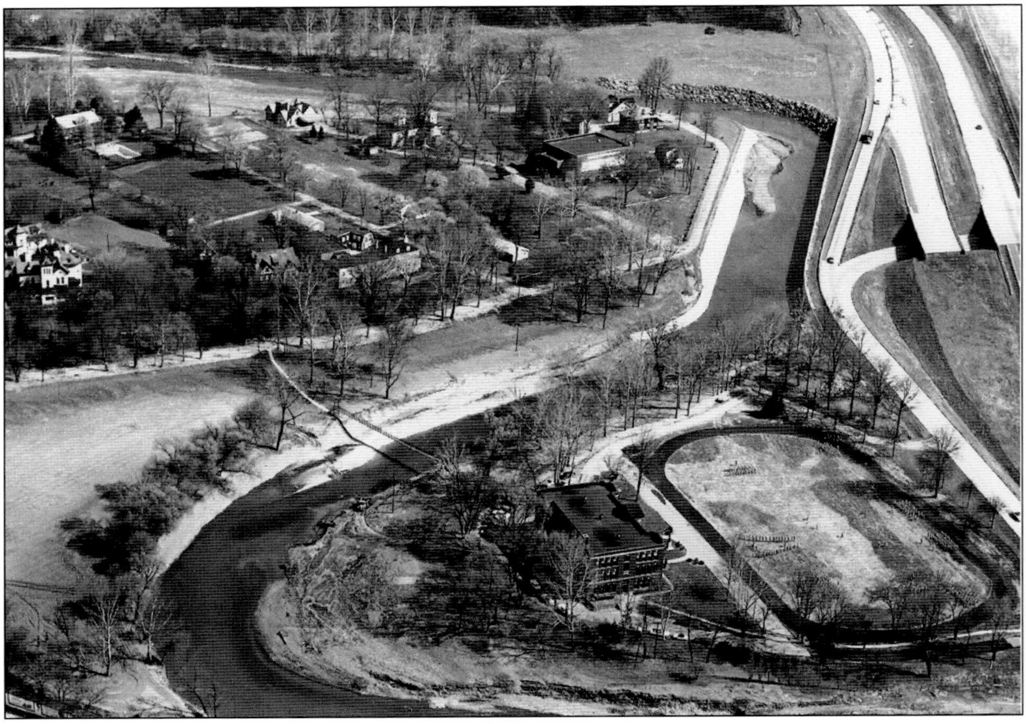

Aerial Photograph, Thedah Place, 1963. Construction of Interstate 70 can be seen in the upper right. The interstate highway was to pass close to Linsly's Campus and required the redirection of Wheeling Creek. This resulted in the loss of Weiss Hall and the property surrounding it, but a new dormitory was quickly constructed in a different location. The new Weiss Hall was completed in 1959 long before I-70 was completed.

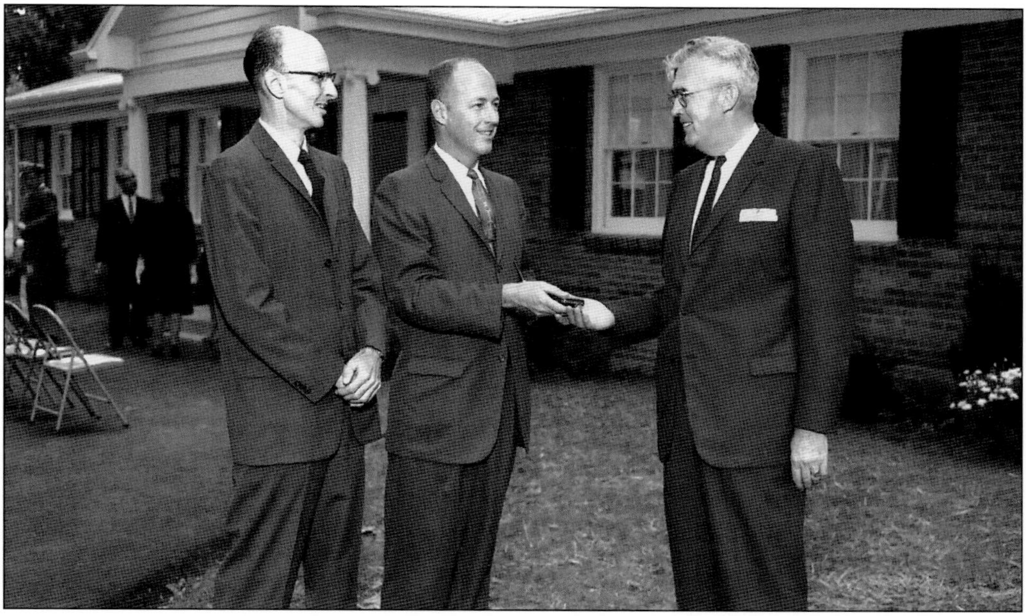

Dedication of the Fawcett Infirmary, 1961. From left to right are Mr. York Fawcett, Dr. R. Alan Fawcett, and Basil G. Lockhart. As a memorial to Ivan Fawcett (Class of 1906), a member of the board from 1941 to 1958, the Fawcett family donated an 18-bed infirmary to the school. Fawcett Hall was completed in 1961.

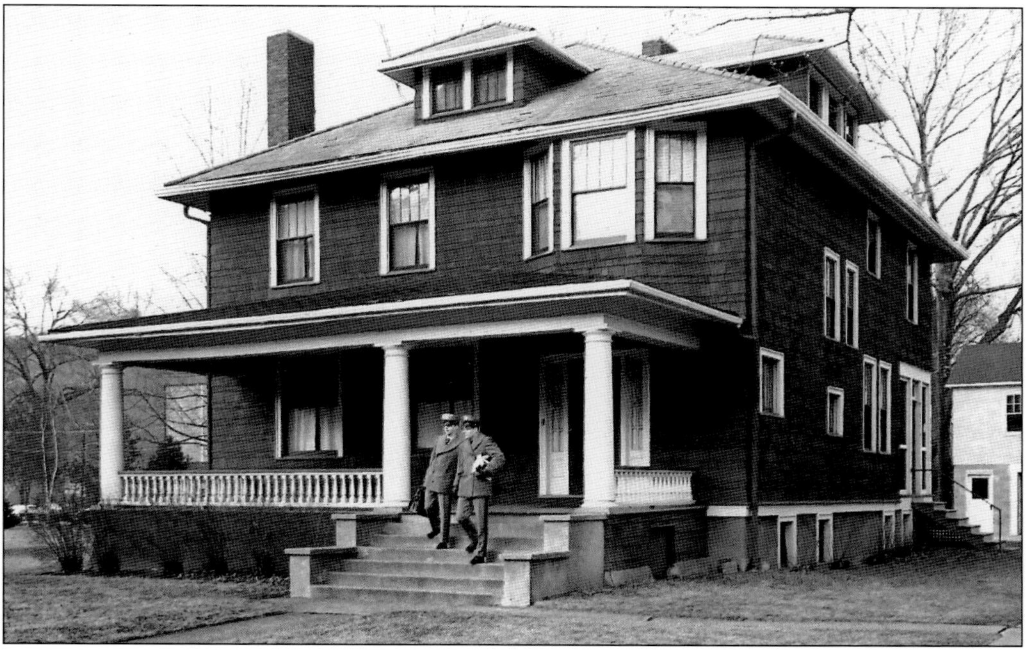

Coudon Hall, 1969. Coudon Hall was acquired by Linsly in 1969 and the Coudon family endowed the upkeep of the building. It was originally used as a faculty residence but later became the Headmaster's home. As the school neared its 150th anniversary in 1964, the school's swelling enrollment had reached 375 students, more than Old Main could comfortably accommodate. This prompted the board to begin a capital-funds campaign in order to enlarge and modernize the classroom facilities.

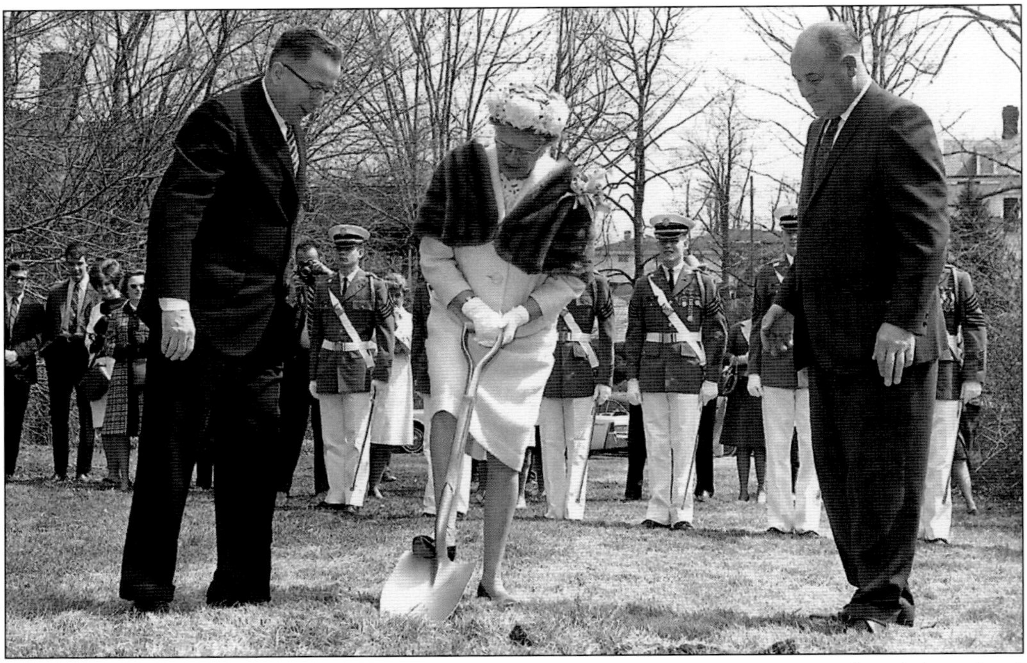

Sophie Banes Breaking Ground, 1966. About this time, Sophie Banes (center) offered the school a challenge grant of one million dollars to be matched by the school, alumni, and friends. The challenge was met and, with such a generous gift, the board decided to construct a new main building across the creek from Old Main, thus consolidating the entire campus on one side of Wheeling Creek. Groundbreaking was held in 1966 and Banes Hall was dedicated in 1968.

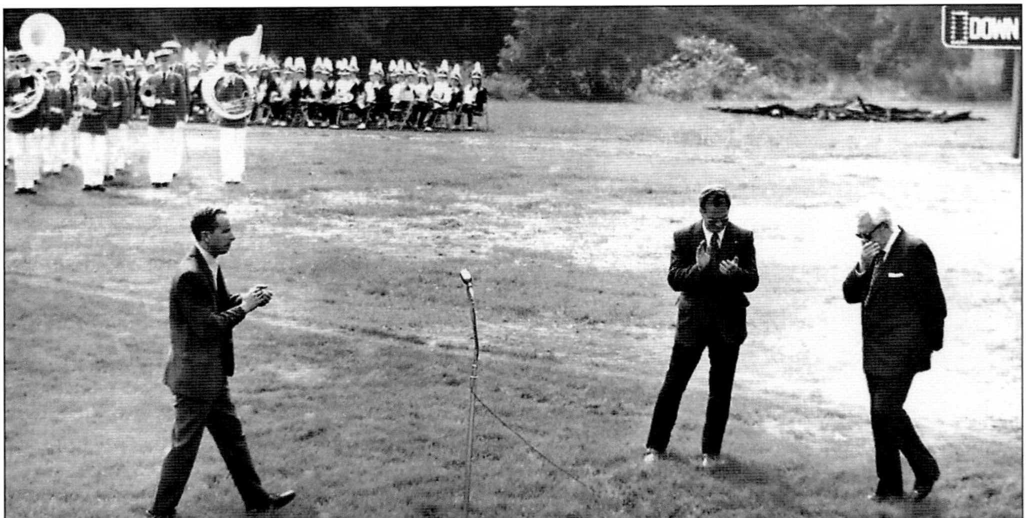

Dedication of Lockhart Field, 1973. From left to right are Dr. Donald Hofreuter, Harry A. Chorpenning, and Basil G. Lockhart. In 1972, Basil Lockhart retired after 33 years of dedicated service. As an administrator he had encouraged competence, cooperation, and loyalty within his faculty, whom he constantly urged to "treat each boy as if he were his own." Lockhart was a strong leader who saw the school through an era of extraordinary growth, but a new era was dawning. Linsly was about to change, but the basic principles upon which the school was founded did not.

Five

The New Linsly

Certainly the acquisition of Banes Hall and the highest enrollment in Linsly's history, which occurred shortly after Banes Hall opened, enabled Linsly to modernize its curriculum. However, two changes made by the board during the next two decades were to alter the nature of the school. The first was the decision to discontinue the military program in 1979 when Reno DiOrio became Headmaster. In the 1927 Catalog the aim of the military program as stated was "not to produce conquestive, bloodthirsty soldiers . . . but to instill habits of punctuality, neatness, and obedience to constituted authority." The second was the decision, in 1988, to make the school into a coeducational institution once again. Although neither of these changes was popular with some of the alumni, they were not capriciously made. The board had sound reasons for making them. In many ways, this time period may also be considered the second age of building, for beginning in the 1980s numerous additions were made to Linsly's campus.

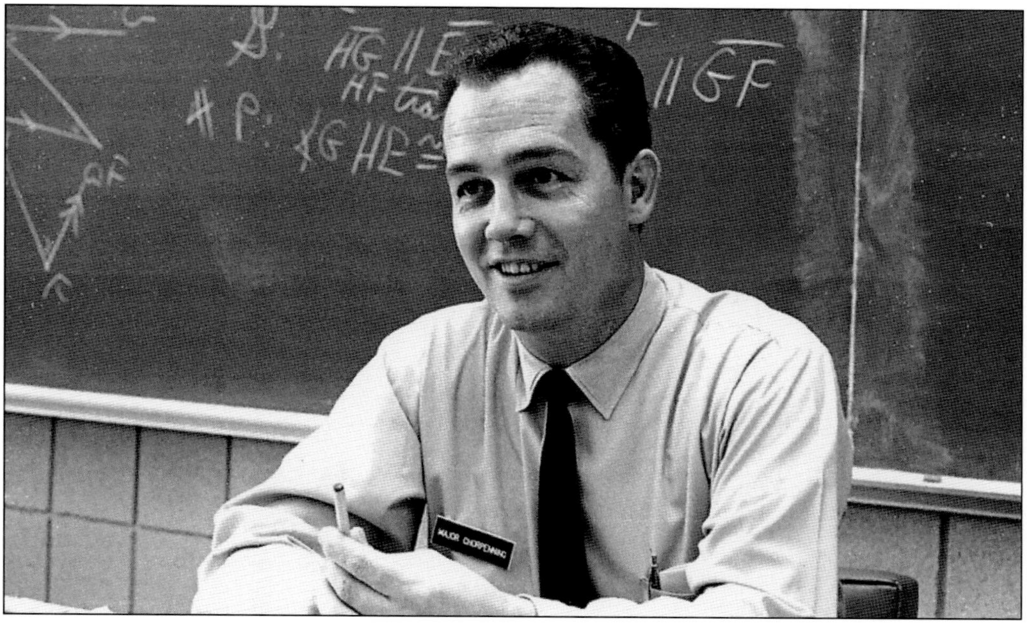

Harry A. Chorpenning. When Chorpenning became Headmaster in 1972, daily drill was reduced to twice a week. Chorpenning was left in the difficult position of maintaining the military program at a time when the increasing unpopularity of the Vietnam War caused inner conflicts for many of the cadets and their parents. At Linsly, the military program had provided an opportunity for students to hold leadership positions of authority and responsibility. Linsly believed than one had to learn to obey before one could lead.

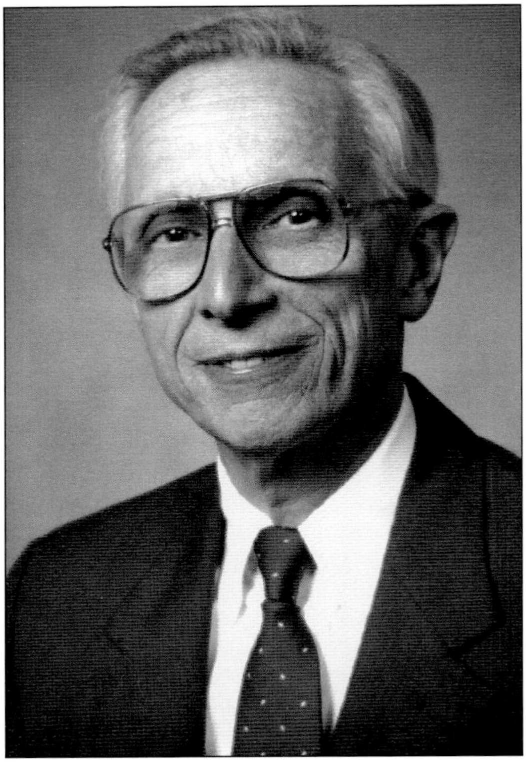

Dr. Donald Hofreuter, President, Linsly Board of Trustees. In an interview by Dorothy Parlett of the *Wheeling Intelligencer* staff in 1978, Dr. Donald Hofreuter, president of the board of trustees, explained that leadership opportunities could be provided by means of a prefect system, used in many private schools. Hofreuter said, "Right now, we believe time in a secondary school maybe can be better spent than in close-order drill." The traditional uniform worn by cadets was replaced by a coat and tie suitable to a private, independent school for boys.

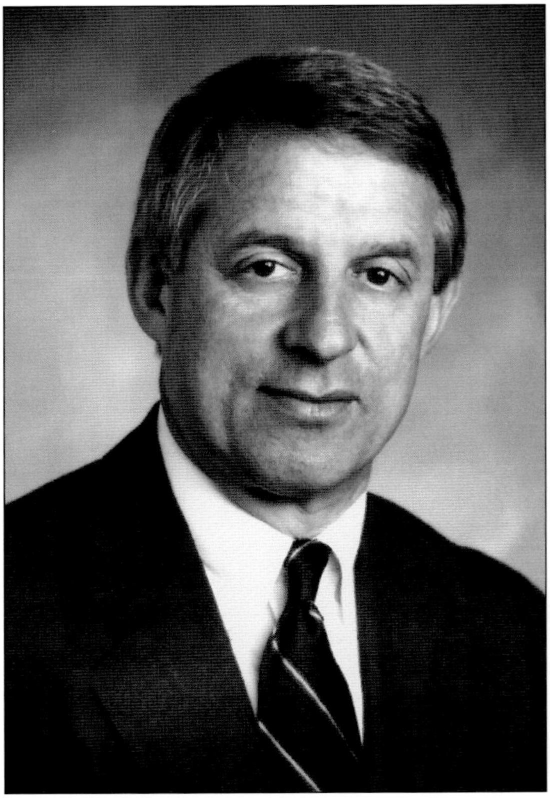

Reno DiOrio. Headmaster DiOrio initiated the "no quit" policy, which required students participating in extracurricular activities to complete what they started. Students were not permitted to quit. Likewise, they could not be "cut." Thus, Linsly students learned the importance of completing what one has started, and not giving up when the first difficulty is encountered. When DiOrio became headmaster, the board had no plans for making the school coeducational; however, beginning with the first minstrels in the 1930s and, thereafter, young ladies from surrounding high schools had participated in the shows.

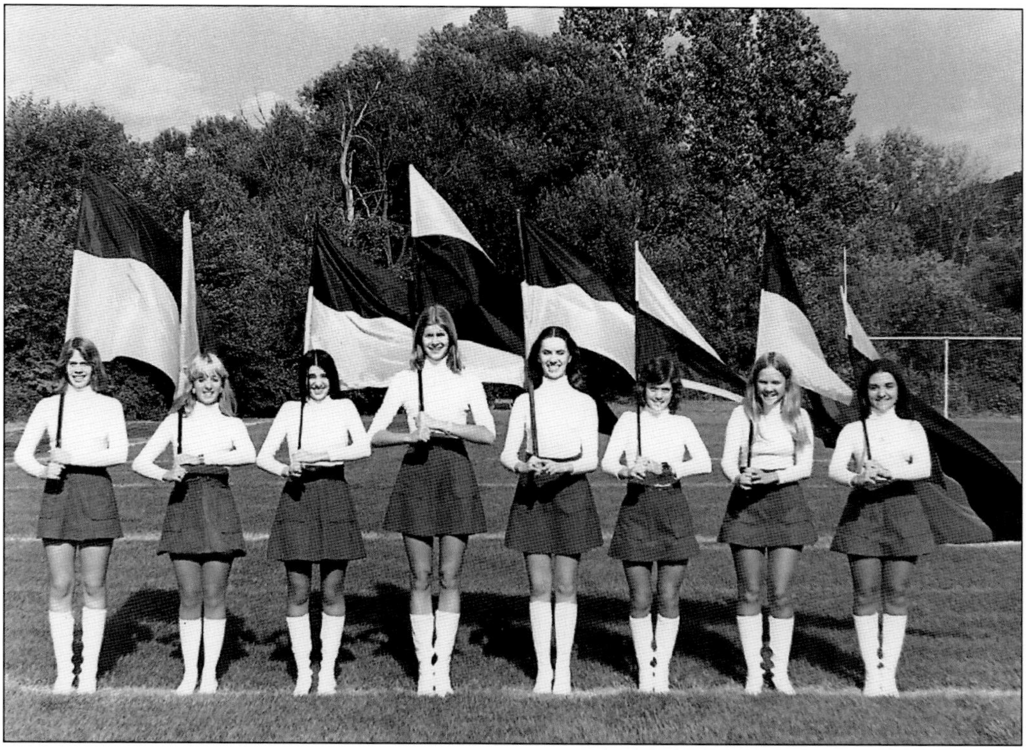

Flag Girls, 1974. In the decades of the 1960s and 1970s, Mount de Chantal girls were Linsly's flag girls. During this period the glee clubs and choirs of Linsly and Mount de Chantal combined for an annual Christmas program.

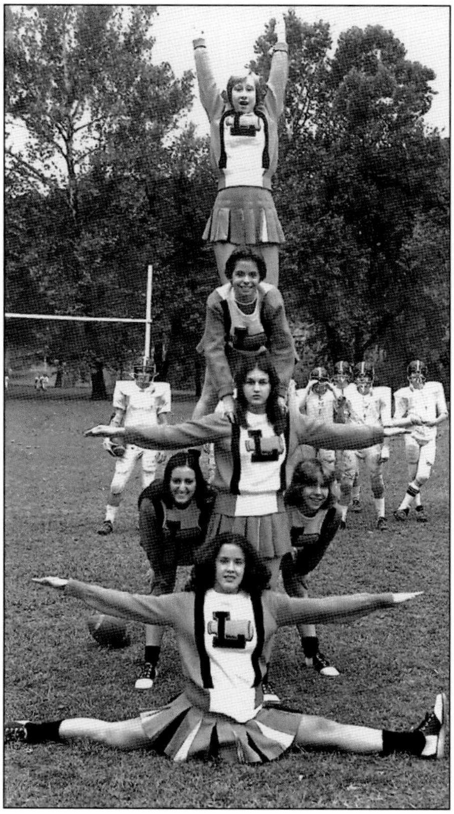

Mount de Chantal Cheerleaders. During this era Mount de Chantal girls were the Linsly cheerleaders and wore Linsly cheerleader uniforms. This arrangement continued for several years until Linsly became coeducational.

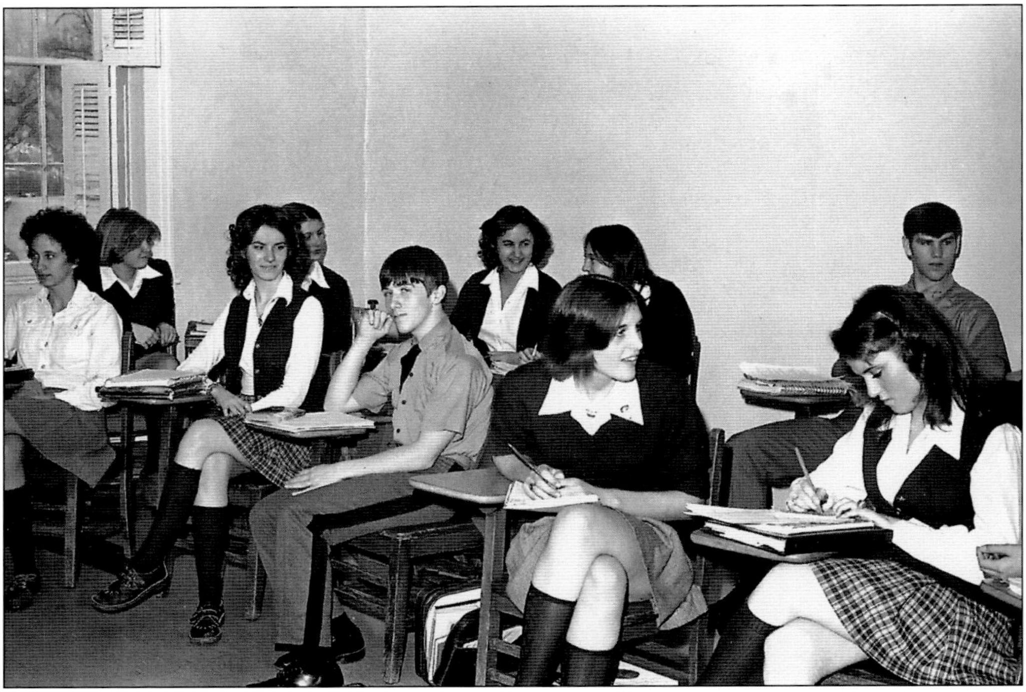

A Philosophy Class at Mount de Chantal. In 1976, Linsly students attended some classes at Mount de Chantal that were not offered at Linsly. Students are shown here in a philosophy class at the Mount. Likewise Mount de Chantal girls attended some classes at Linsly.

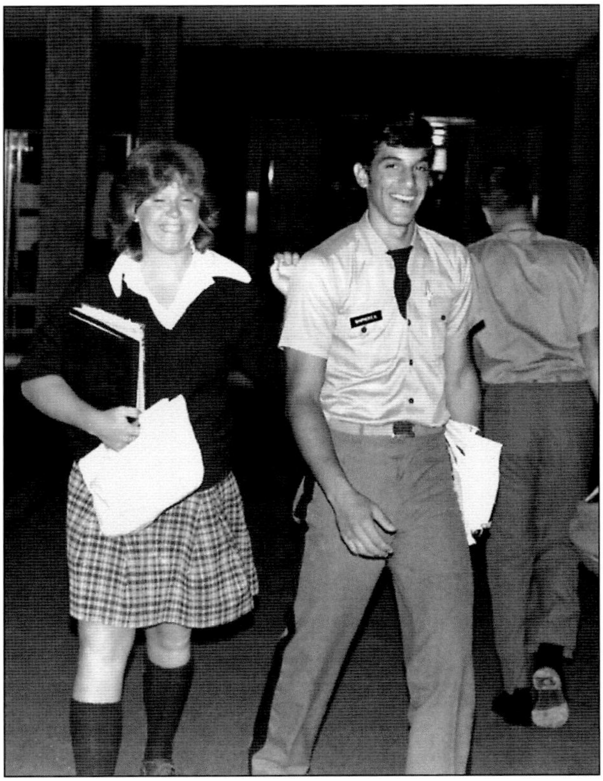

Mount Girls "Invade" Linsly, 1977. In January of 1977, there was a natural gas shortage due to extreme weather conditions. This resulted in the gas heating at Mount de Chantal being turned off. Linsly loaned its unused, electrically-heated areas to the Mount so they could conduct classes as usual.

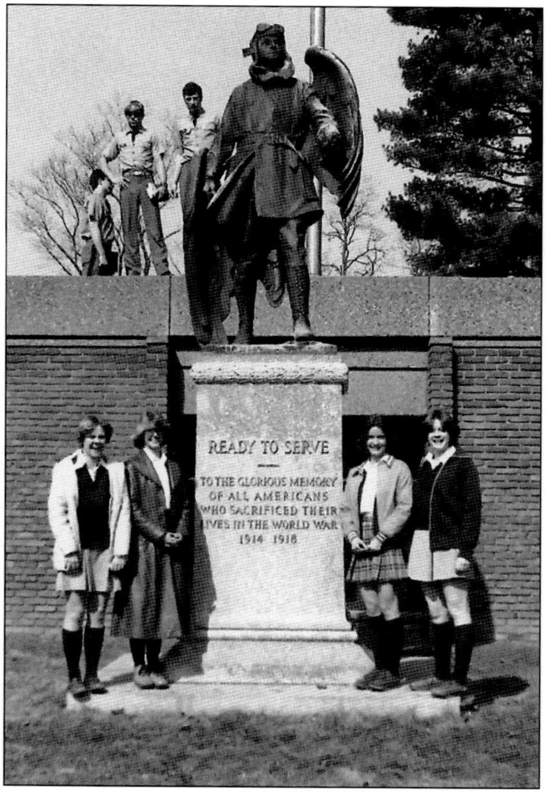

Mount Girls Visit *The Aviator*. For three weeks in January of 1977, Linsly became temporarily coeducational as the Mount girls and the cadets intermingled. Everything went smoothly. The cadets and the Mount girls enjoyed the unusual situation. Thus Linsly gained some insight into how well coeducation might work were it to be considered in the future.

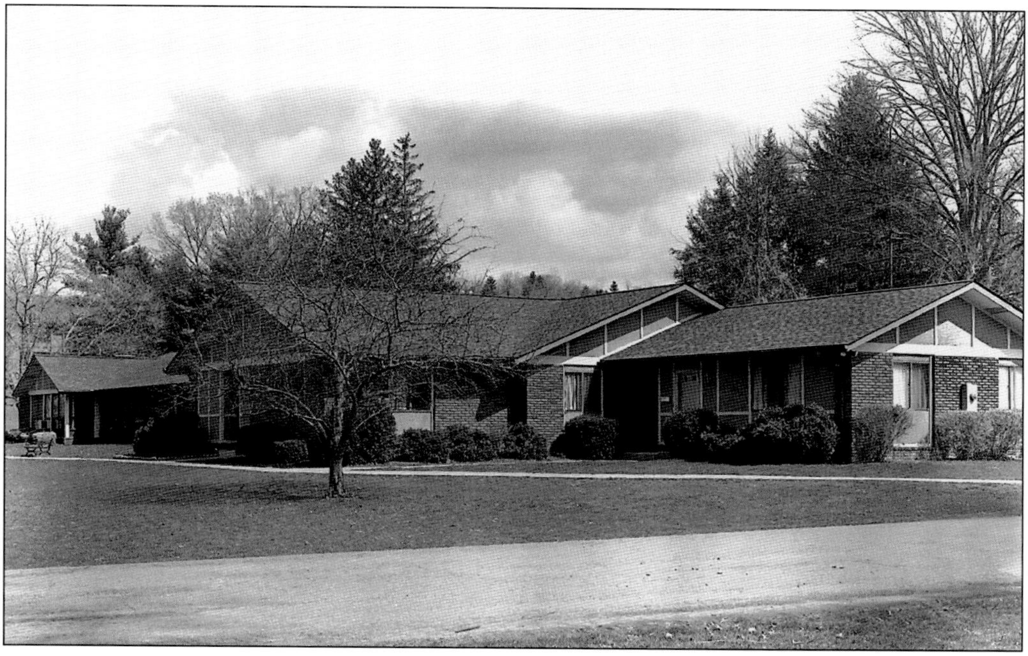

East Hall. More room was needed as the enrollment of boarding students increased so that a new dormitory was constructed in 1983. East Hall became the dormitory for older boys and Weiss Hall was used for younger boys.

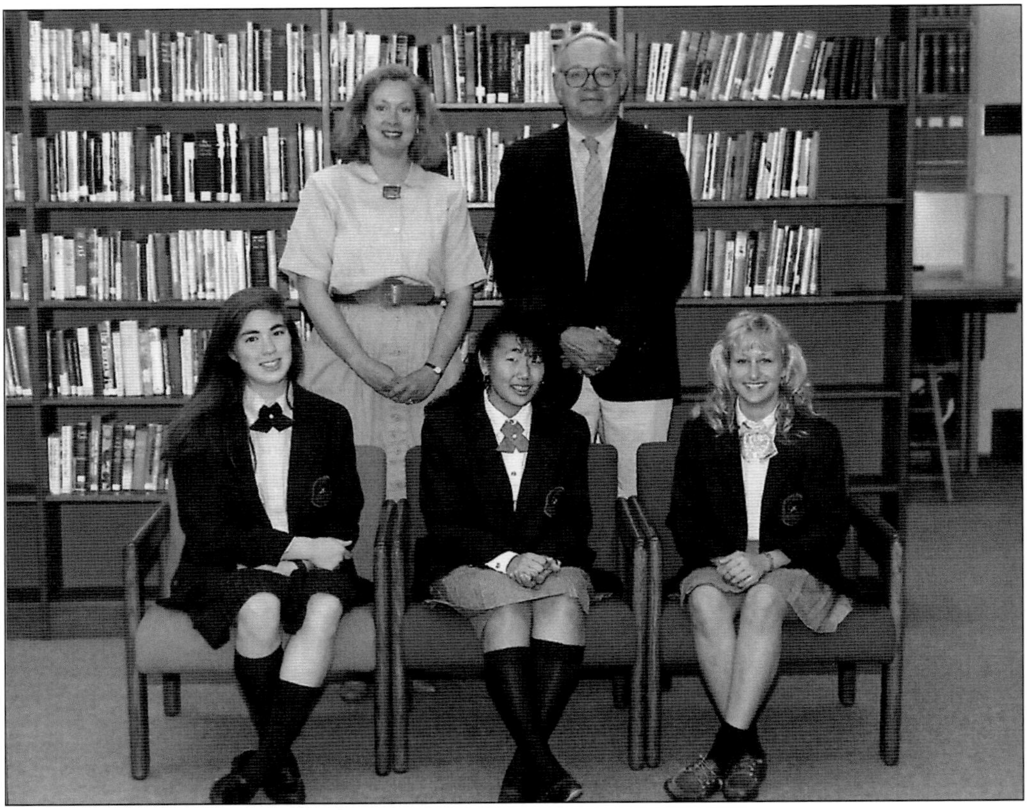

The First Three Girls to Enroll at Linsly, 1988. From left to right are (seated) Samantha Perrin, Jennifer Yoon, and Janice Shellhase; (standing) Cheryl Sprague, dean of women, and James Hawkins, admissions director. By the late 1980s, the growing role of women in the workforce, in politics, and in society in general was a factor in the decision of the board to make the school coeducational. Central to their decision was the conviction that Linsly's opportunities should be extended equally to men and women. In practical terms, it also meant a doubling of the available prospective student pool.

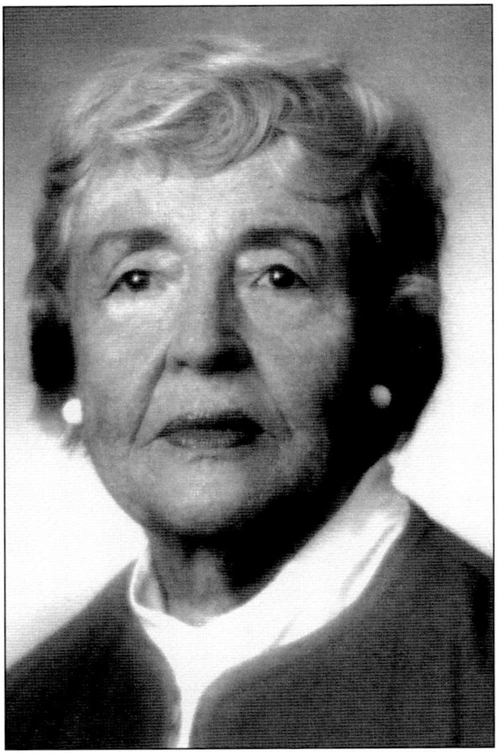

"Pinkie" Williams. Frances "Pinkie" Williams, wife of John R. Williams, who served as a trustee at Linsly for many years, was named to the board of trustees. She was the first woman to serve on the board in the history of the school. Williams said, "Coeducation will enrich student life at Linsly, and it will provide both boys and girls the opportunity of an excellent education."

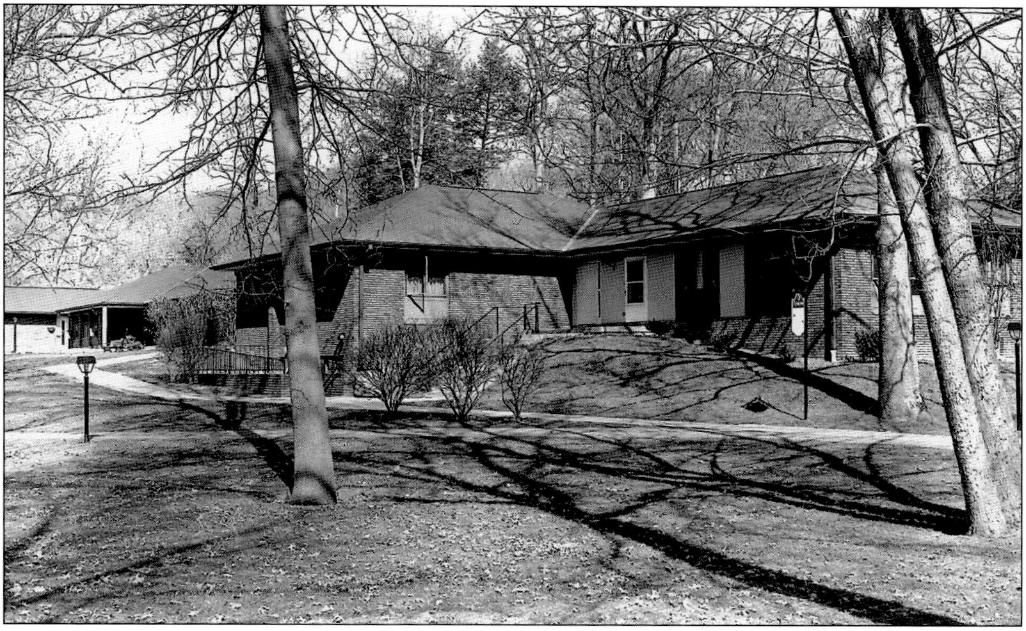

West Hall. In order to provide room for female boarding students, West Hall was constructed in 1988. Merriman Hall was then used for older girls while the younger girls were located in the new dormitory. President of the board, Donald H. Hofreuter, remarked, "A coeducational environment best prepares young people intellectually, socially, and psychologically for the world in which they live and the colleges they will attend."

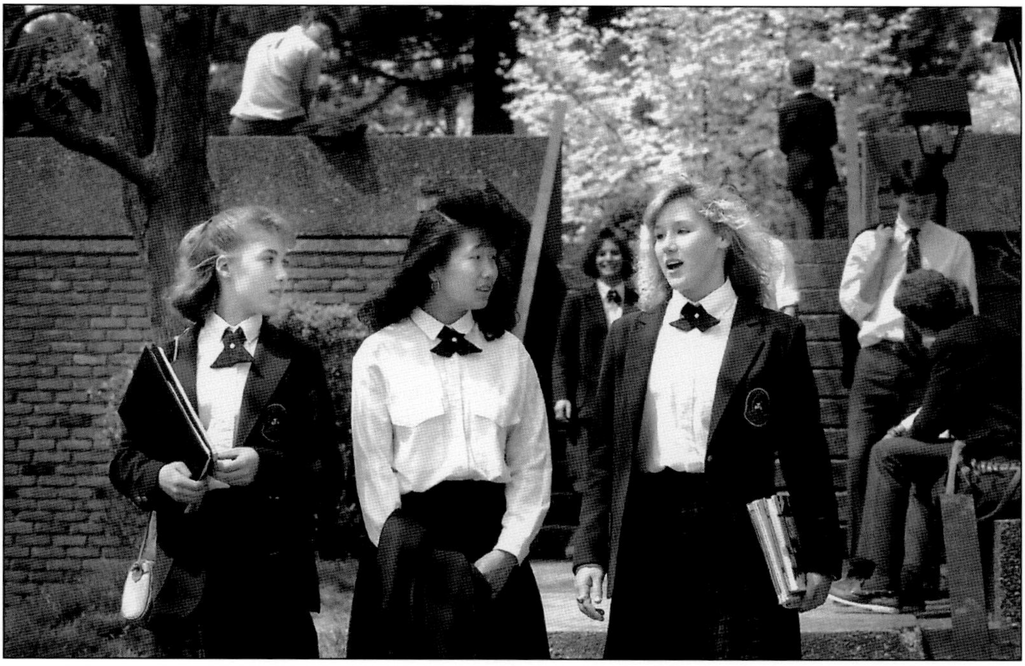

Coeds on Campus, 1989. Headmaster DiOrio said that the decision to become coeducational was reached after a lengthy study by a committee of alumni, parents, board members, and faculty. DiOrio said, "Boys and girls need to work together . . . . We are going to be a better school in the future because of this move."

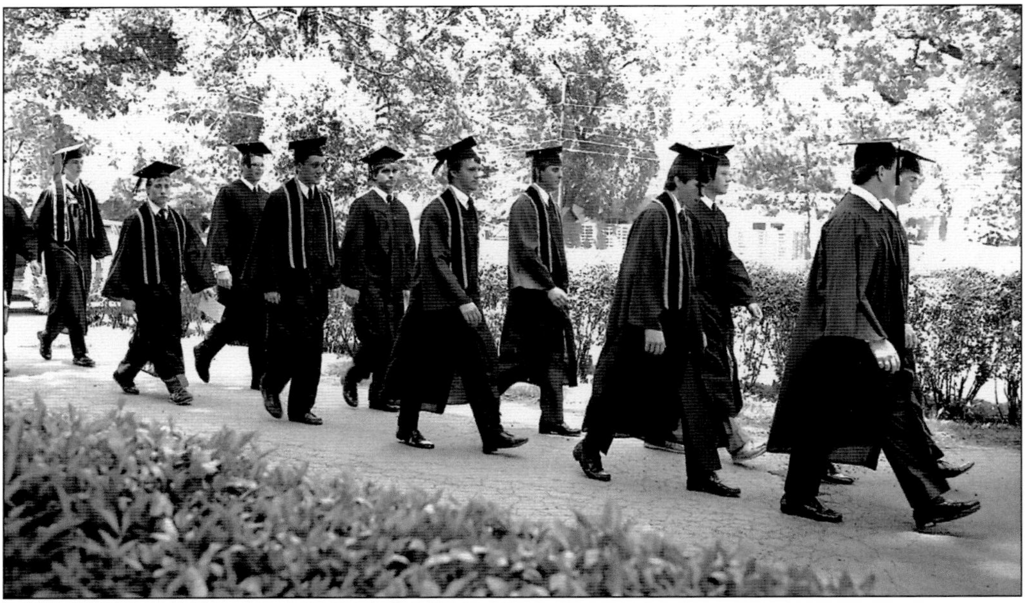

Last All-Male Graduation, 1989. Tim Finch, a Linsly student, said in reaction to girls enrolling at Linsly, "When I heard they were coming I thought we were going to have coed gym classes and I almost jumped out of my chair." While at the time this seemed like a radical move, historically Linsly was just returning to its roots since the school was a coeducational institution from its inception in 1814 until 1861.

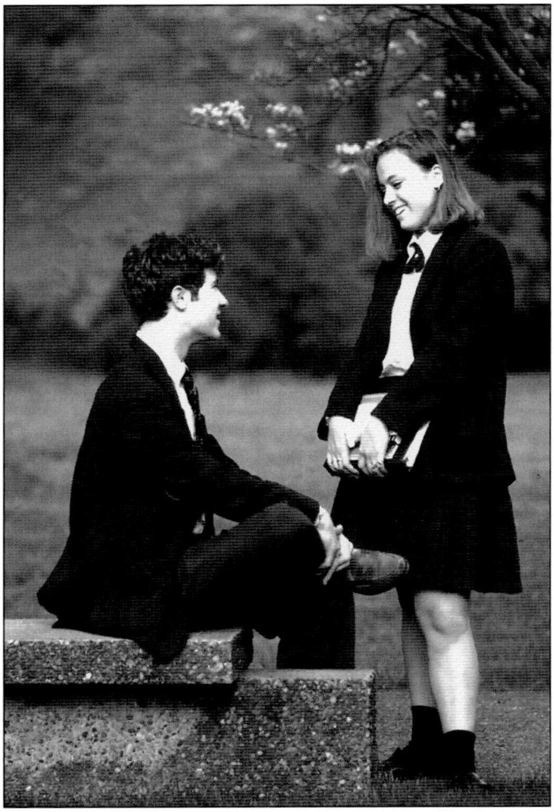

Students on Campus, 1992. One benefit from coeducation was that Linsly now had its own supply of young ladies who could be cheerleaders, flag girls, and homecoming queen candidates. Also, women's sports added a new dimension to Linsly's athletic program.

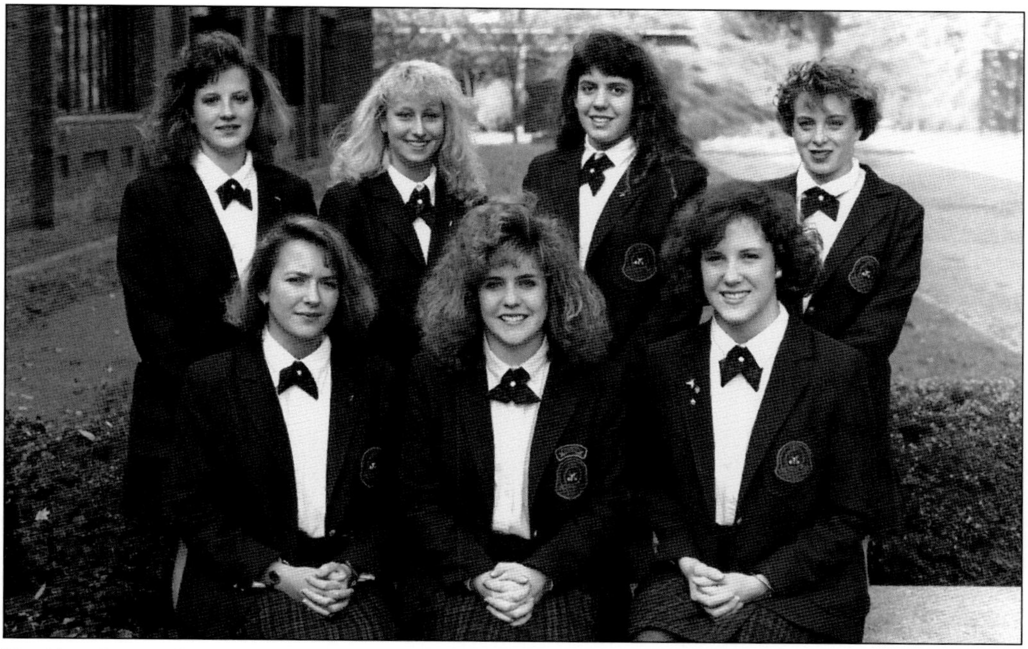

THE FIRST FEMALE STUDENTS TO GRADUATE IN 129 YEARS, 1990. From left to right are (front row) Wendy Lynn McAtee, Anyia Leigh Boroski, and Jessica Susan Clymer; (back row) Emily Spaulding Carter, Janice Kitson Shellhase, Tonya Hadjis, and Holly Kristin Keefer.

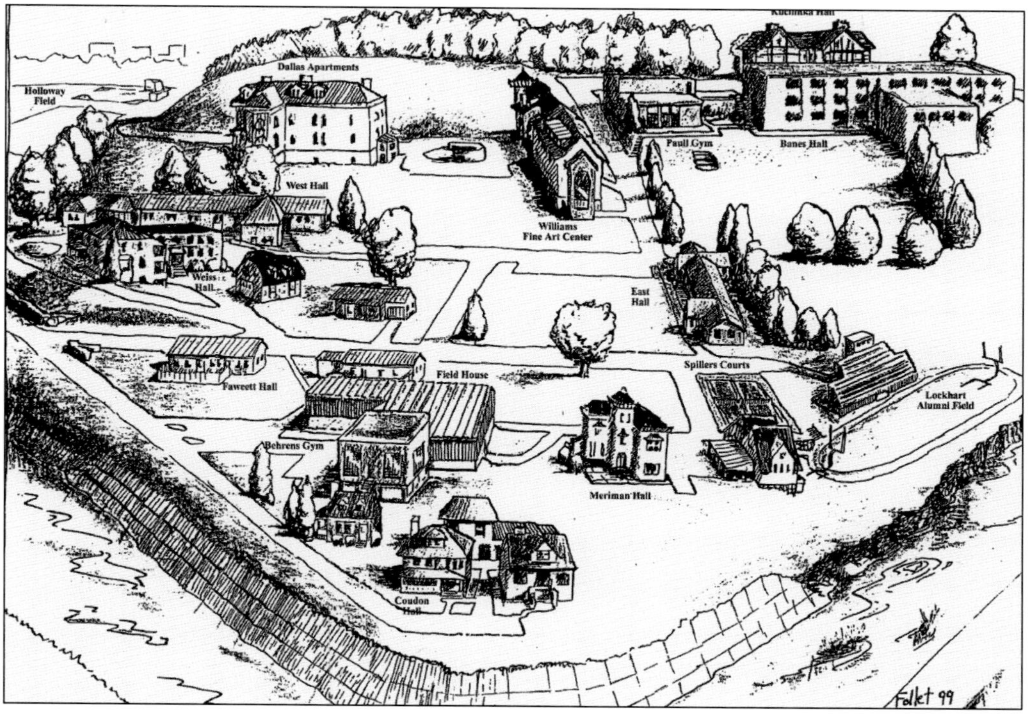

MAP OF THE CAMPUS BY ROBIN FOLLET, 1999. In 1992, a field house was constructed as an adjunct to Behrens Gymnasium that not only provided much-needed additional athletic facilities but also served as a location for graduation, honors ceremonies, Extravaganza practice, and an aerobics center. The field house can be seen in the foreground in front of the old gym.

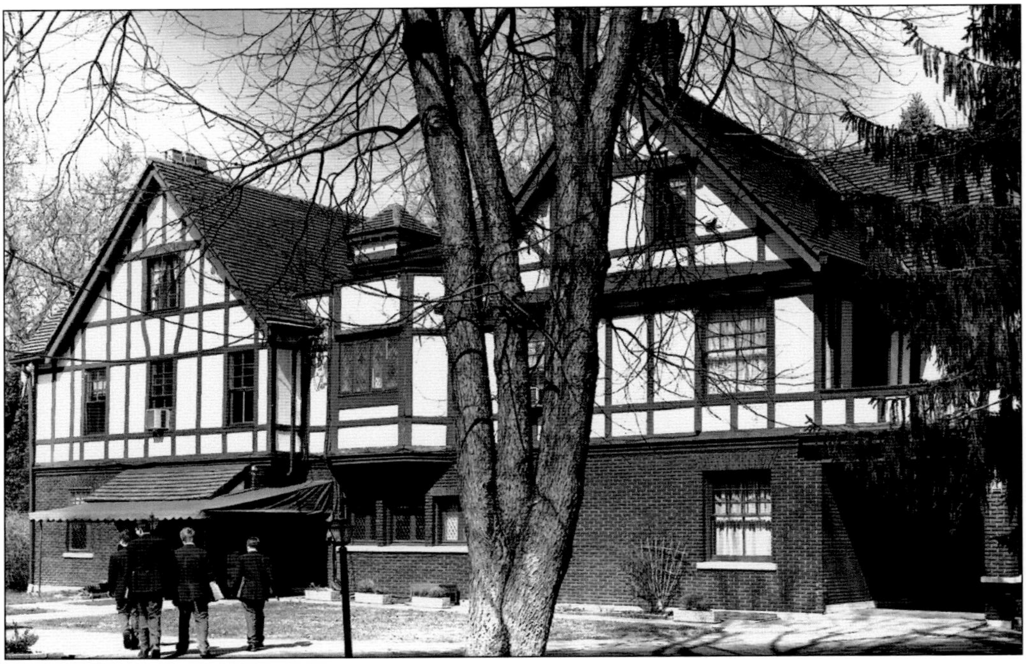

Kuchinka Hall. Hearnlee Place was acquired in 1992 and funds for a complete restoration were donated by Anna Kuchinka. The building provided administrative offices, classrooms, a board room, and an infirmary.

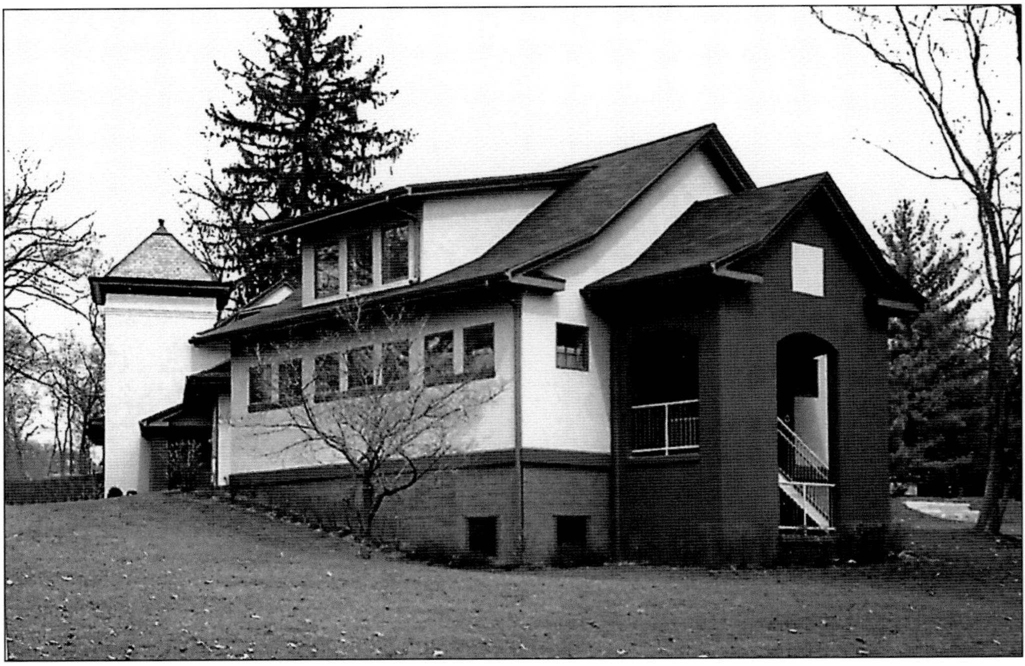

Williams Visual Arts Center. A generous donation by Pinkie Williams and a matching campaign resulted in the construction of the Williams Visual Arts Center in 1999. This building provided art studios, classrooms, and gallery areas. Some prominent local artists have donated works, which are displayed in this building. Specialized areas for ceramics and photography are included in the facility.

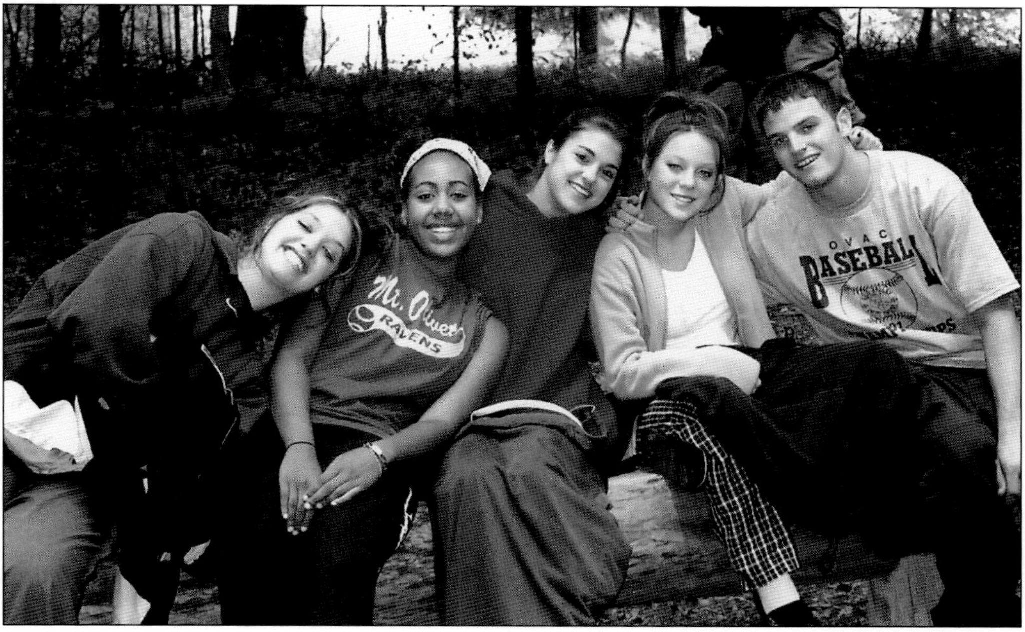

LINSLY STUDENTS AT THE LOC. The *Linsly Outdoor Center*, known as the LOC, was developed through a cooperative effort of The Linsly School and the Pennsylvania Department of Environmental Resources. In September 1987, Linsly acquired a long-term lease on 35 acres in Raccoon State Park in Pennsylvania, which also included some buildings. The concept, which was originated by Headmaster DiOrio, is based on what is known as experiential education—learning experiences that fall outside the classroom.

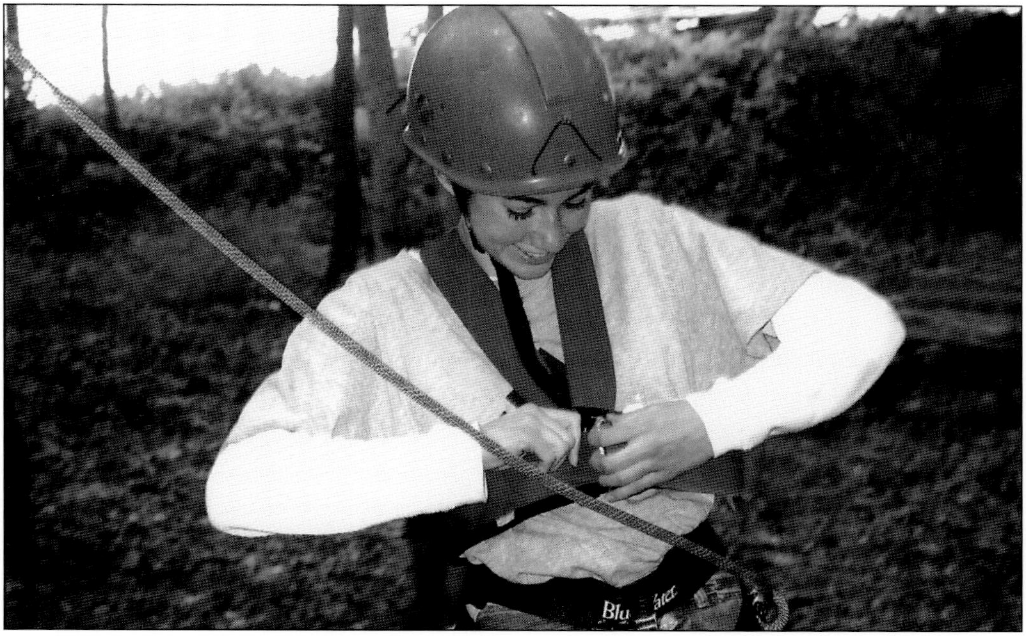

GETTING READY FOR A CHALLENGE. These experiences are aimed at building trust, responsibility, teamwork, and leadership through a variety of programs that provide adventure, environmental education, and unique outdoor experiences. Students are challenged to do what they might not think themselves capable of doing, thus building confidence.

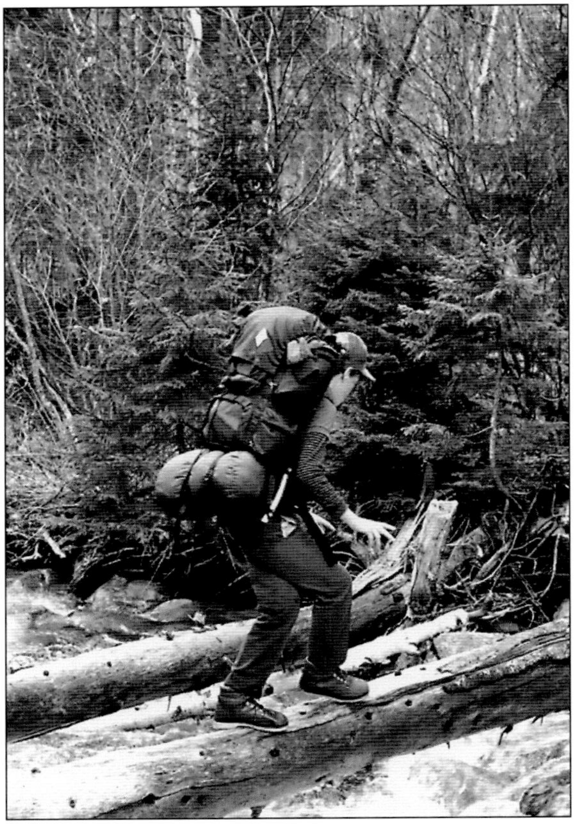

Backpacking. The qualities needed for a group to work together successfully are not talked about—they are experienced, felt, and visualized. Programs are targeted to specific groups and may include a variety of activities such as caving, canoeing, rock climbing, and backpacking.

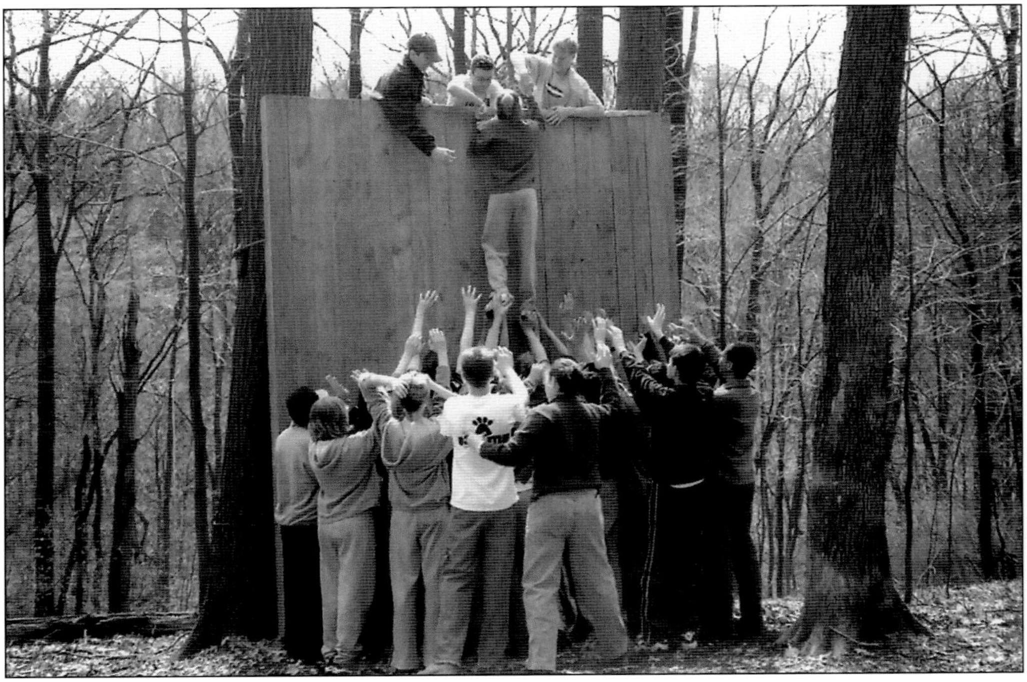

The Wall. Each program assumes that an individual has unique abilities and, as part of a group, these abilities form combinations of strengths, which are the basis for growth.

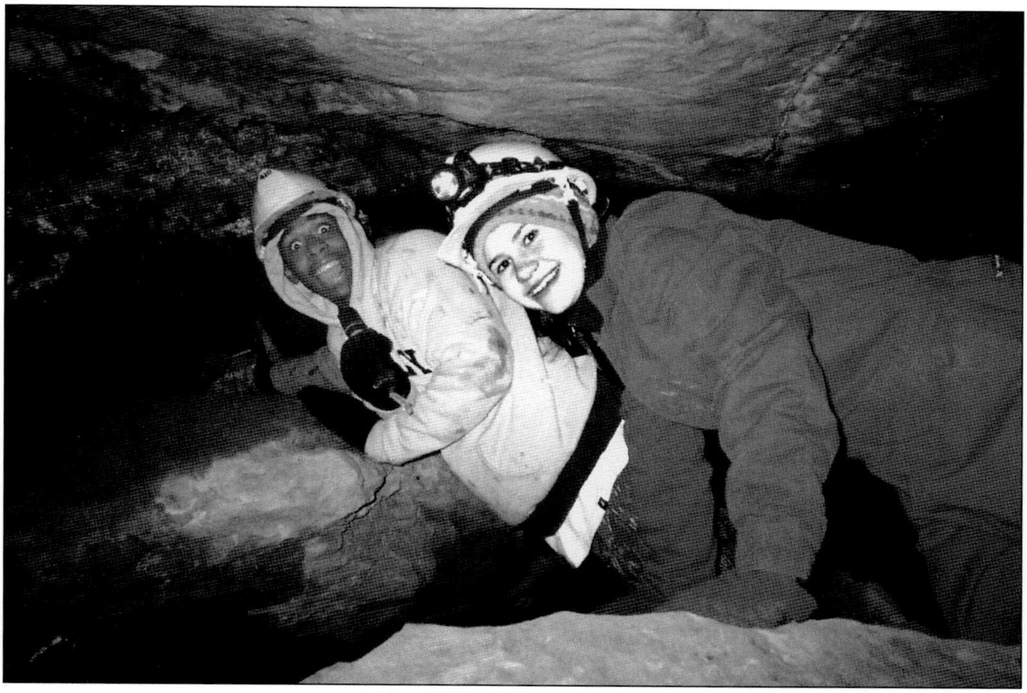

Caving. Using a method known in outdoor education circles as *Challenge by Choice*, individuals choose an activity in which they feel personally challenged.

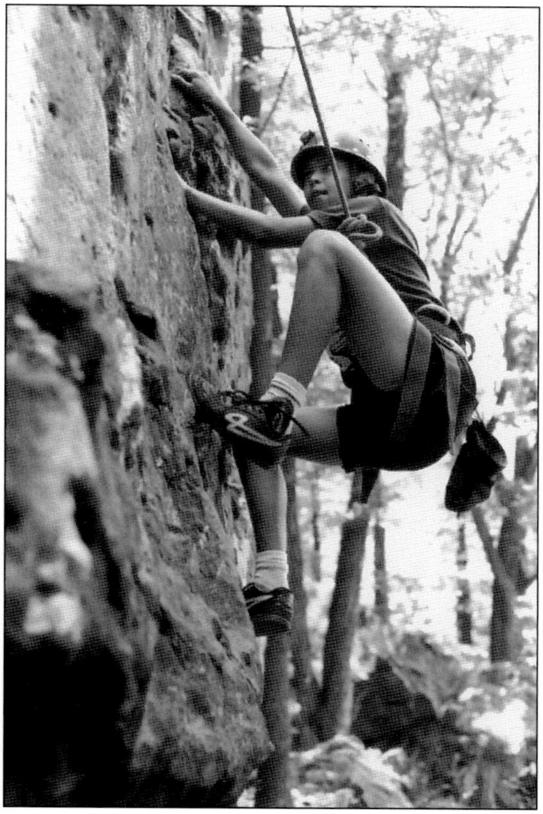

Rock Climbing. In utilizing the group's strength, students find that their own successes are more readily attainable. By conquering their own chosen challenges— doing something they believe themselves incapable of doing— individuals succeed on a personal level, while enabling the group to achieve its goals. *Challenge by Choice* is part of the philosophy of the LOC as is the previously mentioned "no quit" policy. Every class at Linsly spends a week each year at the LOC.

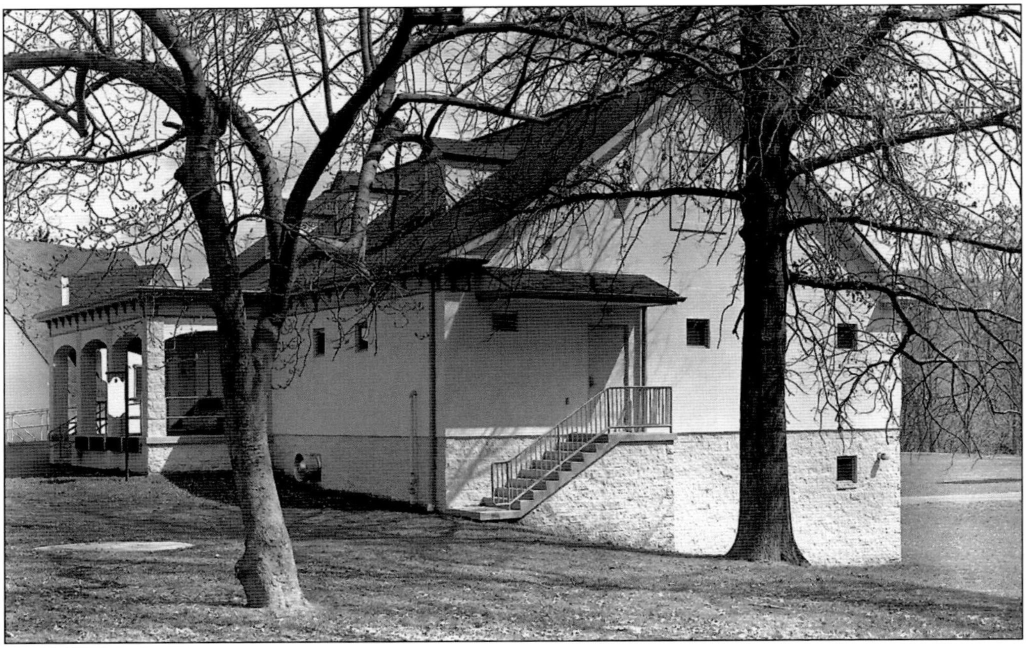

The Hess Center. Thanks to an endowment by Andrew Hess, a 60-by-40 foot, completely equipped wood shop was constructed in 2001, thus providing facilities for Linsly students interested in woodworking. This building, which is located near Lockhart Field, also contains locker rooms for visiting teams.

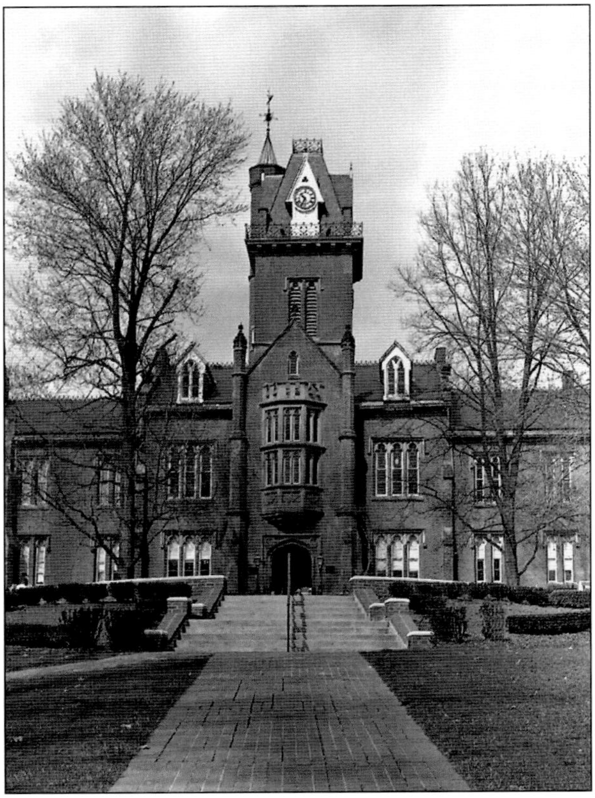

Bethany College's Old Main, a National Historic Landmark. A relatively new program, the *Linsly to Bethany Honors Summer Program*, was initiated in 2002.This educational opportunity bridges the gap between high school and college. It was originated by Chad Barnett, Linsly's assistant director of admissions. Two full weeks of study in film, literature, and music at Bethany College, under the guidance of award-winning professors and dedicated college preparatory school instructors, give Linsly sophomore, junior, and senior students the opportunity to experience college-level instruction. (Time spent at the LOC is also a part of this unique summer program.)

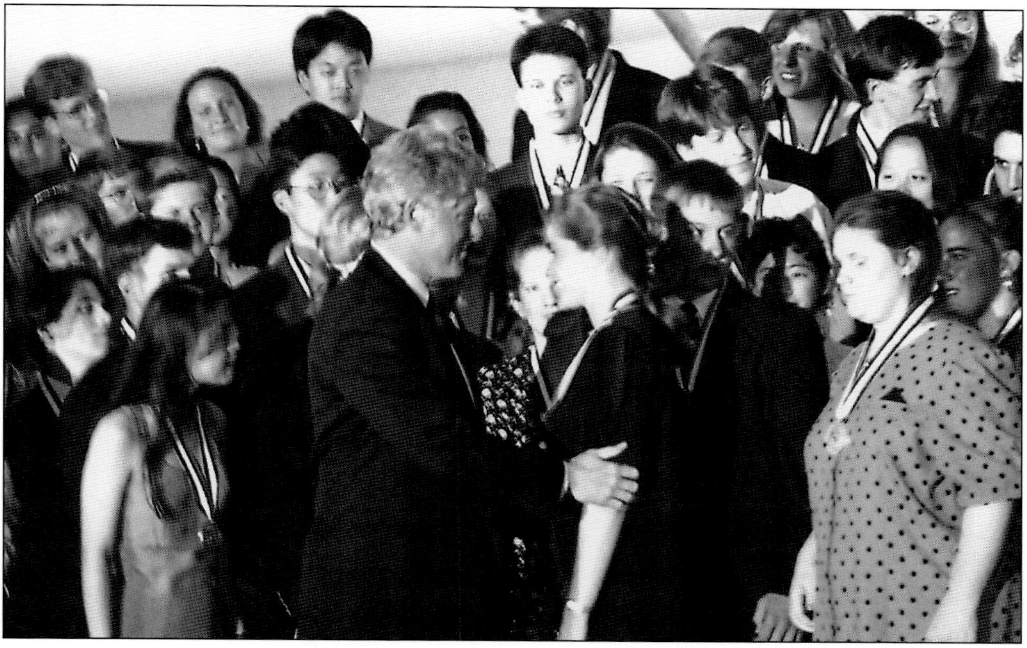

Kathryn Hamilton Bodkin, Presidential Scholar, 1993. Linsly's female students have brought many honors to the school since 1988. Perhaps one of the most impressive was the selection of three Linsly women as presidential scholars. This program is one of the highest honors bestowed on graduating high school seniors.

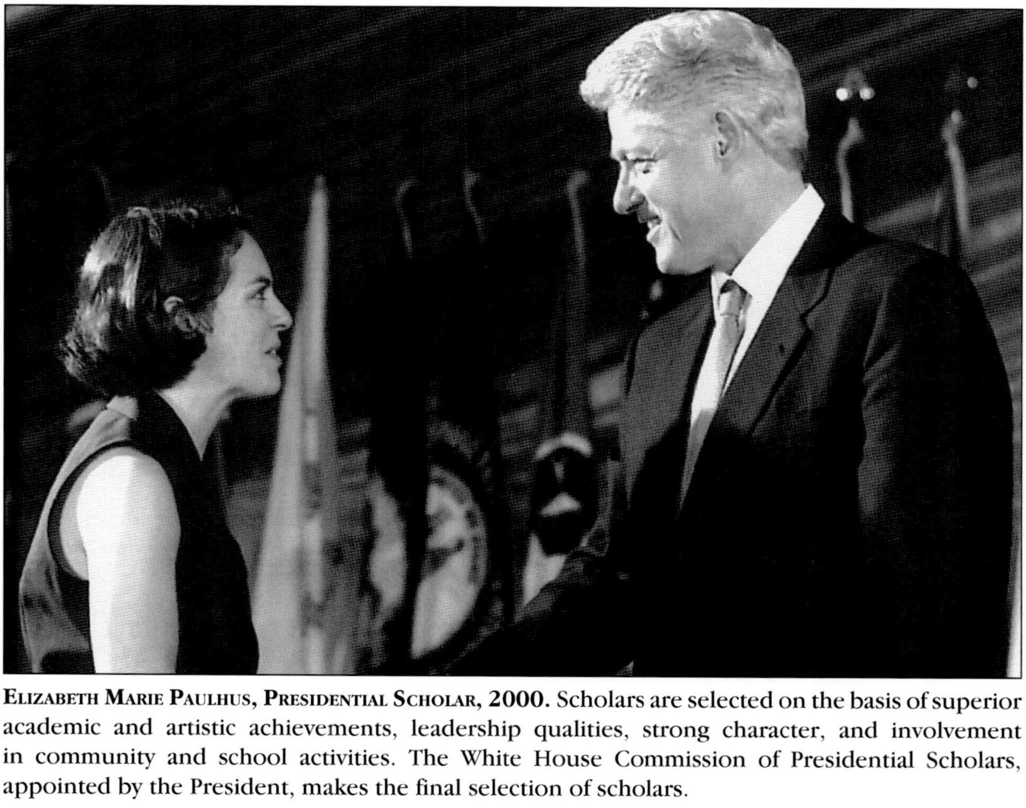

Elizabeth Marie Paulhus, Presidential Scholar, 2000. Scholars are selected on the basis of superior academic and artistic achievements, leadership qualities, strong character, and involvement in community and school activities. The White House Commission of Presidential Scholars, appointed by the President, makes the final selection of scholars.

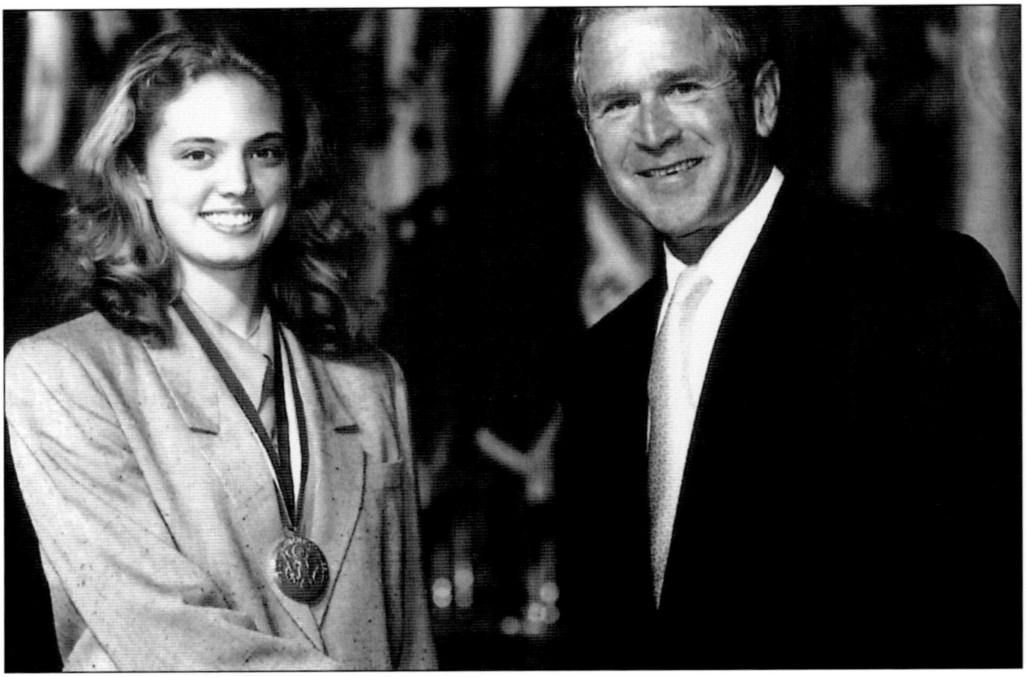

Ashley Michelle Hinnerman-Mulroy, Presidential Scholar, 2001. This commission selects one young man and one young woman from each state, the District of Columbia, Puerto Rico, and United States students living abroad. Scholars are invited to Washington, D.C. to receive the Presidential Medallion at a recognition ceremony.

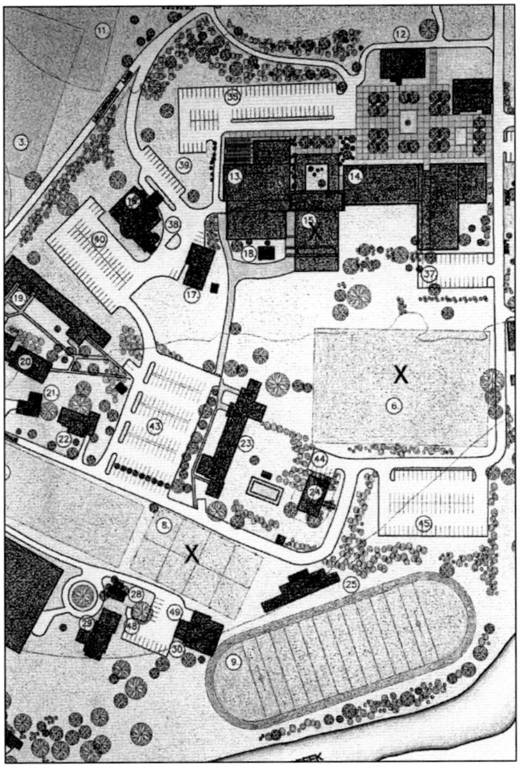

Vision 2020. The future for Linsly looks bright. Enrollment has never been higher and the school has plans for expansion of the campus. The "Xs" on this map show areas for future development and include additional classroom space, a soccer field and new tennis courts, as well as a number of smaller improvements. The school's many successes demonstrate that The Linsly School could serve as a model for secondary schools throughout the country.

Six

Athletics
A Brief History

While calisthenics were incorporated as part of the military program, which began in 1876, the first reference to any athletic competition can be found in a field day program printed in 1892. Individual competitions listed include such activities as broad jump, high jump, 100-yard dash, and shot put. The same year, the minutes of the board indicate that gymnastic equipment was purchased to be placed in the Armory. The earliest record of team sports is a reference to a football team in 1898. This may have been the first secondary school football team in the Ohio Valley, but the team did play Wheeling High School that year three times. Linsly forfeited the first game of the season (because they did not show up), but they defeated Wheeling 5-0 in the second game. The last game was played on Thanksgiving Day and was won by Wheeling High. Linsly's 1899 football team achieved a record of 5-1-1 and held their opponents scoreless for each win. On the basis of this record they claimed the city championship. Most local schools did not sponsor teams until the turn of the century, so Linsly looked to Washington and Jefferson College and Bethany College for competition. By then, Linsly had baseball and basketball teams in addition to a football squad. Many of the same students played on all three teams.

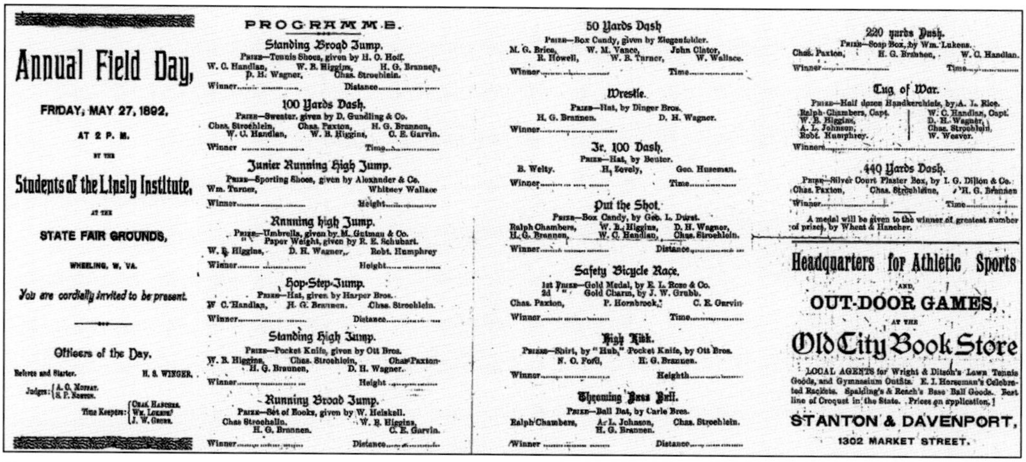
Annual Field Day,
FRIDAY, MAY 27, 1892,
AT 2 P. M.
BY THE
Students of the Linsly Institute,
AT THE
STATE FAIR GROUNDS,
WHEELING, W. VA.
You are cordially invited to be present.

Officers of the Day.
Referee and Starter. H. S. WINGER.
Time Keepers: Chas. Hancher, Wm. Lukens, J. W. Grubb.

PROGRAMME.

Standing Broad Jump.
Prize—Tennis Shoes, given by H. O. Hoff.
W. C. Handlan, W. B. Higgins, H. G. Brannen, D. H. Wagner, Chas. Stroehlein.
Winner........ Distance........

100 Yards Dash.
Prize—Sweater, given by D. Gundling & Co.
Chas. Stroehlein, Chas. Paxton, H. G. Brannen, W. C. Handlan, W. B. Higgins, C. E. Garvin.
Winner........ Time........

Junior Running High Jump.
Prize—Sporting Shoes, given by Alexander & Co.
Wm. Turner, Whitney Wallace
Winner........ Height........

Running High Jump.
Prize—Umbrella, given by M. Gutman & Co.
" Paper Weight, given by R. E. Schubart.
W. B. Higgins, D. H. Wagner, Robt. Humphrey
Winner........ Height........

Hop-Step-Jump.
Prize—Hat, given by Harper Bros.
W. C. Handlan, H. G. Brannen. Chas. Stroehlein.
Winner........ Distance........

Standing High Jump.
Prize—Pocket Knife, given by Ott Bros.
W. B. Higgins, Chas. Stroehlein, Chas. Paxton, H. G. Brannen, D. H. Wagner.
Winner........ Height........

Running Broad Jump.
Prize—Set of Books, given by W. Heiskell.
Chas Stroehlein, W. B. Higgins, H. G. Brannen. C. E. Garvin.
Winner........ Distance........

50 Yards Dash
Prize—Box Candy, given by Ziegenfelder.
M. G. Brice, W. M. Vance, John Clator, R. Howell, W. B. Turner, W. Wallace.
Winner........ Time........

Wrestle.
Prize—Hat, by Dinger Bros.
H. G. Brannen. D. H. Wagner.
Winner........

Jr. 100 Dash.
Prize—Hat, by Beuter.
B. Welty. H. Eovely, Geo. Huseman.
Winner........ Time........

Put the Shot.
Prize—Box Candy, by Geo. L. Durst.
Ralph Chambers, W. B. Higgins, D. H. Wagner, H. G. Brannen, W. C. Handlan, Chas. Stroehlein.
Winner........ Distance........

Safety Bicycle Race.
1st Prize—Gold Medal, by E. L. Rose & Co.
2d " Gold Charm, by J. W. Grubb.
Chas. Paxton, P. Hornbrook, C. E. Garvin
Winner........ Time........

High Kick.
Prize—Shirt, by "Hub," Pocket Knife, by Ott Bros.
N. O. Ford, H. G. Brannen.
Winner........ Heighth........

Throwing Base Ball.
Prize—Ball Bat, by Carle Bros.
Ralph Chambers, A. L. Johnson, Chas. Stroehlein. H. G. Brannen.
Winner........ Distance........

220 Yards Dash.
Prize—Soap Box, by Wm. Lukens.
Chas. Paxton, H. G. Brannen, W. C. Handlan.
Winner........ Time........

Tug of War.
Prize—Half dozen Handkerchiefs, by A. L. Rice.
Ralph Chambers, Capt. W. B. Higgins, A. L. Johnson, Robt. Humphrey.
W. C. Handlan, Capt. D. H. Wagner, Chas. Stroehlein, W. Weaver.
Winners........

440 Yards Dash.
Prize—Silver Court Plaster Box, by I. G. Dillon & Co.
Chas. Paxton, Chas. Stroehleine, H. G. Brannen
Winner........ Time........

A medal will be given to the winner of greatest number of prizes, by Wheat & Hancher.

Headquarters for Athletic Sports
AND
OUT-DOOR GAMES,
AT THE
Old City Book Store
LOCAL AGENTS for Wright & Ditson's Lawn Tennis Goods, and Gymnasium Outfits. E. I. Horseman's Celebrated Rackets. Spalding's & Reach's Base Ball Goods. Best line of Croquet in the State. Prices on application.
STANTON & DAVENPORT,
1302 MARKET STREET.

Field Day Program, 1892. In 1913, the Wheeling High football team ended the season with a 11-0-1 record and claimed the state championship. They beat Linsly that year 52-0 and their coach was Guy Holden who, at the time, was the headmaster at Linsly. While this seems unusual by today's standards, at that time team sports were not as organized as they are today and the rules were very loose.

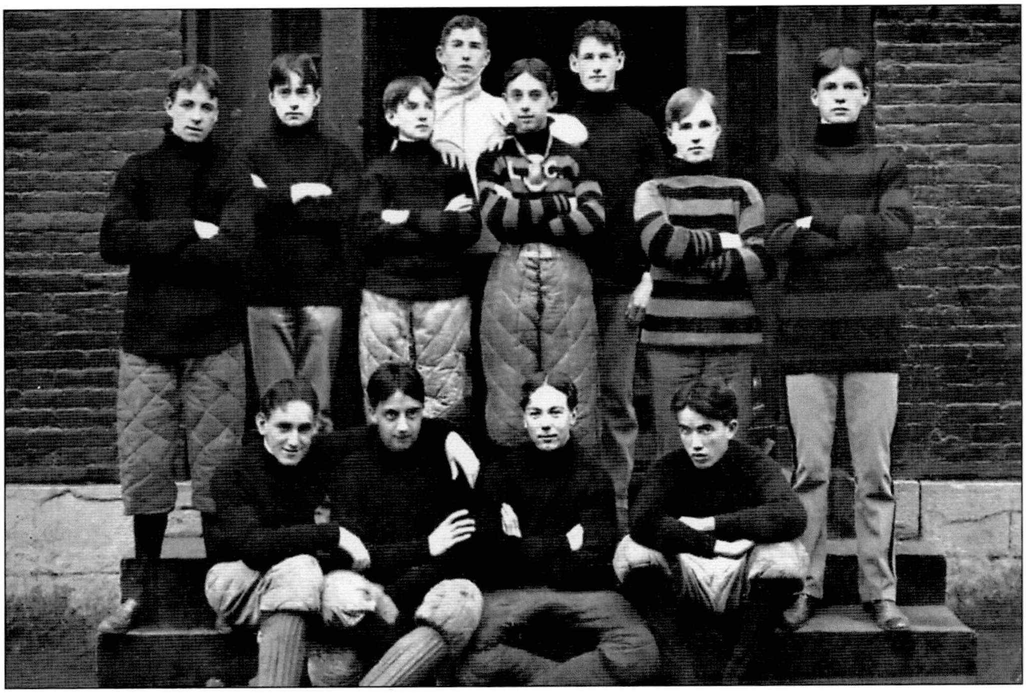

Football Team, 1899. In 1916, Linsly's football team played Franklin College and won by a score of 105-0; in the same year they beat Morris Harvey College 13-7. Also in 1916, 11 schools (including Linsly) became charter members of the State High School Athletic Association. Prior to that time high school sports had few rules and regulations. In 1918, Linsly's football squad managed an impressive 9-1 season record.

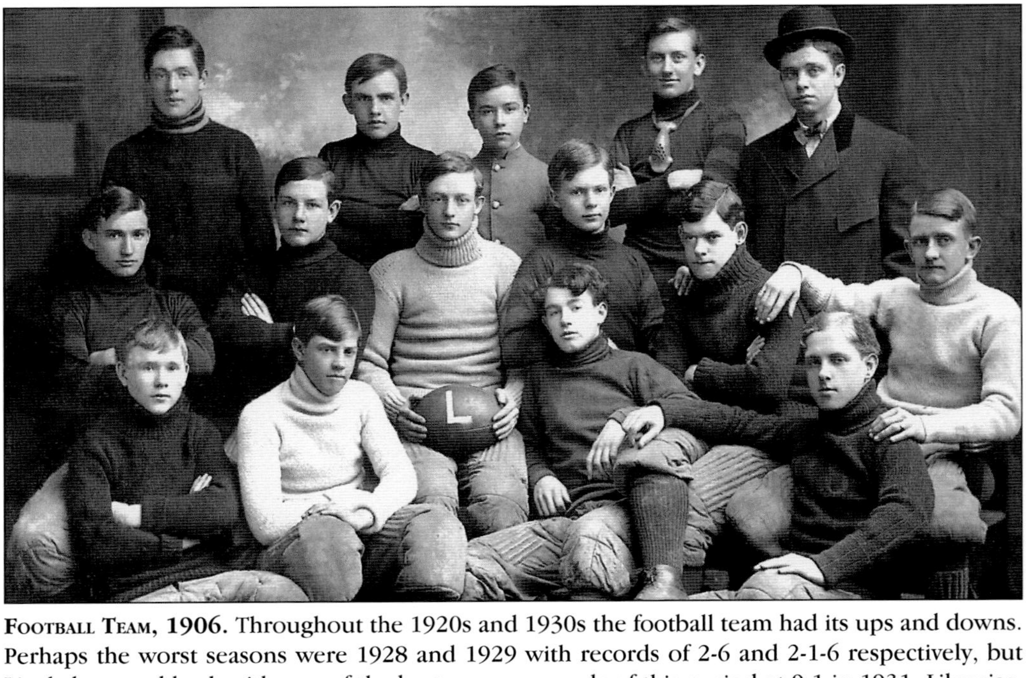

Football Team, 1906. Throughout the 1920s and 1930s the football team had its ups and downs. Perhaps the worst seasons were 1928 and 1929 with records of 2-6 and 2-1-6 respectively, but Linsly bounced back with one of the best season records of this period at 9-1 in 1931. Likewise, Linsly's basketball team had good and bad seasons during the 1920s and 1930s.

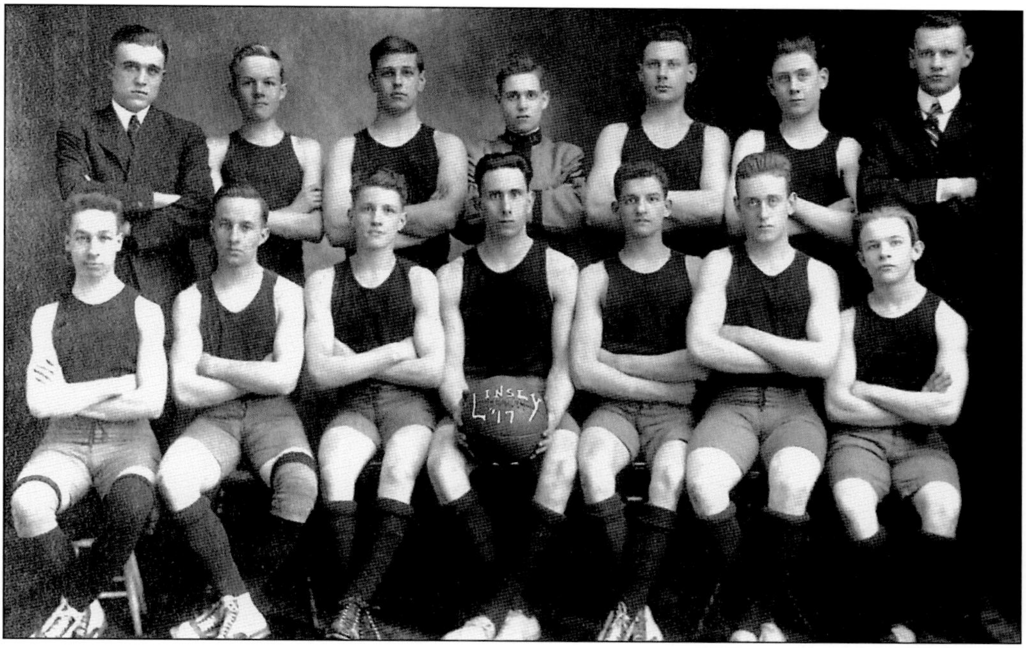

Basketball Team, 1917. Records are sparse, but it is known that the 1918 team went 12-3 for the season, and the 1926 squad had an unbeaten season with a record of 17-0. From 1917 to 1930, Amos Alonzo Stagg of the University of Chicago promoted a National High School Basketball Tournament (NHSB).

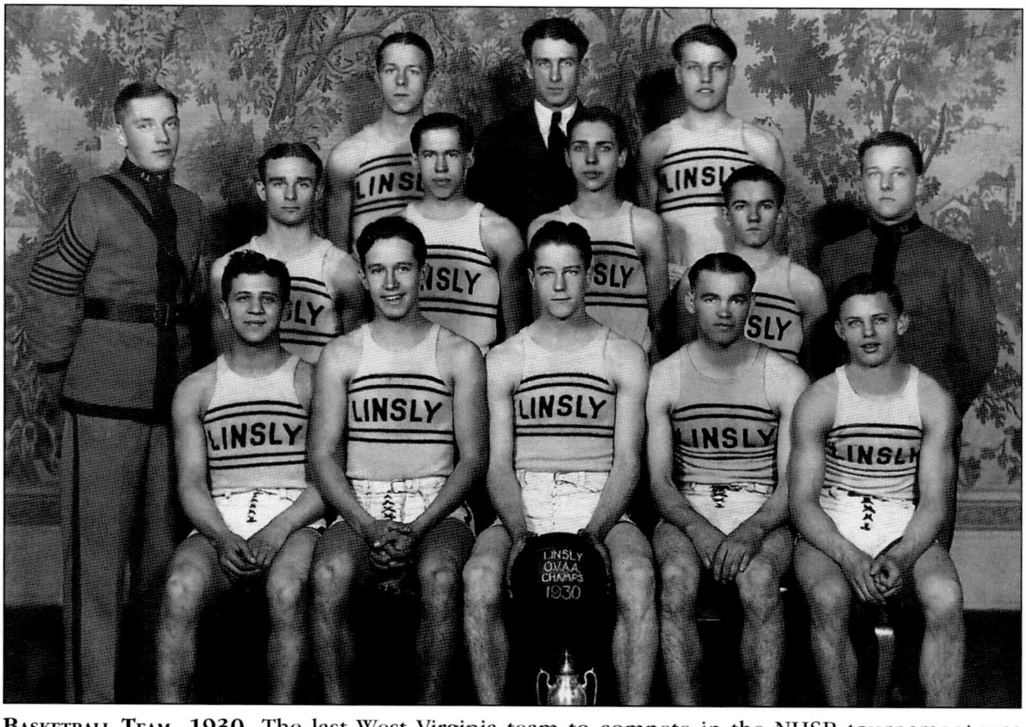

Basketball Team, 1930. The last West Virginia team to compete in the NHSB tournament was Linsly's 1930 squad, which had an unbeaten season of 17-0. The Linsly team won the first two games but lost in the third. The boys' basketball team won the Class A Championship in 2001.

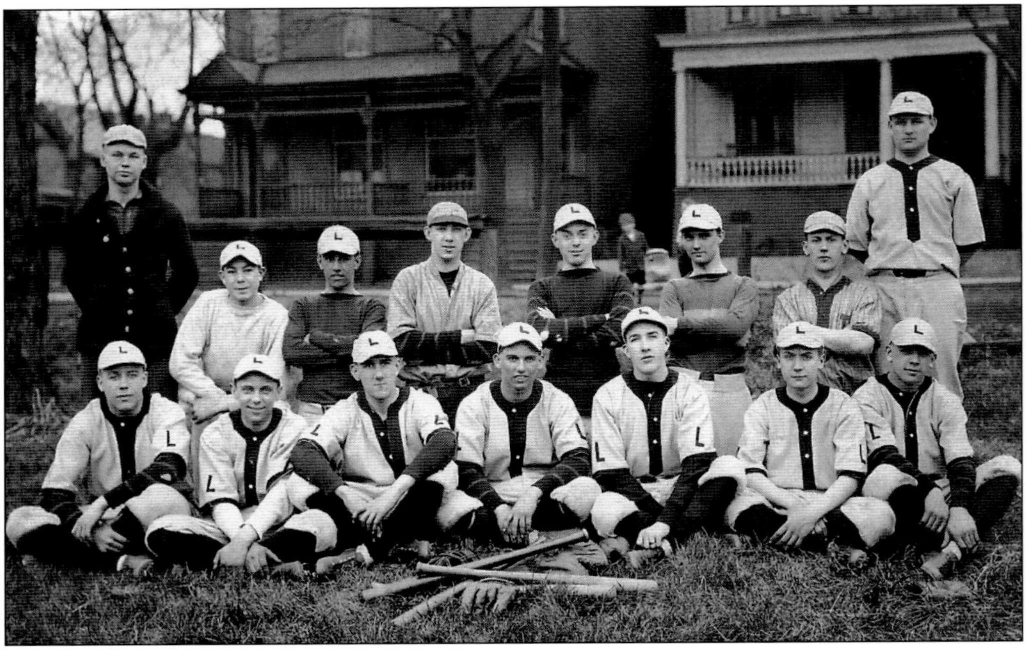

BASEBALL TEAM, *C.* 1925. By 1943, a demand had risen for a conference that would help stimulate and promote a competitive program of high school athletics in the Ohio Valley. There was also a need to formalize and standardize rules and procedures. The Ohio Valley Athletic Conference (OVAC) was organized in 1943 by F.W. Bowen, J.E. Ewing, M.S. Hattala, B.G. Lockhart, J.V. Nelson, C. Petty, and C.F. Walker with C.S. Wiseman as the first president.

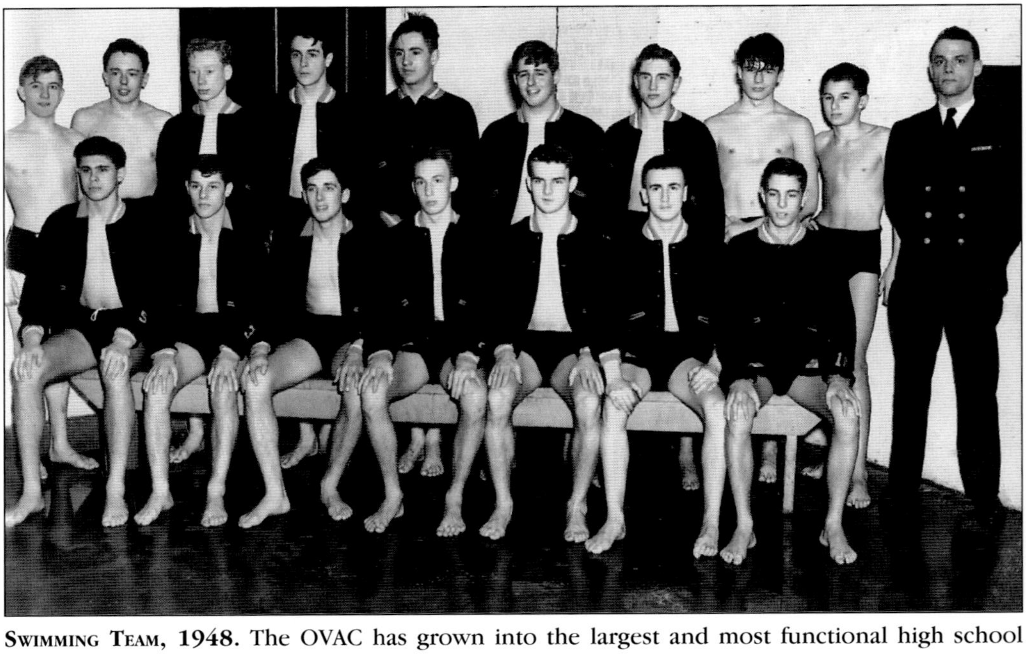

SWIMMING TEAM, 1948. The OVAC has grown into the largest and most functional high school conference of its kind in the United States. Perhaps Linsly's most notable sports team achievement was winning 36 consecutive OVAC swimming championships. This winning streak began in 1948 and ended in 1983 when the conference stopped the competition because there were too few teams. The competition was resumed later.

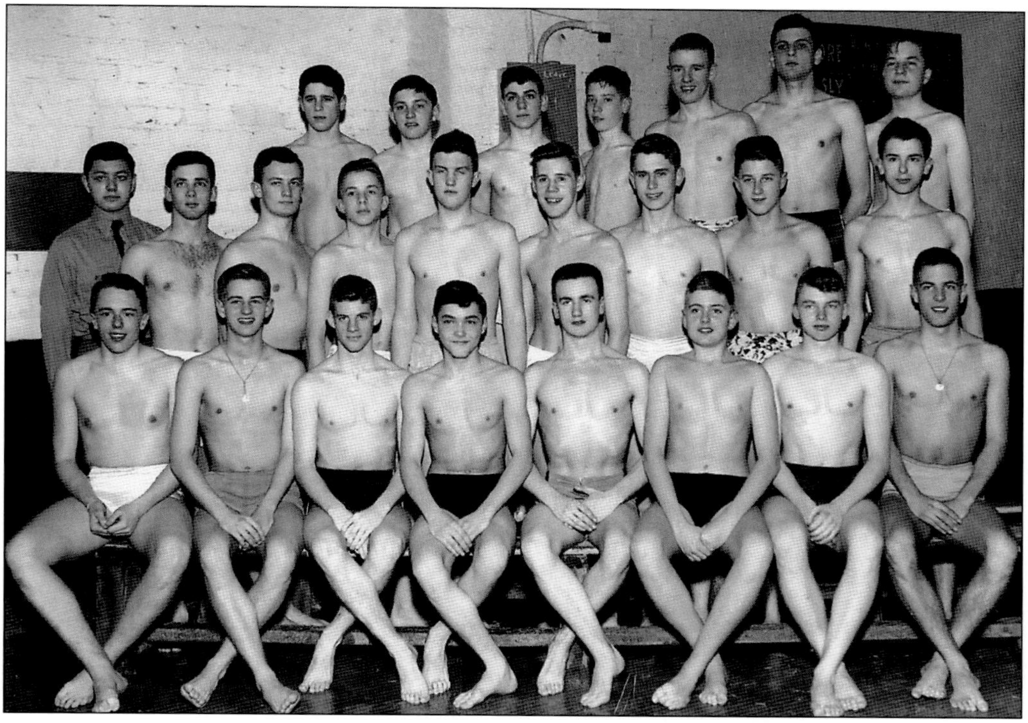

Swimming Team, 1950. In the 1990s, an Ohio Valley Swim League was formed and Linsly's boys' team won the championship in 1990, 1992, and 1993. The girls' swim team won the championship in this league in 1993 and 1994. In 1998, Linsly was invited to the West Virginia State High School Invitational Swimming Championship where they captured first place for the boys' and girls' teams, and first place for the combined team. Also in 1998, Linsly won the OVAC overall team title and in 2002, the OVAC small schools title.

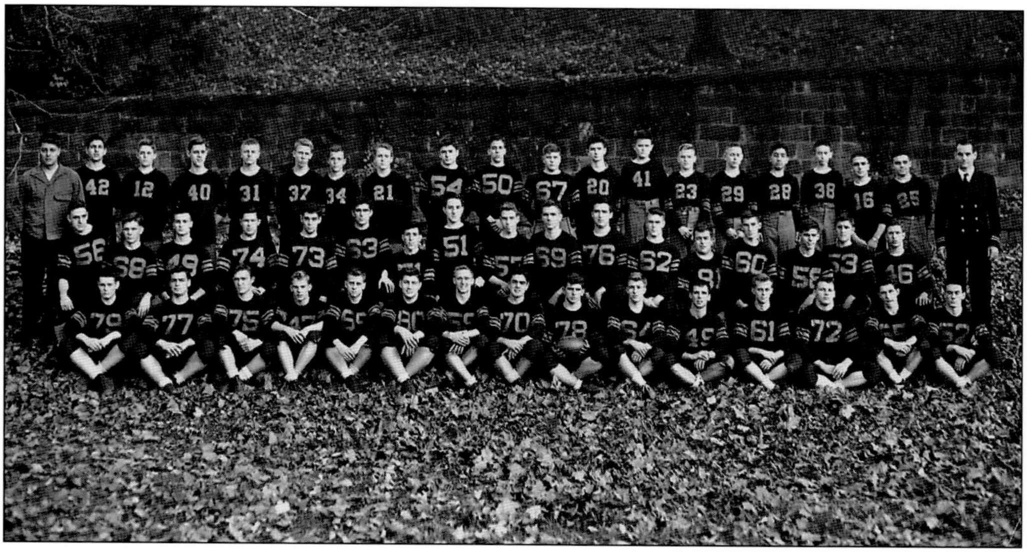

Football Team, 1949. Linsly's football team took its share of OVAC titles as well, winning the championship in 1949, 1951, 1952, 1987, 1989, and 1996. Linsly's first undefeated football team was the 1986 squad, which had a 10-0 record. The 1987 (9-0) and 1996 (10-0) teams were also undefeated.

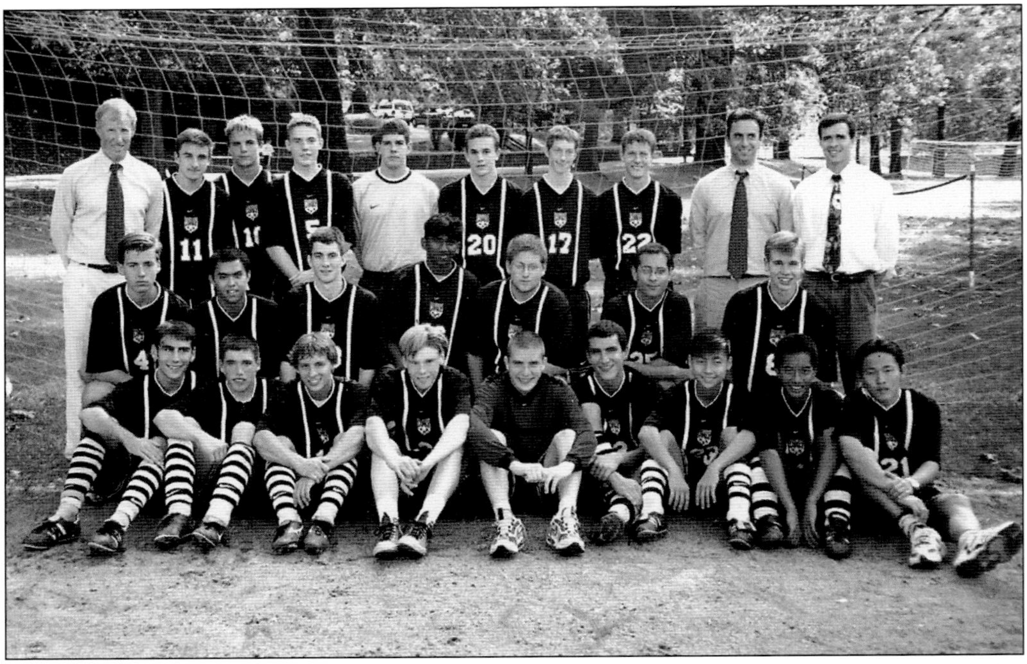

Soccer Team, 1986, Interstate Prep School League (IPSL) Champs. Linsly's soccer team is the second oldest in the state. This sport began in 1975 at Linsly and initially the team played Pittsburgh area schools because there were no local soccer teams. Since then, more Ohio Valley schools have added soccer teams so that the OVAC now includes soccer in its program.

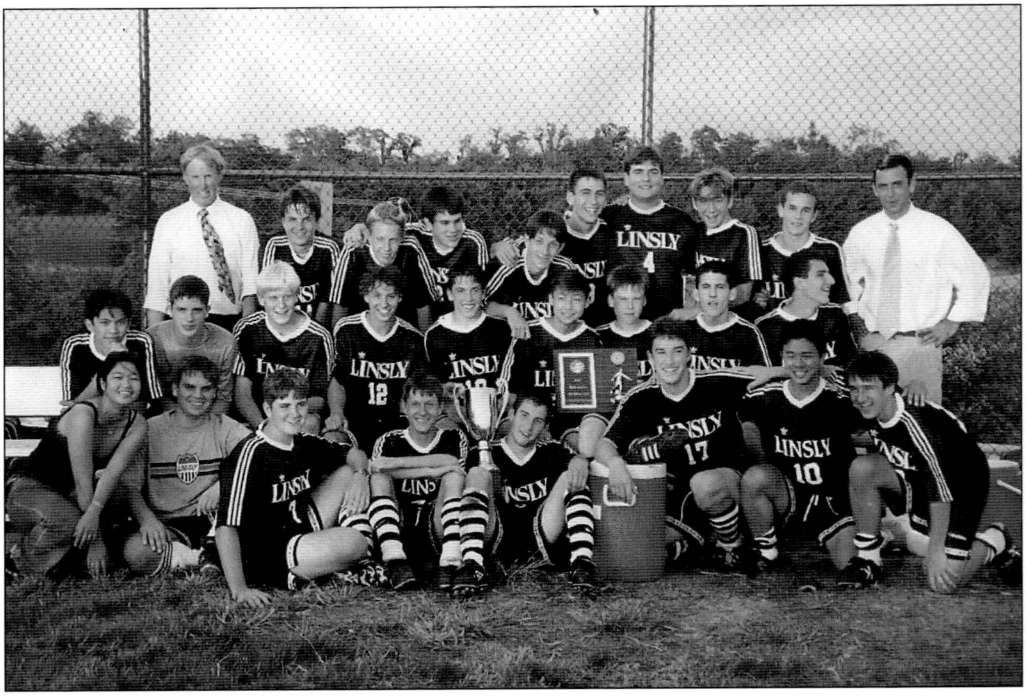

Memorial Cup Champions, 1997. Linsly's soccer team won the OVAC Division I championship in 1991, 1992, 1994, 1998, 2000, 2001, and 2002. These teams also played in the IPSL Championships in 2001 and 2002 and won.

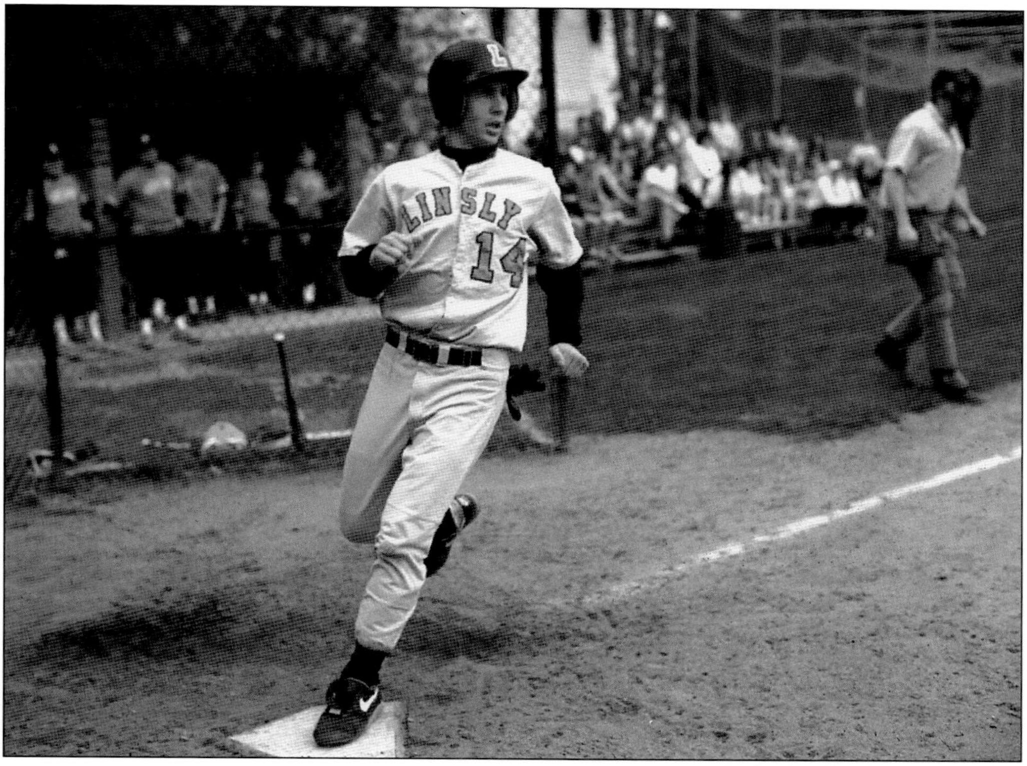

LINSLY SCORES! 1992. In baseball, Linsly has racked up an impressive record by winning the OVAC championship in 1982, 1985, 1986, 1987, 1989, 1991, 1994, 1995, 1997, 2000, and 2001. Linsly had baseball teams from the early 1900s onward but few records of the early years are available.

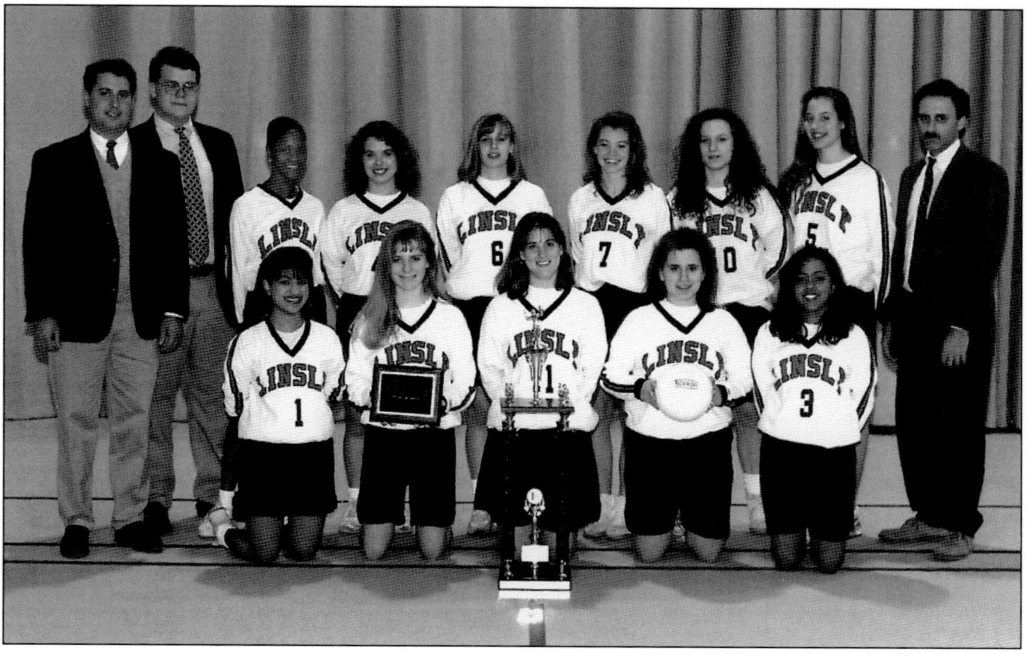

VOLLEYBALL TEAM, 1992. Likewise the volleyball team won the OVAC season championship in 1991, 1992, 1994, and 1997, as well as the tournament championship in 1992.

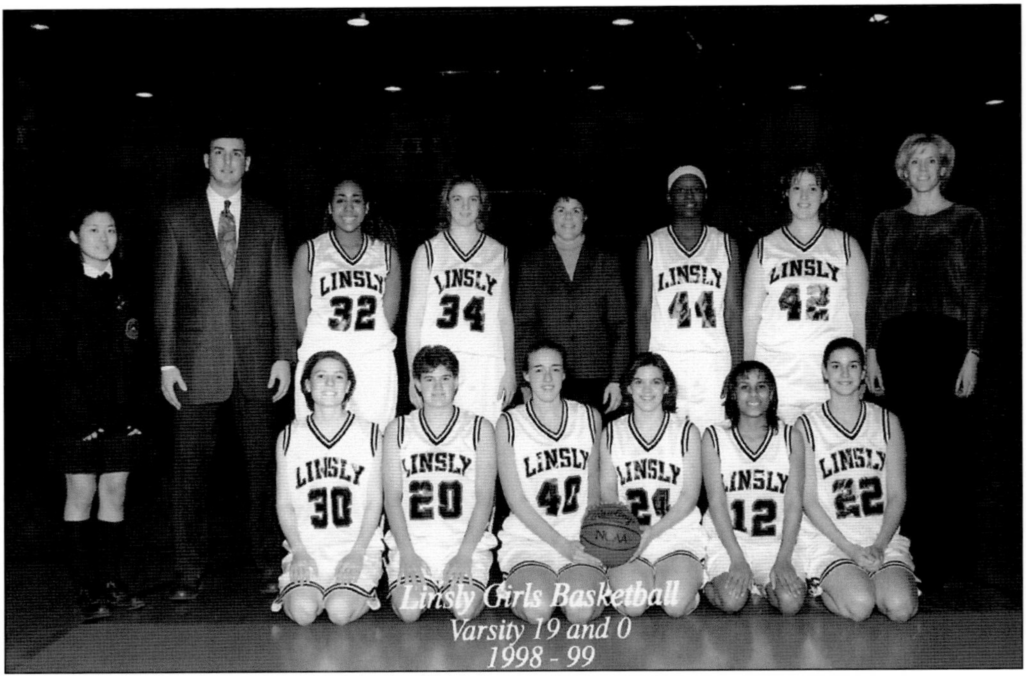

GIRLS' BASKETBALL TEAM (19-0), 1998. In basketball, the OVAC championship title went to the boys' team in 1971 and 1998, and to the undefeated (19-0) girls' team in 1998.

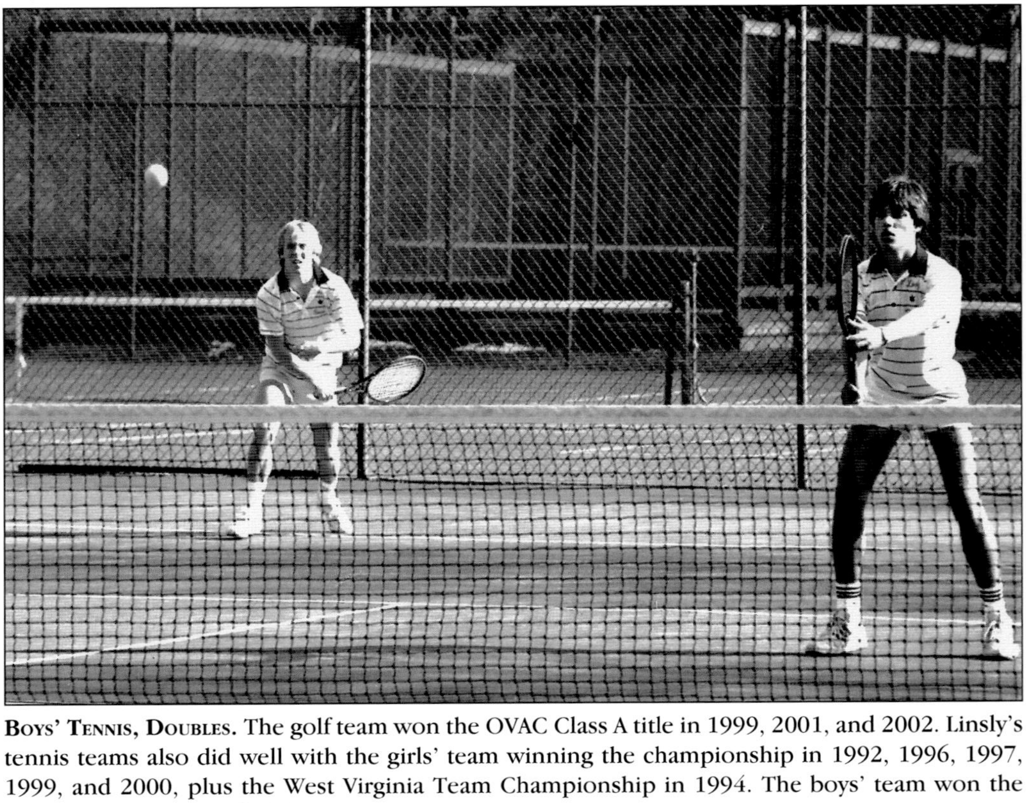

BOYS' TENNIS, DOUBLES. The golf team won the OVAC Class A title in 1999, 2001, and 2002. Linsly's tennis teams also did well with the girls' team winning the championship in 1992, 1996, 1997, 1999, and 2000, plus the West Virginia Team Championship in 1994. The boys' team won the OVAC title in 1991 and 1997.

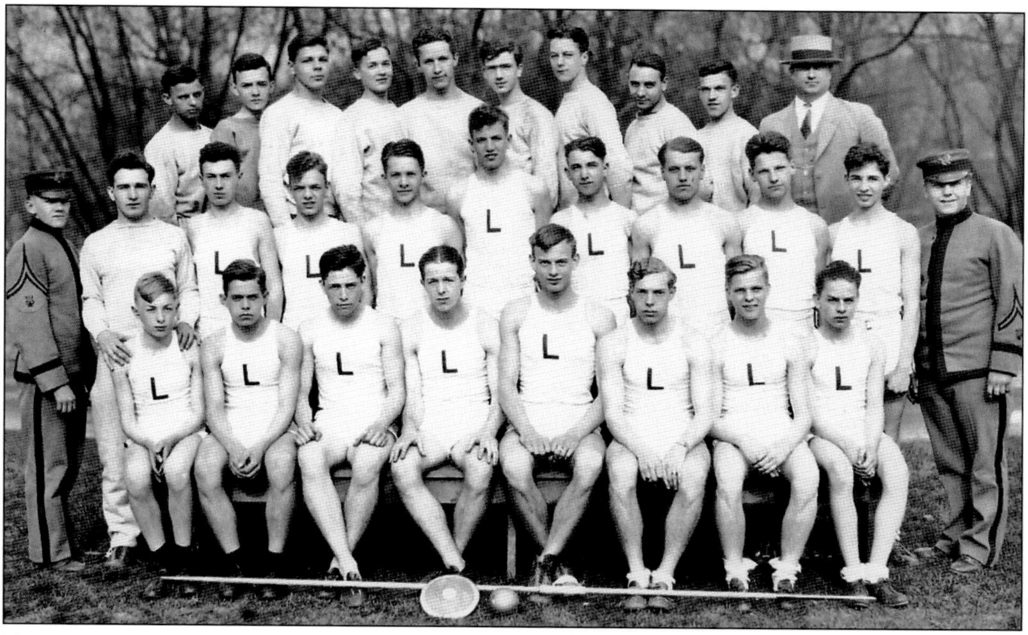

Track Team, 1925. Linsly has excelled in track as well. The boys' team won Class A championship trophies in 2000 and 2002 and made OVAC team champs in 1994 and 1995. They also won the championship title in the Ohio Valley Track League in 1987, 1997, and 2001. The girls' team was the OVAC Champions in 1999.

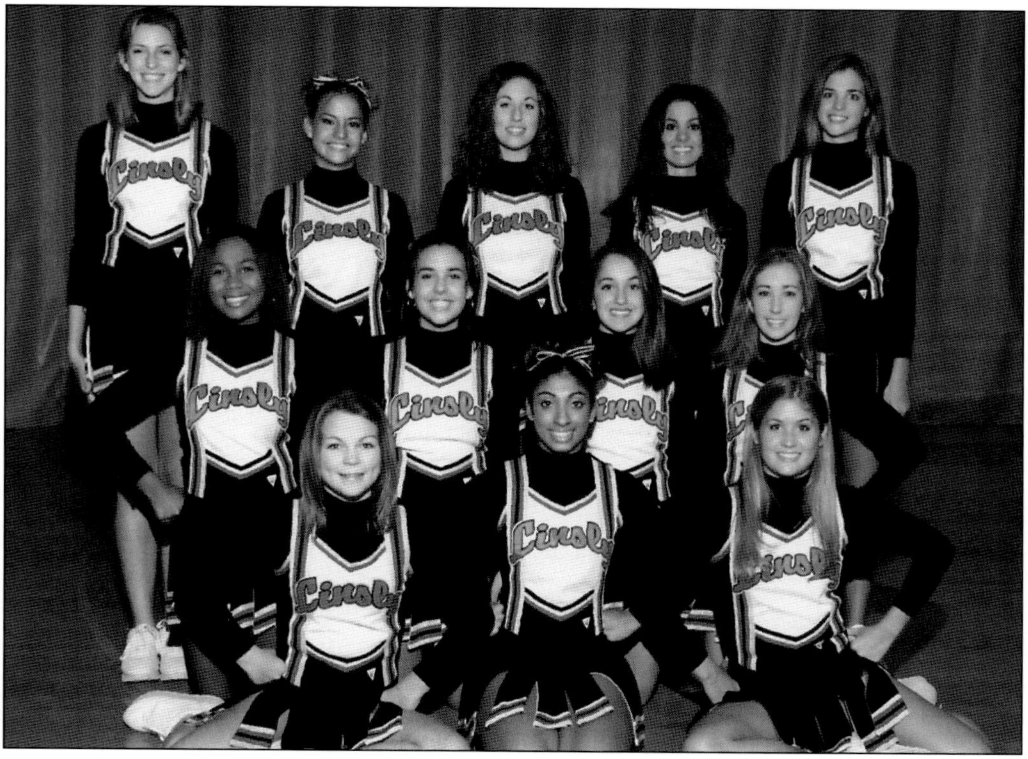

Cheerleaders, 2003. In cheerleading, Linsly's team won the 1996 OVAC Class A title and the championship in 1990 and 1991 at the International Cheerleading Foundation Camp.

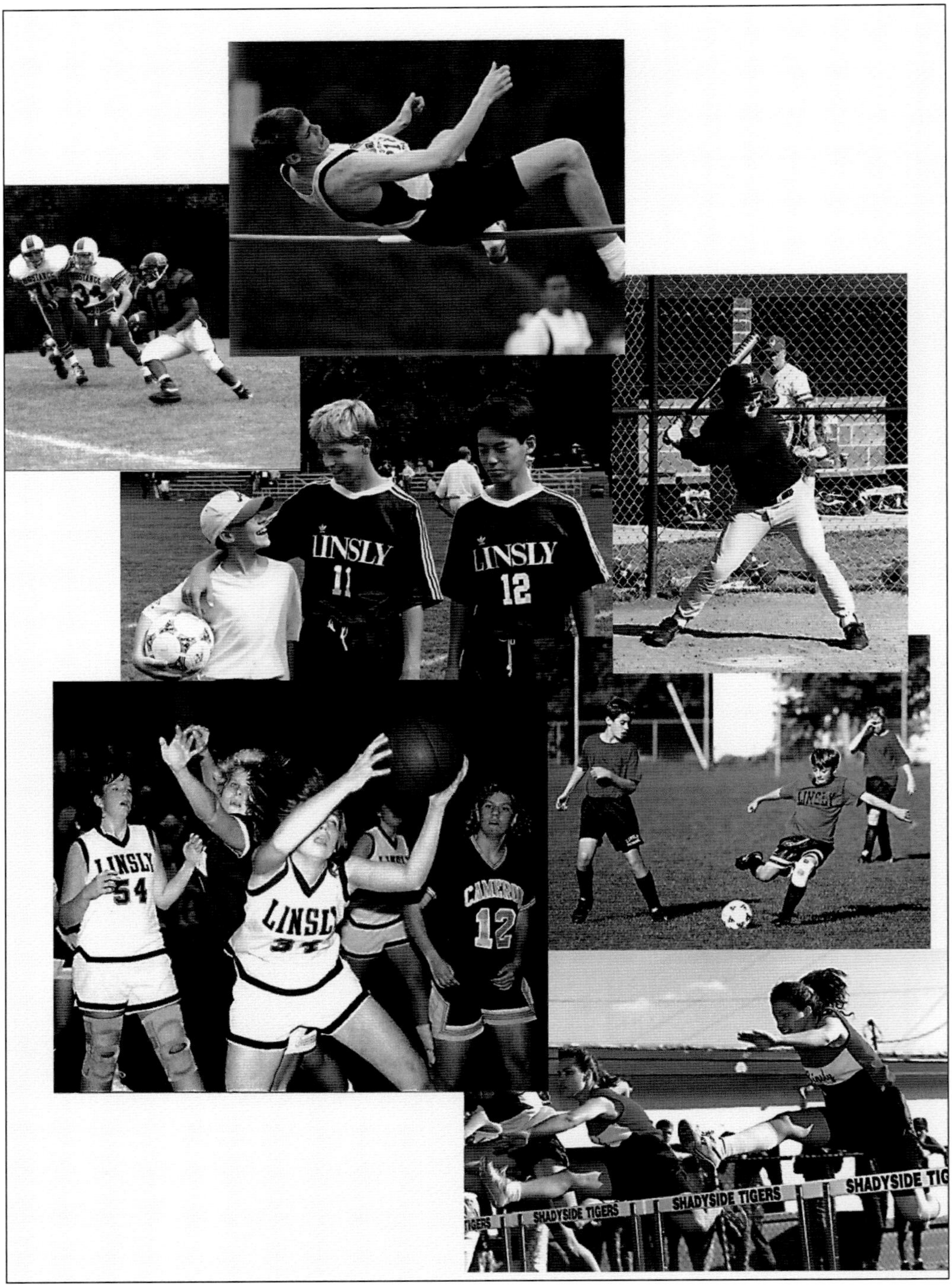

The Cadets in Action. All in all, Linsly's athletic record can only be described as amazing in view of its small enrollment, which has varied from less than 100 students to around 400 students today. When asked, Linsly's coaches attribute this to what can be called the "Linsly Spirit," an ethereal and difficult-to-describe quality discussed in the next chapter. Linsly's athletic program has changed over the years to meet the needs of the students. In 2003, Linsly began a new program in boys' ice hockey and looks forward to a girls' team in the near future.

Seven

Traditions Old and New

Traditions are the strings that tie the alumni to the institution. Linsly is a very old institution and, as such, has acquired many traditions in its 189-year history. Many of these are associated with the military period and are no longer observed, but several, such as the school colors (orange and black), The Aviator *monument, and the nickname of the sports teams ("the cadets"), have endured. But more importantly, those qualities that are harder to define and have made Linsly what it is today are still a part of the institution. The traditions and symbols help to define the school in terms of what it was in the past and what it is today*

The Lamp of Learning, 1896. The "lamp of learning" first appeared in advertisements for the school in the 1870s and, subsequently, in all of the school seals and flags.

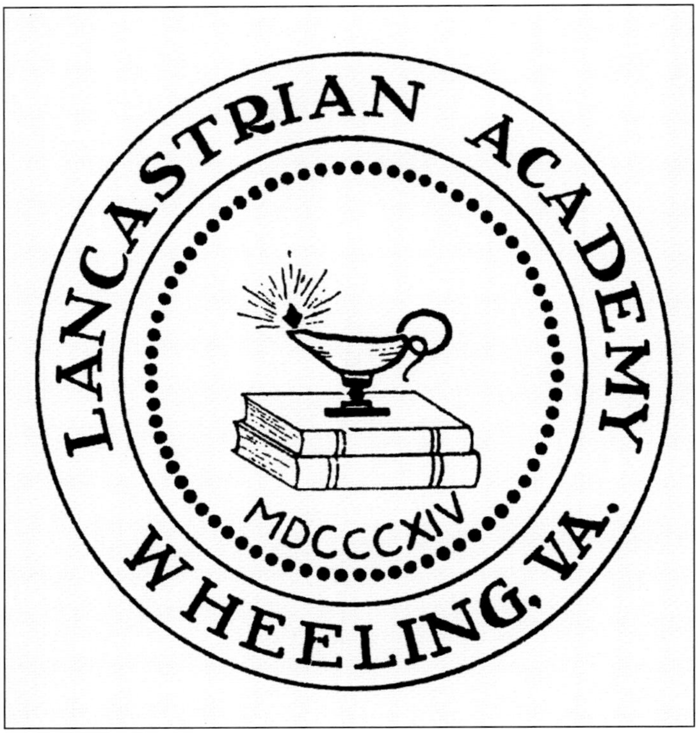

The Lancastrian Academy Seal. The "Lancastrian Academy" seal was used until 1942 when the official name of the school was changed to "Linsly Institute." The school name, "Linsly Military Institute," never appeared on a seal but it was used as the name of the school from the 1940s up until the time when the military program was discontinued.

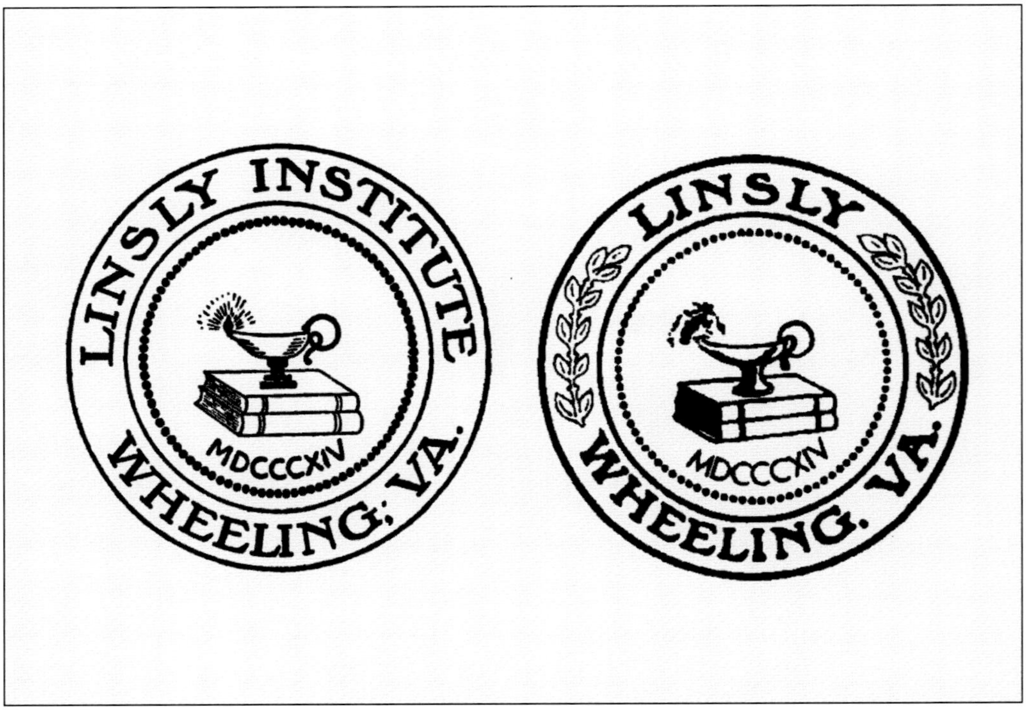

The Linsly Institute Seal (left) and the Linsly Seal (right). The seal was changed to read "Linsly" in 1979 and is the one in use today. All of the seals have also included "Wheeling, Va." and "MDCCCXIV" (1814).

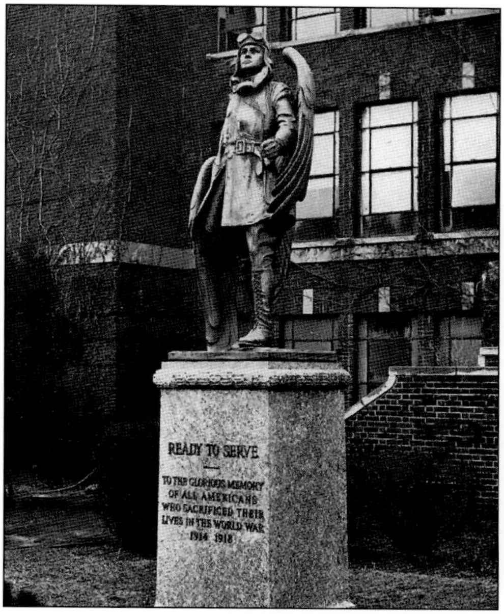

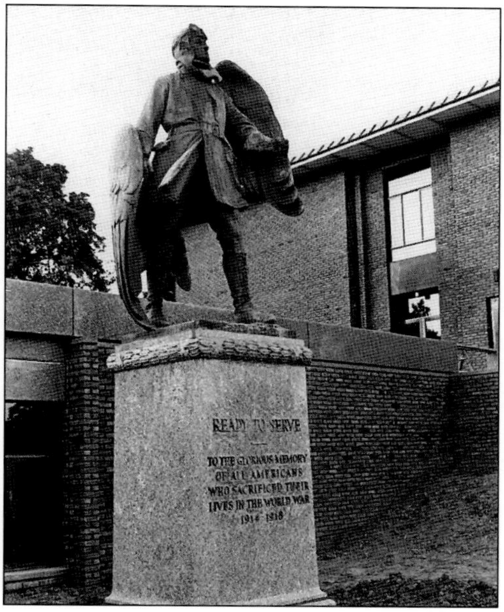

***The Aviator*, 1961 (left) and 1968 (right).** *The Aviator* monument is the only artifact that survived the demolition of Old Main. It was moved to a location near Banes Hall in 1968. For many years *The Aviator* served as a touchstone of courage and sacrifice for generations of cadets who drilled in its shadow, and as a place to honor the nation's servicemen and women on Memorial Day. The internationally known sculptor Augustus Lukeman was commissioned by Sallie Maxwell Bennett to create this lasting memorial to her son.

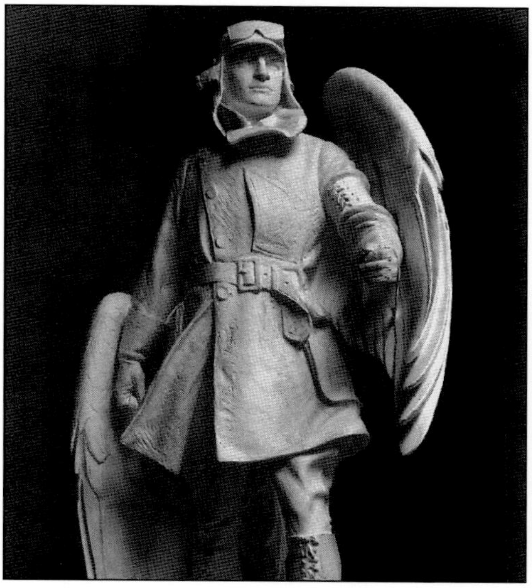

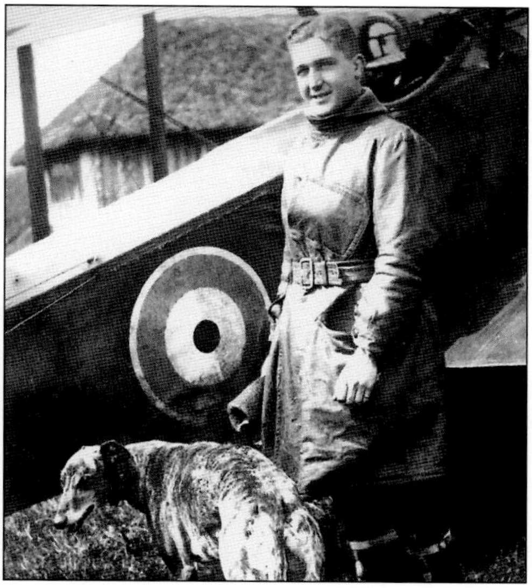

***The Aviator* in Plaster Before Casting (left) and Lt. Louis Bennett Jr. RAF (right).** Lukeman's beautiful statue of a winged aviator, whose likeness is that of Louis Bennett, was desired by the War Department to place in front of the Treasury Building in Washington, D.C. Mrs. Bennett elected instead to place it on a granite pedestal in front of Old Main at Linsly. The statue stands as a symbol of service—service by cadets and faculty of Linsly who served in this nation's wars, service by graduates of Linsly who contributed their talents to the betterment of the community and the country, and service by Linsly's educators who served the students and the school, much as Bennett had served his country with dedication and sacrifice when necessary.

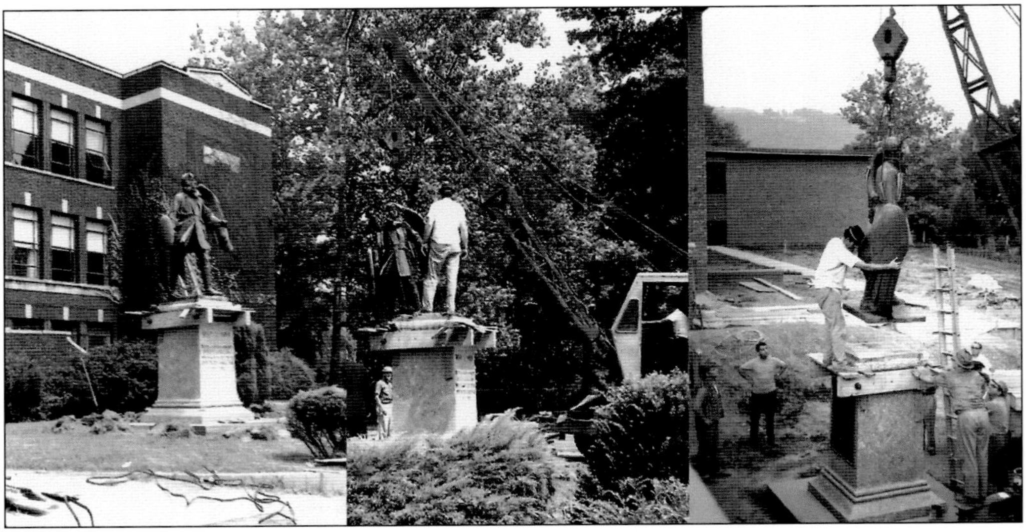

Moving *The Aviator*, 1968. *The Aviator* remains a symbol that defines Linsly's past and present. It appeared on decals and uniform pins in the past and on class rings even today. Students on Linsly's campus walk past *The Aviator* every day on their way across Linsly's campus.

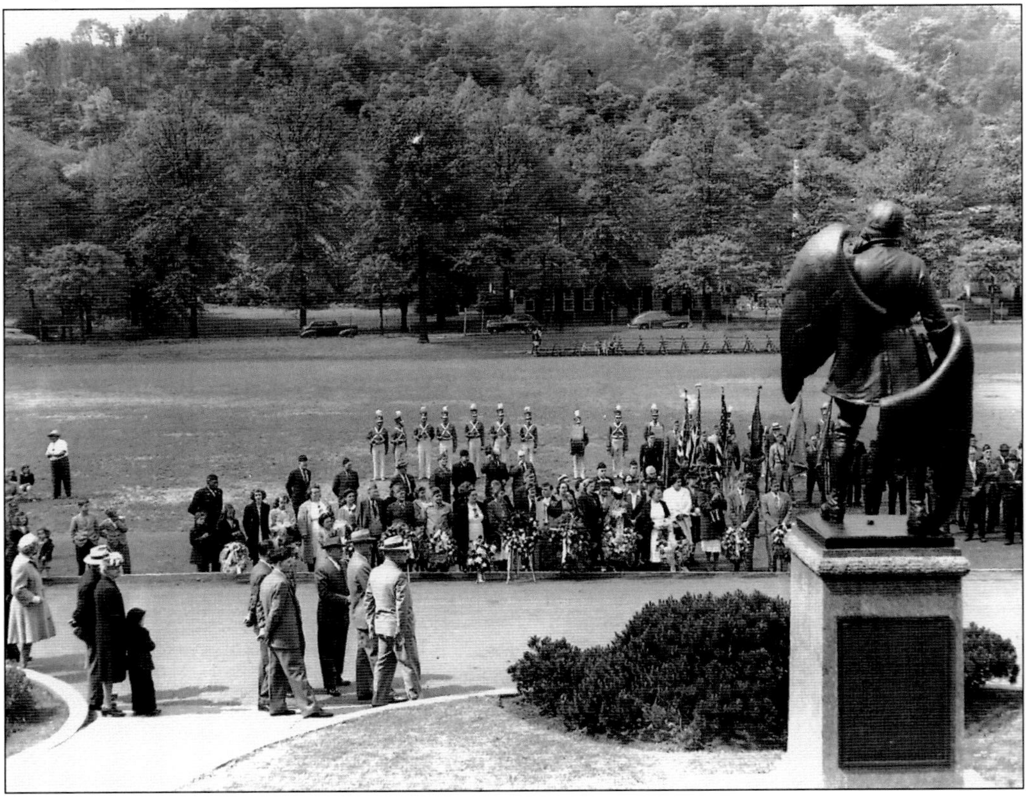

Armistice Day Celebration, *c.* 1940. Alumni who have been graduated from Linsly for 50 or more years are automatically inducted into the Aviator Society, an informal group that meets once a month for lunch and conversation. It is the aim of the society to offer help in various forms to the school and to keep memories and traditions alive so that the history of the institution will not be forgotten.

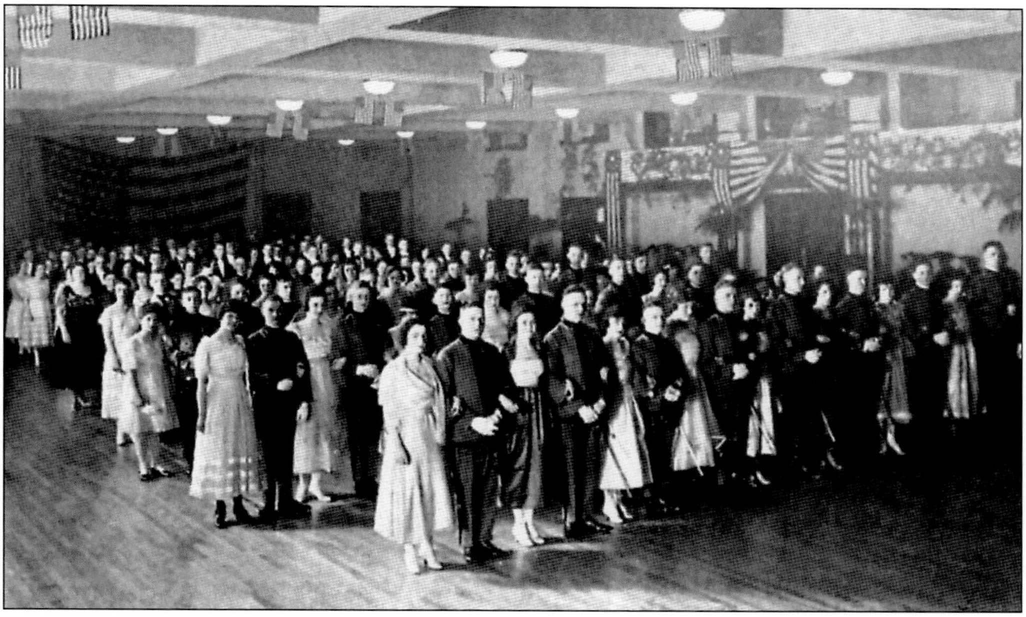

Military Ball, 1918. Records of a military ball go back to the early 1900s. In this photograph of the ball that was held in 1918, the cadet officers in the front row are wearing their sabers, which may have made dancing awkward. All during the military period it was the social event of the year. The first military balls were held in the Scottish Rite Cathedral and always opened with a "Grand March" of all the couples in attendance led by the cadet officers in order of their rank.

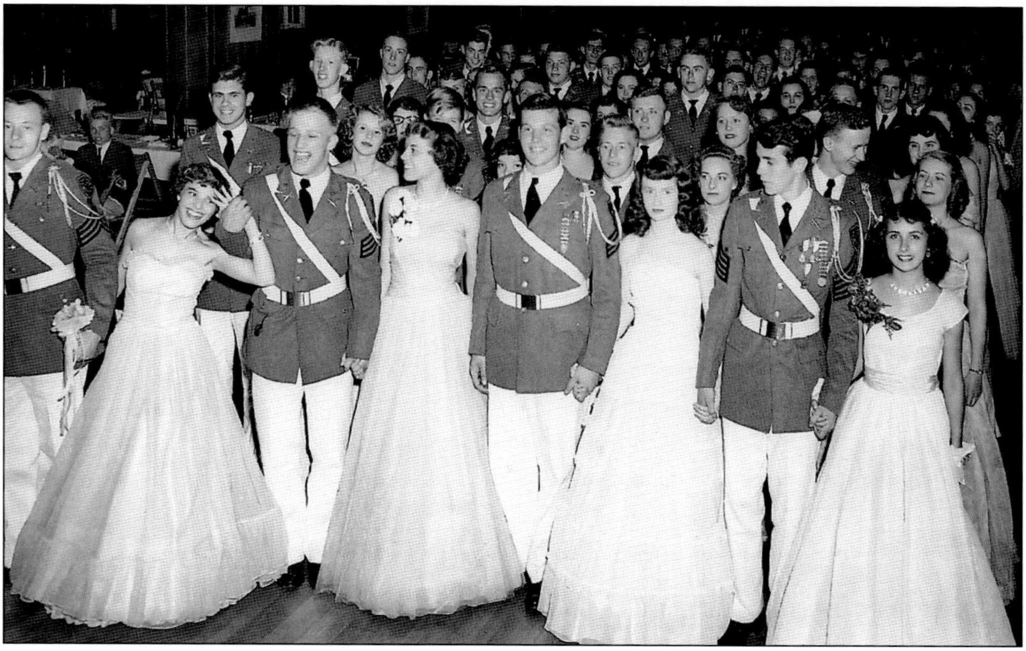

Military Ball, 1949. The cadets wore their formal uniforms and the young ladies wore ball gowns. It was customary for the ladies to carry a dance program wherein young gentlemen signed up for each dance. Later military balls were held in the Pine Room at Oglebay Park. Refreshments, lunches, or dinners were served in different years. At one time, it was traditional for the cadet major to give a dinner party before the ball.

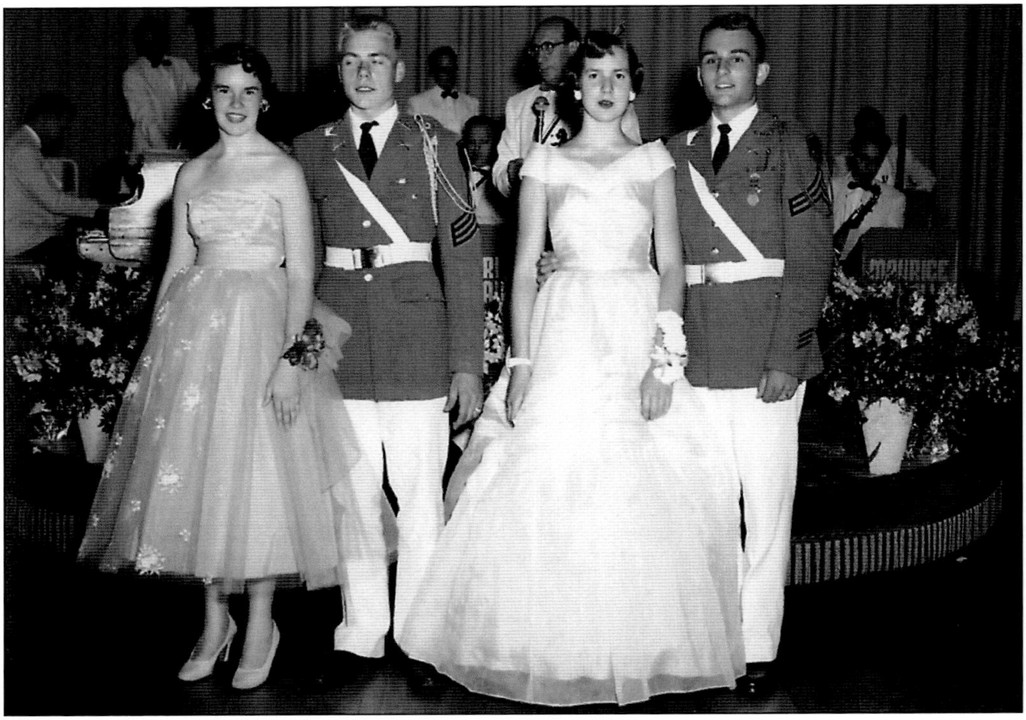

MILITARY BALL, 1954. Of course, once the military program was eliminated, there were no longer any military balls, but proms, which are a lot less formal. The military ball conjures up romantic images of young men in resplendent uniforms and beautiful young ladies in glamorous ball gowns whirling around the floor to the tune of a Strauss waltz.

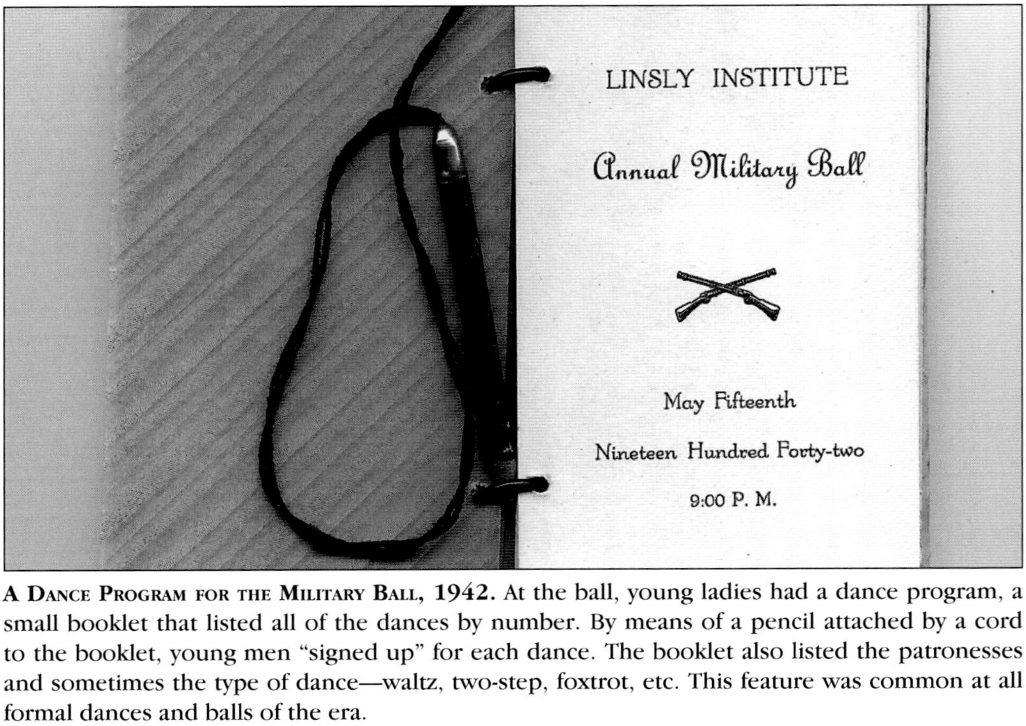

A DANCE PROGRAM FOR THE MILITARY BALL, 1942. At the ball, young ladies had a dance program, a small booklet that listed all of the dances by number. By means of a pencil attached by a cord to the booklet, young men "signed up" for each dance. The booklet also listed the patronesses and sometimes the type of dance—waltz, two-step, foxtrot, etc. This feature was common at all formal dances and balls of the era.

Transferring the Ceremonial Sword. Cadet Maj. Jim Mauer (left) passes the ceremonial sword on to the new Cadet Maj. Tony Giustini. For over 100 years, during the military period, it was traditional to transfer the official sword from the outgoing cadet major to the new cadet major at a small ceremony. The traditional sword is displayed in the school museum

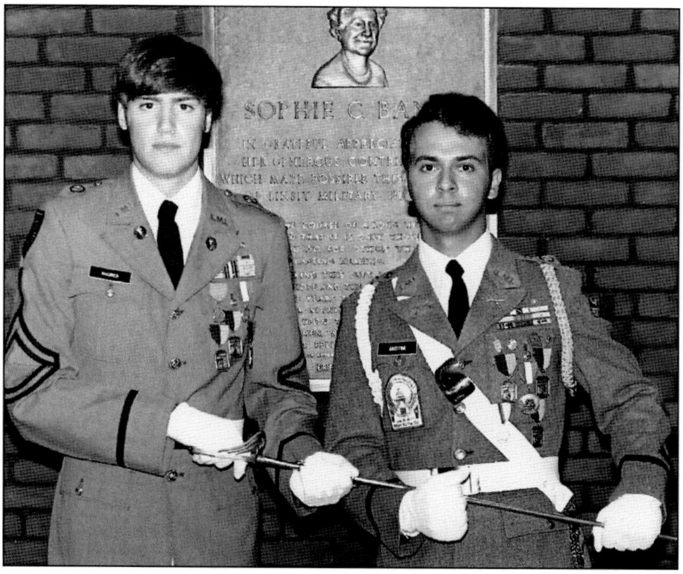

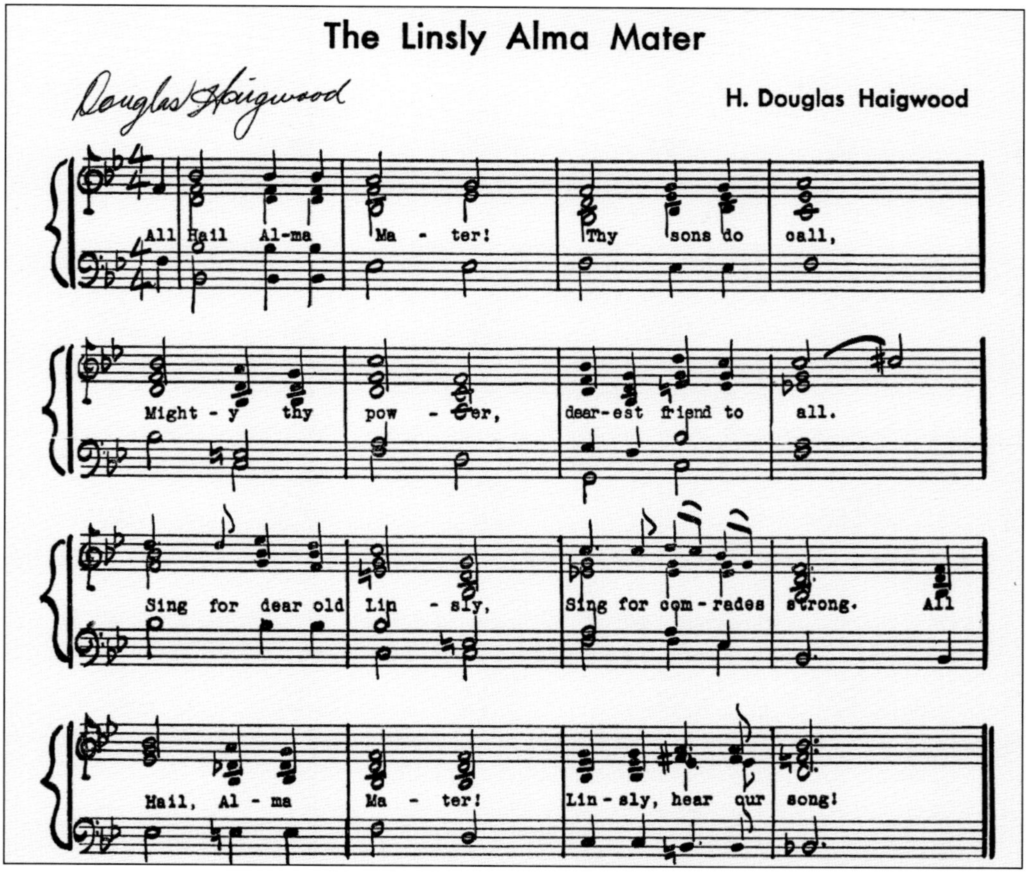

Handwritten Copy of the Alma Mater Signed by H. Douglas Haigwood. It is most fitting that Linsly's alma mater was written by the faculty member with the longest tenure in the history of the school. H. Douglas Haigwood, who served for 45 years, composed both the words and the music.

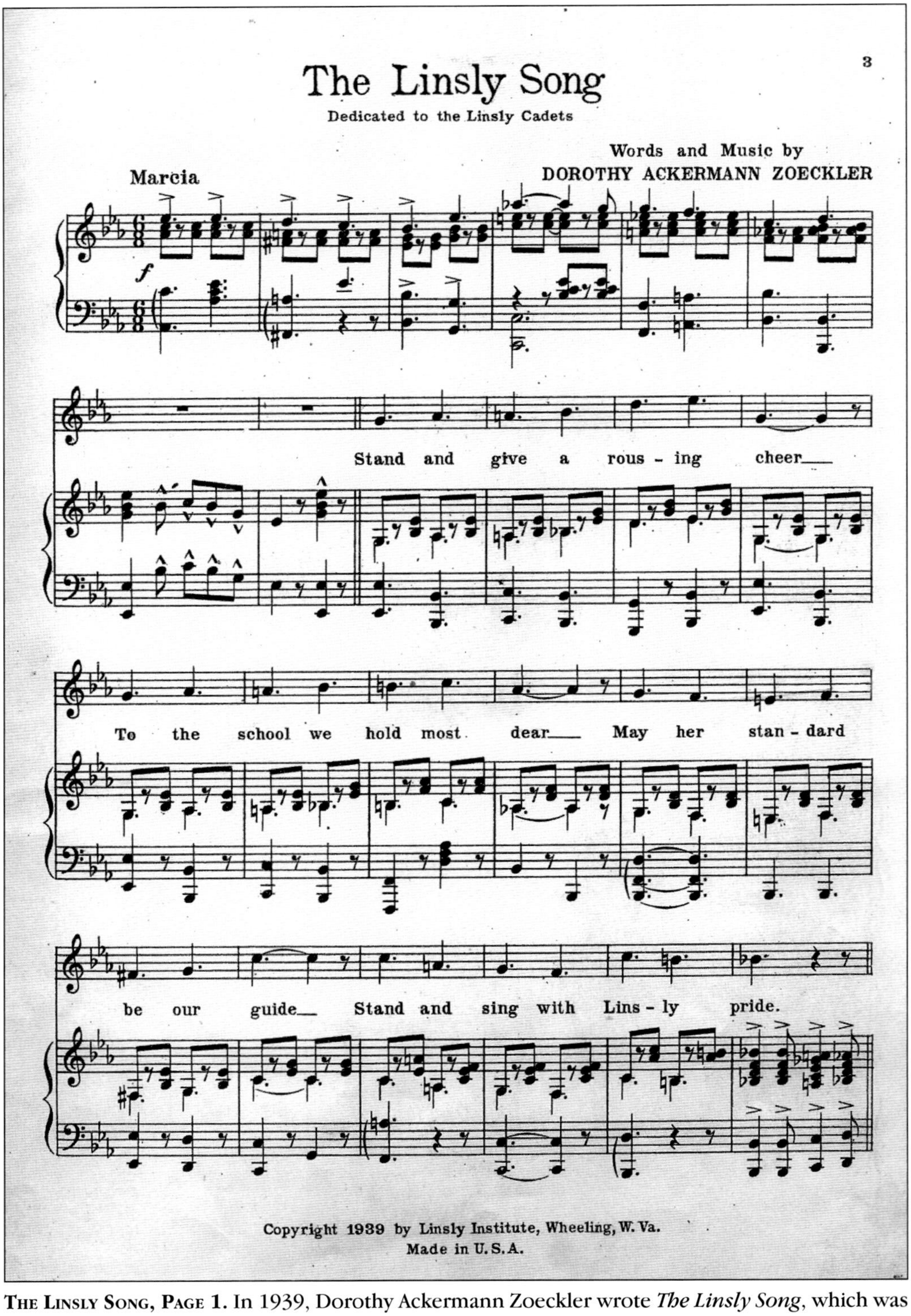

The Linsly Song, Page 1. In 1939, Dorothy Ackermann Zoeckler wrote *The Linsly Song*, which was treated as an official school song but it was not an alma mater. It is a catchy tune with a military flavor that perhaps deserves revival. She also wrote a ballad called *The Military Ball.*

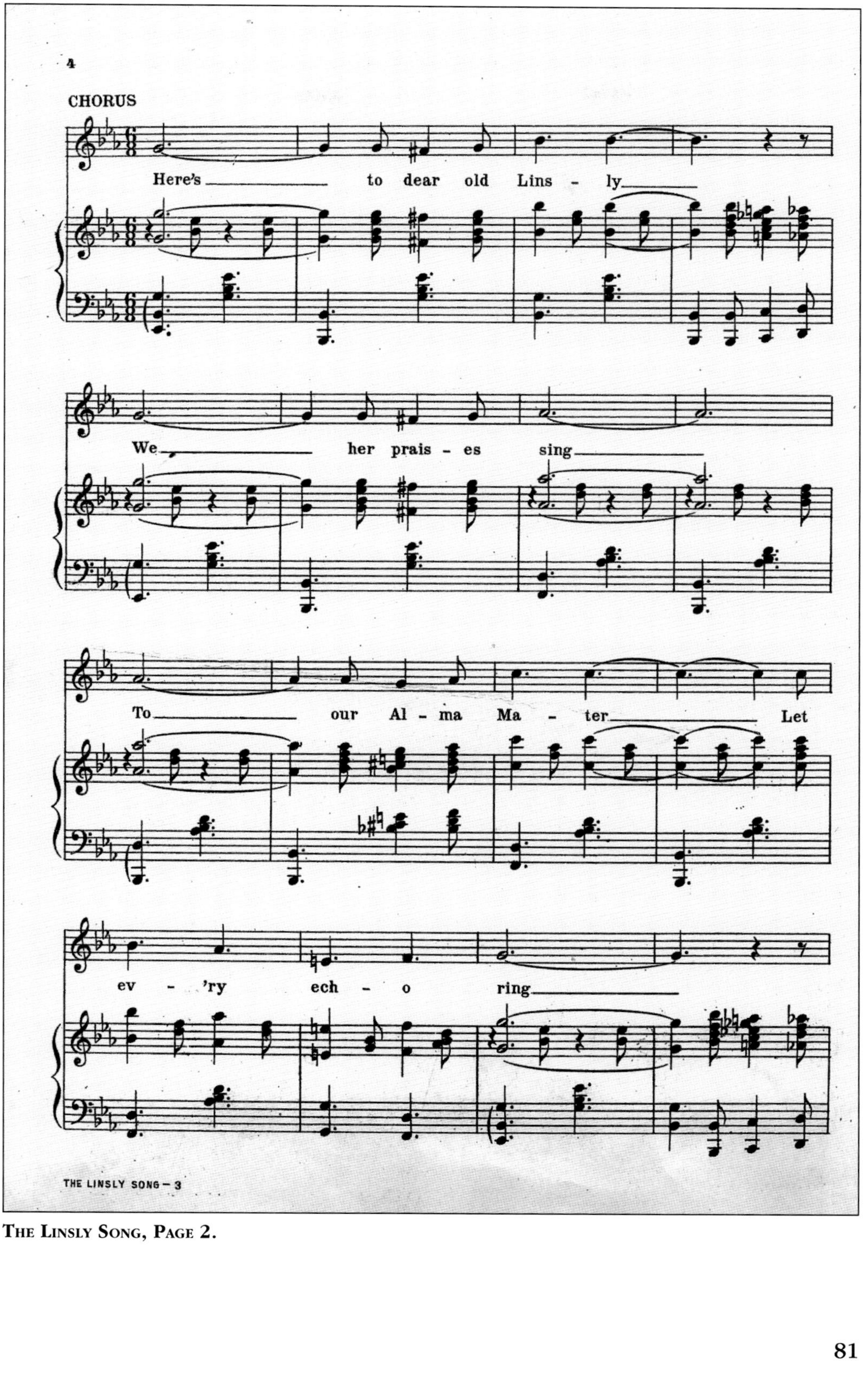

THE LINSLY SONG, PAGE 2.

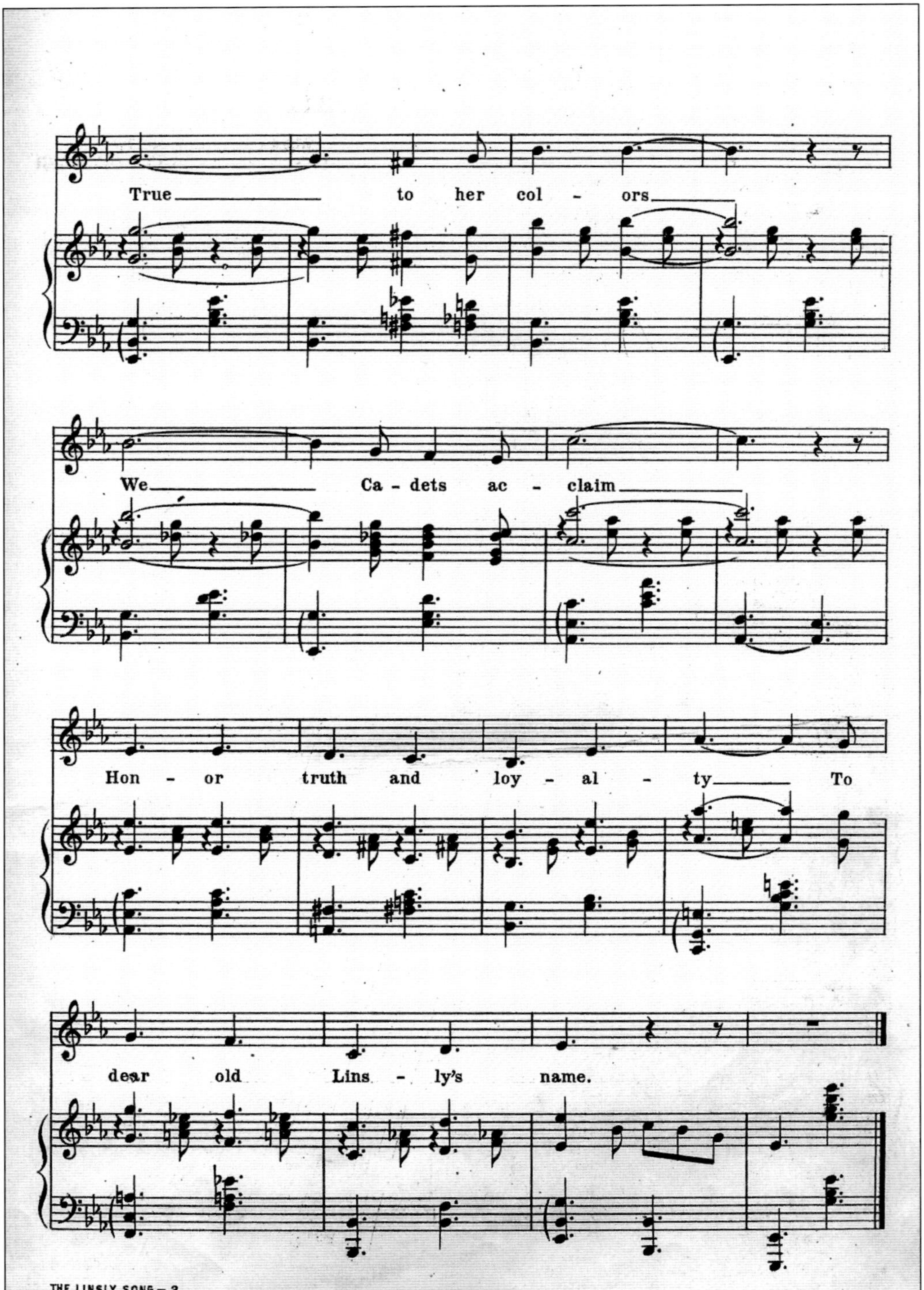

THE LINSLY SONG, PAGE 3.

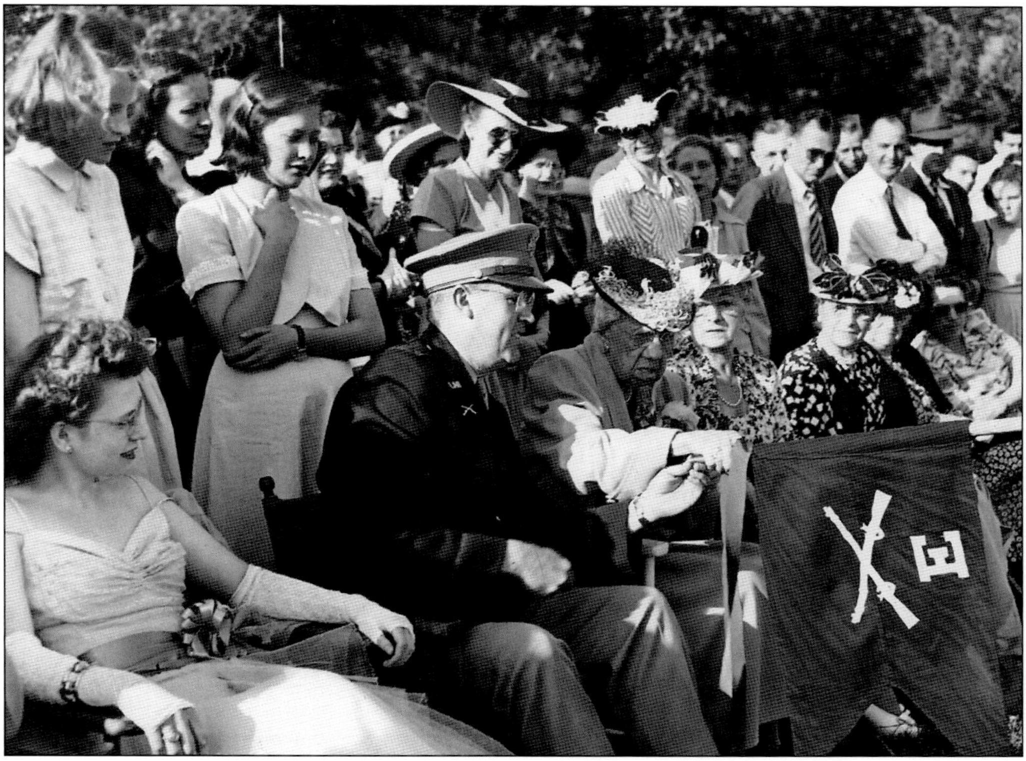

Basil Lockhart and Mrs. Helena Schwertfeger Place a Ribbon on a Winning Company's Guidon Flag, 1948. Final Drills, another tradition that grew in importance through the years, began in the 1870s and lasted until the military program was discontinued in 1979. This was essentially a competition in which individuals and companies competed for awards in close-order drill.

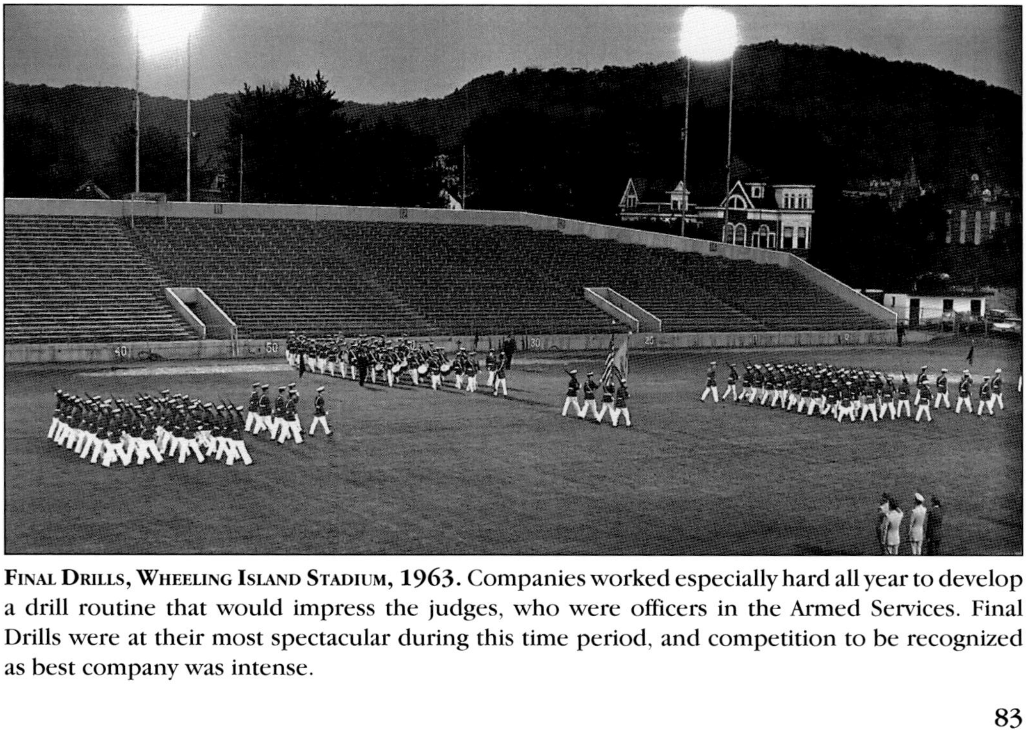

Final Drills, Wheeling Island Stadium, 1963. Companies worked especially hard all year to develop a drill routine that would impress the judges, who were officers in the Armed Services. Final Drills were at their most spectacular during this time period, and competition to be recognized as best company was intense.

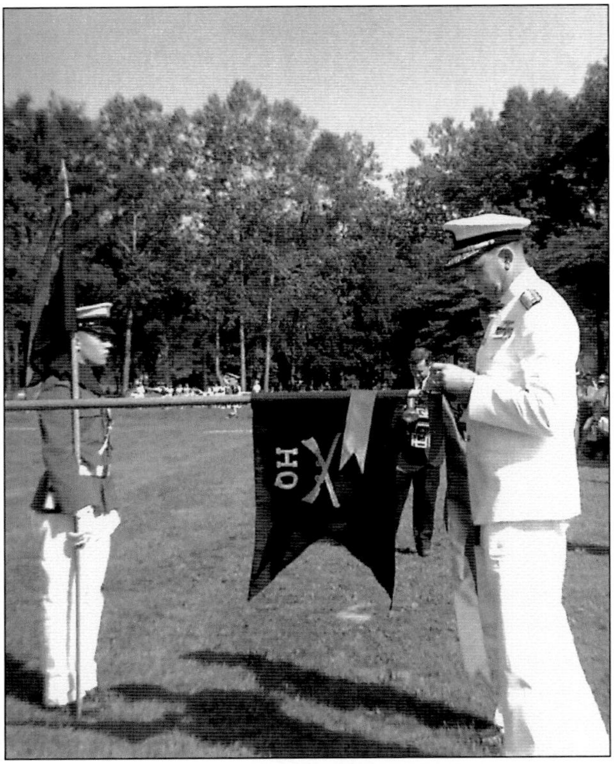

FINAL DRILLS, 1964, ADMIRAL MINTER AWARDS A RIBBON TO HEADQUARTERS COMPANY. It was not uncommon for the commander of the winning companies to invite the members of their company to a local ice cream parlor for a treat at the end of the event.

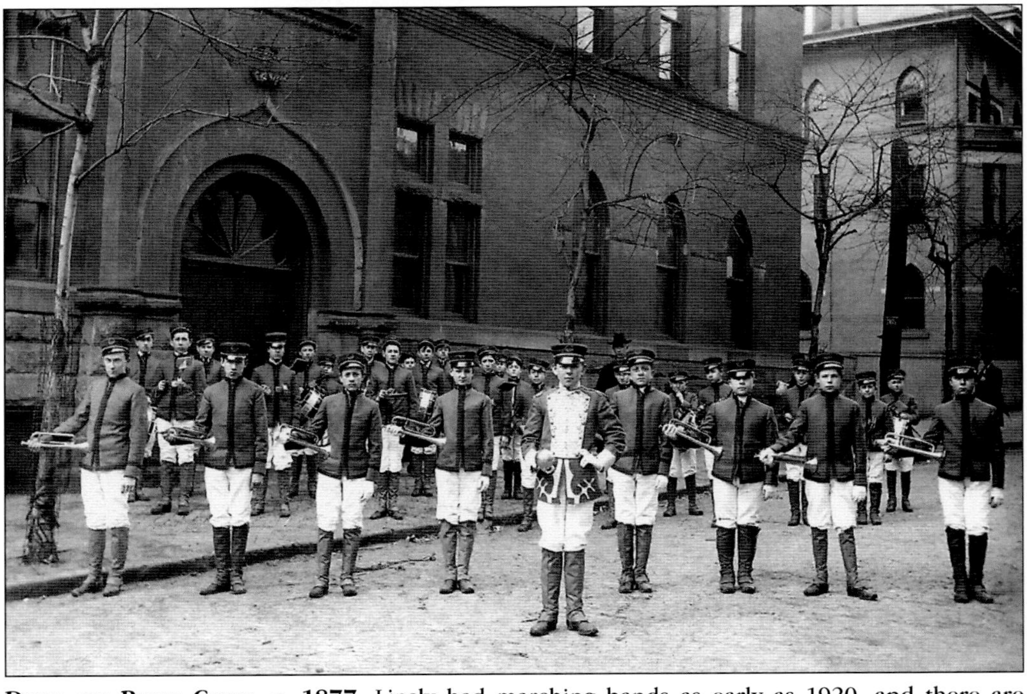

DRUM AND BUGLE CORPS, *c.* 1877. Linsly had marching bands as early as 1920, and there are photographs that indicate some kind of a drum and bugle corps as early as the 1870s. However, the organization that became locally, regionally, and nationally known for its precision drill routines was organized by H. Douglas Haigwood in 1938.

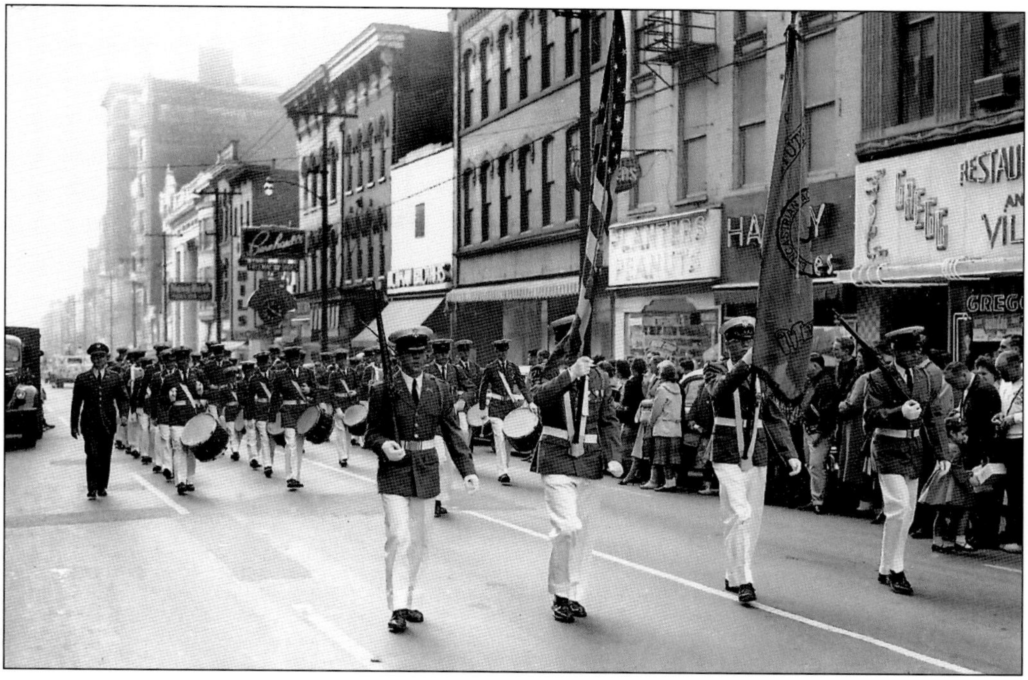

The Color Guard and the Drum and Bugle Corps, 1953. Captain Haigwood can be seen on the left with the Corps in a parade in downtown Wheeling on Market Street. The Corps used soprano and baritone piston bugles, snare drums, tom-toms, bass drums, and cymbals. Haigwood devised a series of amazingly complex routines that probably could not have been carried out by any group who did not have a basic background in close-order drill, and then only after weeks of practice.

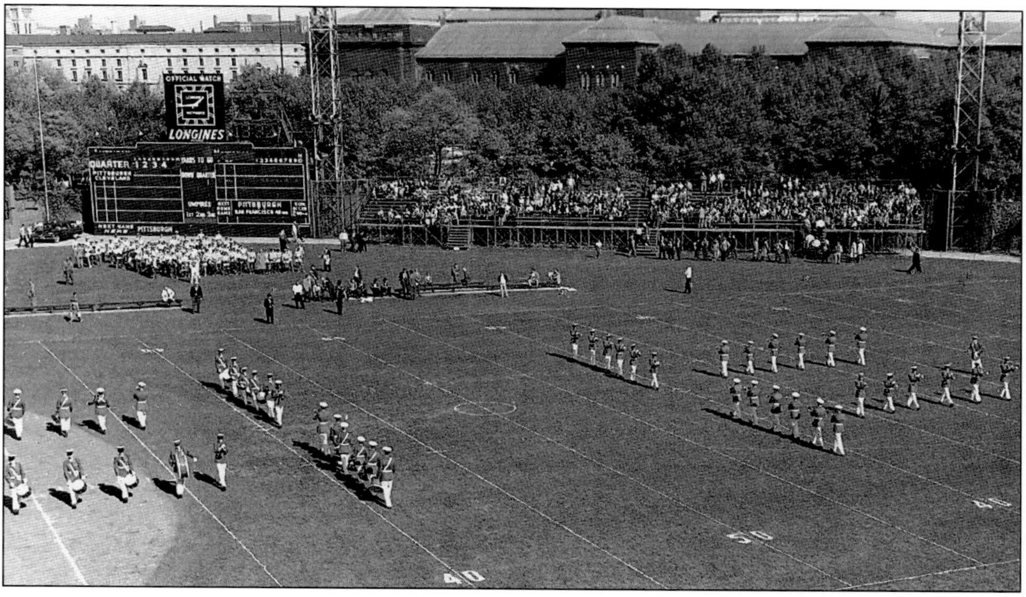

Drum and Bugle Corps at Forbes Field, 1961. The group was well received and participated in all local parades and at numerous events such as baseball games at Forbes Field in Pittsburgh and football games in Cleveland. In 1964, Haigwood switched the bugles to trumpets in order to permit a chromatic scale. He also added a precision rifle squad in the same year.

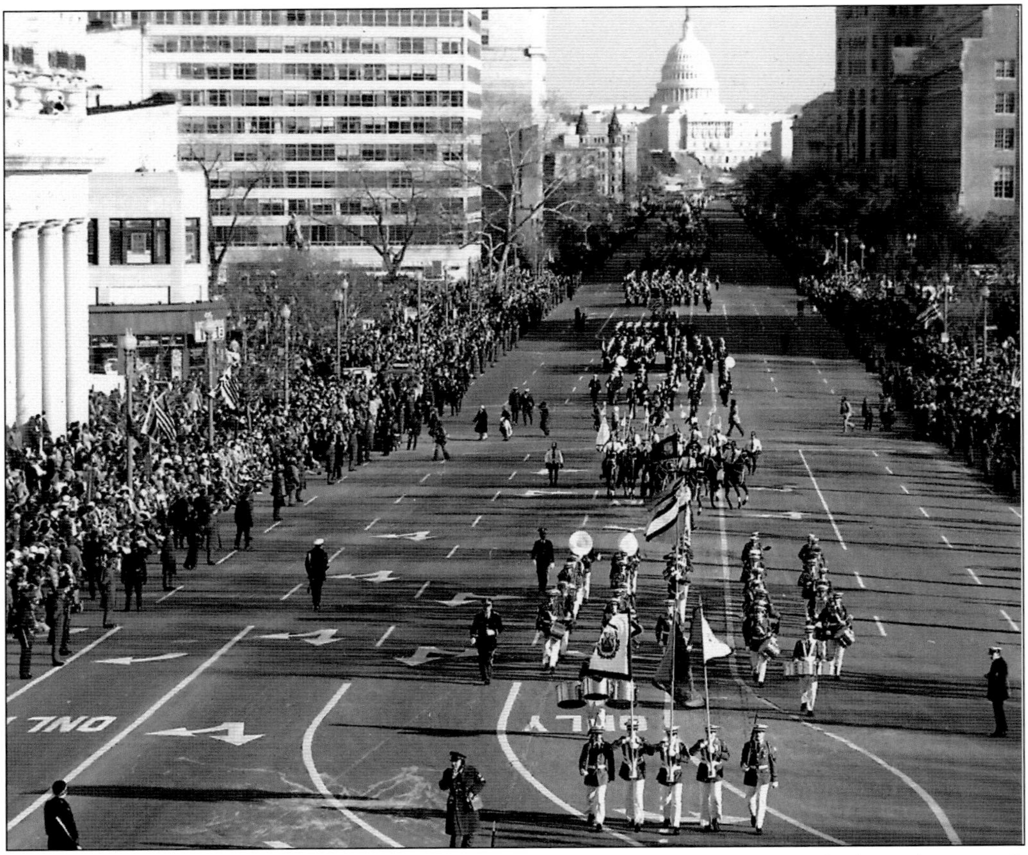

INAUGURAL PARADE, WASHINGTON, D.C., 1977. The cadet precision drill squad, the color guard, and the drum and brass band participated, by invitation, in the inaugural parade in 1977. After Haigwood had directed the corps for 29 years, Peter Donathon became director in 1968. He eventually converted the group to drums and brass in 1974. The marching band lasted until 1979. It became a stage band the following year and strings were added in 1998.

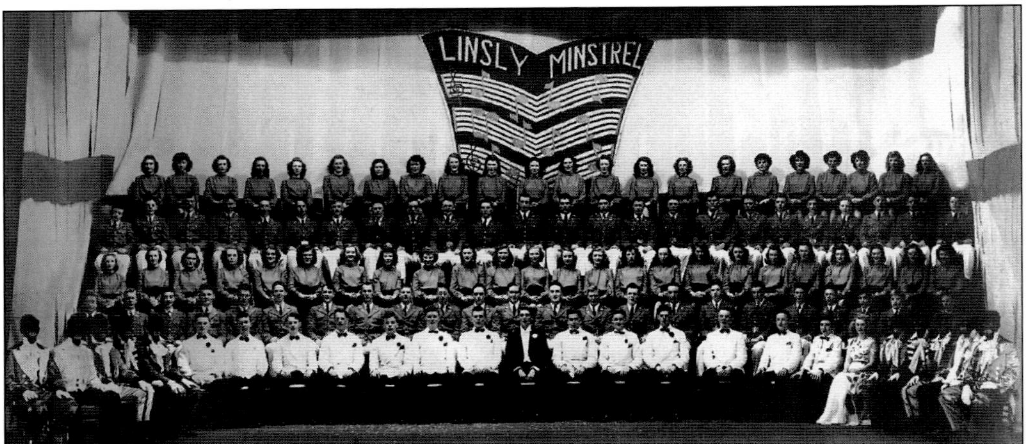

LINSLY MINSTREL, 1946. Perhaps Douglas Haigwood's greatest accomplishment was the annual Linsly Minstrel which he organized in 1946. Prior to this time there had been operettas, but they were not nearly as elaborate as Haigwood's minstrel.

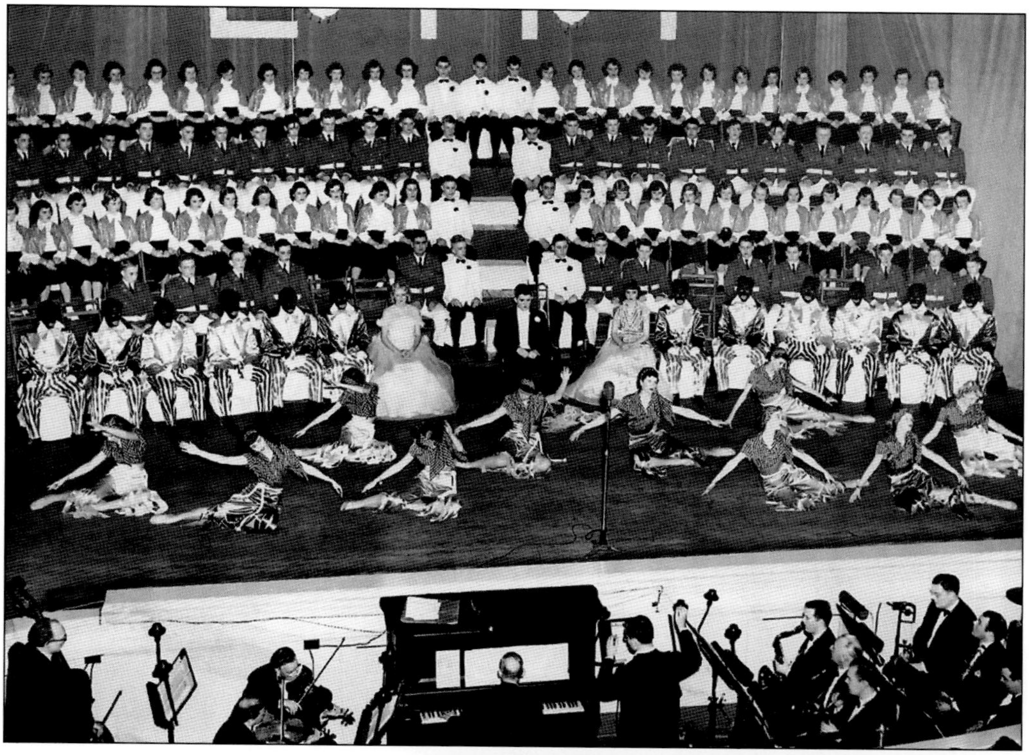

Linsly Minstrel, 1952. From 1939 until 1945, the Minstrel was held in the auditorium of Madison School on Wheeling Island. From 1946 through 1963, it was staged at the Virginia Theater. In 1963, it moved to the Capitol Theater (Capitol Music Hall) and has been there ever since. The minstrel was a traditional old-fashioned production complete with a chorus, soloists, interlocutor, and "end-men" in black-face make-up.

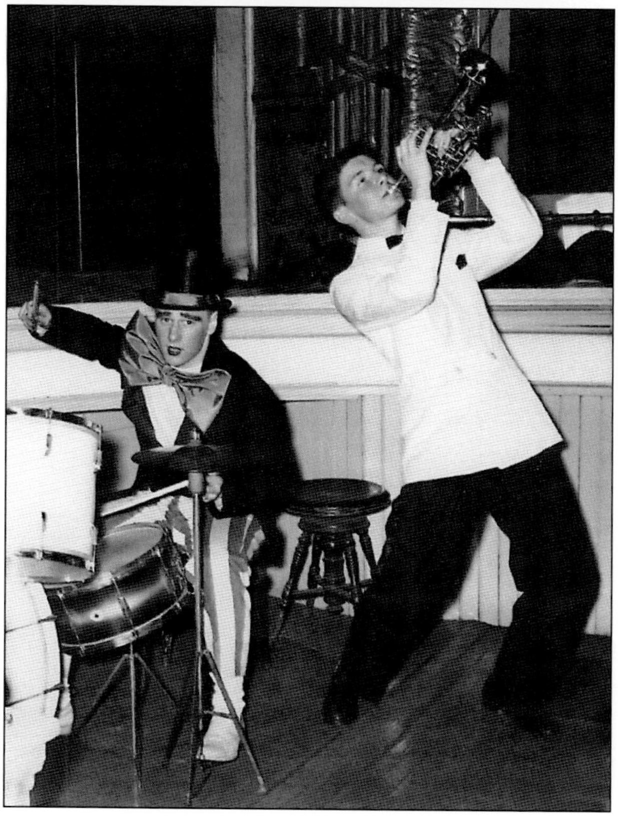

Specialty Act, *c.* 1946. All kinds of specialty acts were included in the Minstrels and Extravaganzas, as well as every kind of music. Many hidden talents are discovered and put to use in this annual event.

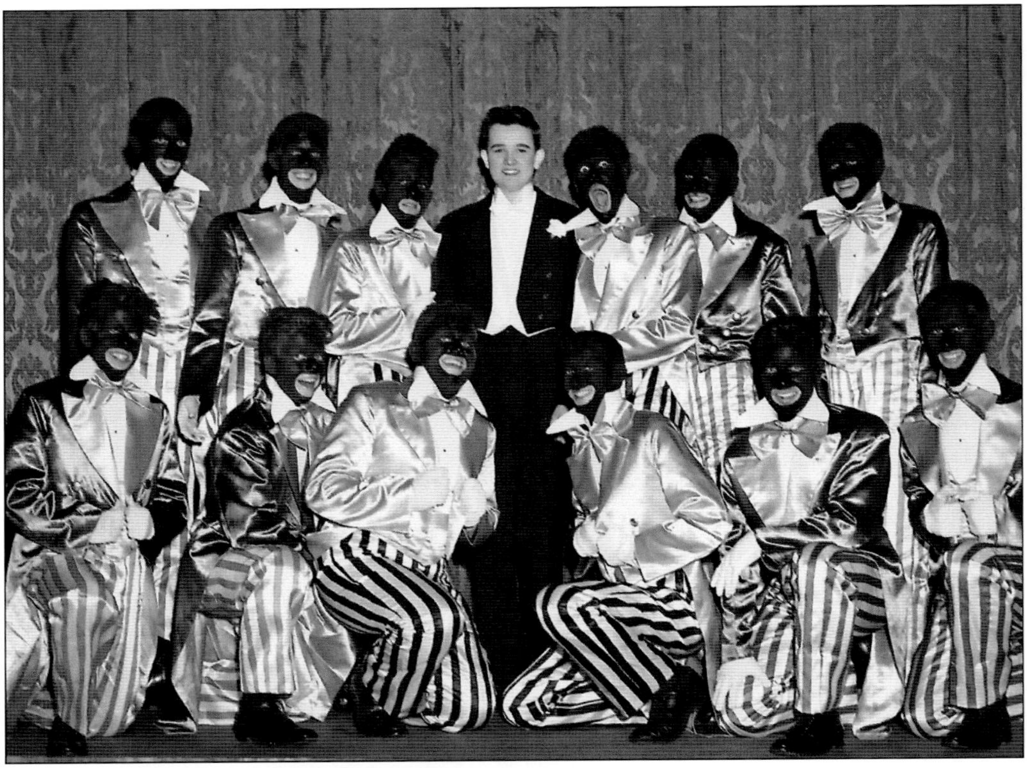

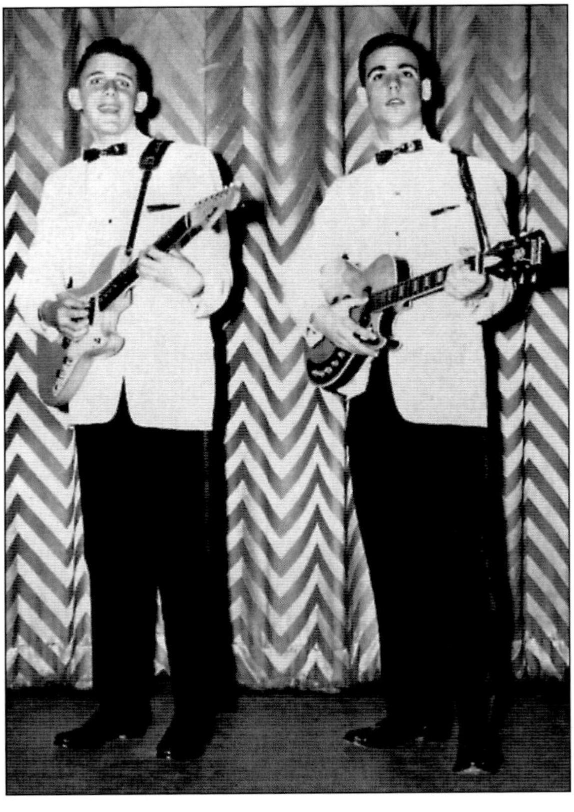

End-men and Bud Lockhart, Interlocutor, 1952. The concept of Blackfaced End Men became increasingly offensive to people, and they were replaced by "bums." This was also considered politically incorrect by an increasingly sensitive society so that the last End Men were "hillbillies."

Wilson and Canfield, Linsly Minstrel, 1961. Speciality acts such as the "Trigger Guards" were very much a part of the minstrel shows. Here, A.D. Wilson and Jack Canfield perform in the 1961 show.

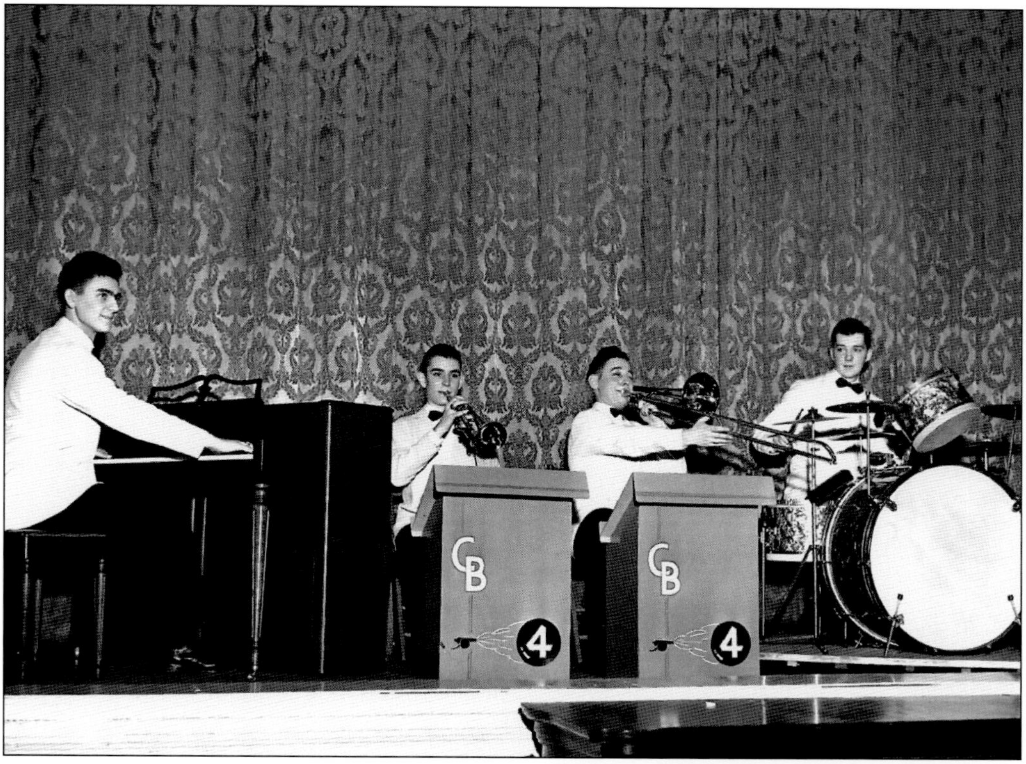

The Cannonball Four, 1952. From left to right are cadets Evan Dadakis, Robert Schramm, Tony Salvatori, and Howard Oliver. Appearing at the Linsly Minstrel and on an early television show in Pittsburgh (WDTV-Channel 3), this group of Linsly students developed quite a following locally in the 1950s where they played for several teen-age dances and performed at the Capitol Theatre in Wheeling and a radio station, WWVA.

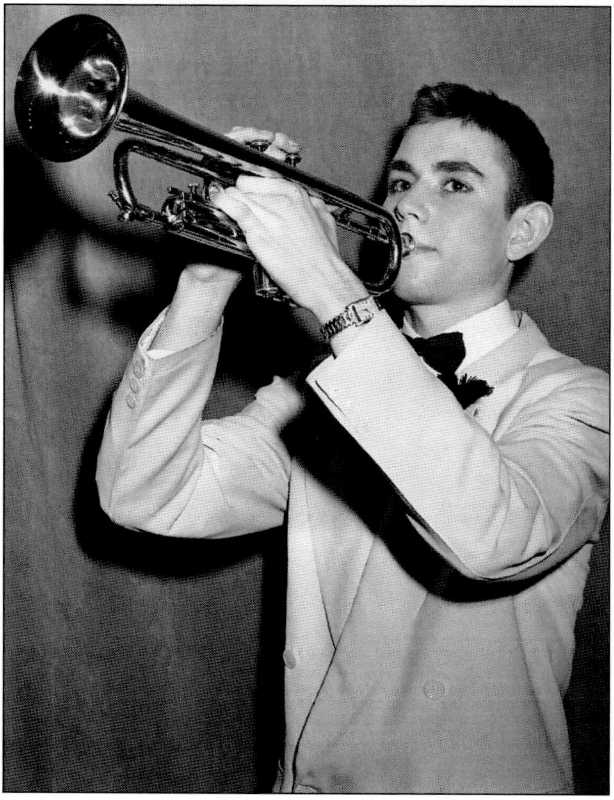

Robert Schramm, 1952. Soloists were also a part of the Linsly Minstrels. In 1952, the author of this book played "Carnival of Venice," a trumpet solo, in the Linsly Minstrel that year.

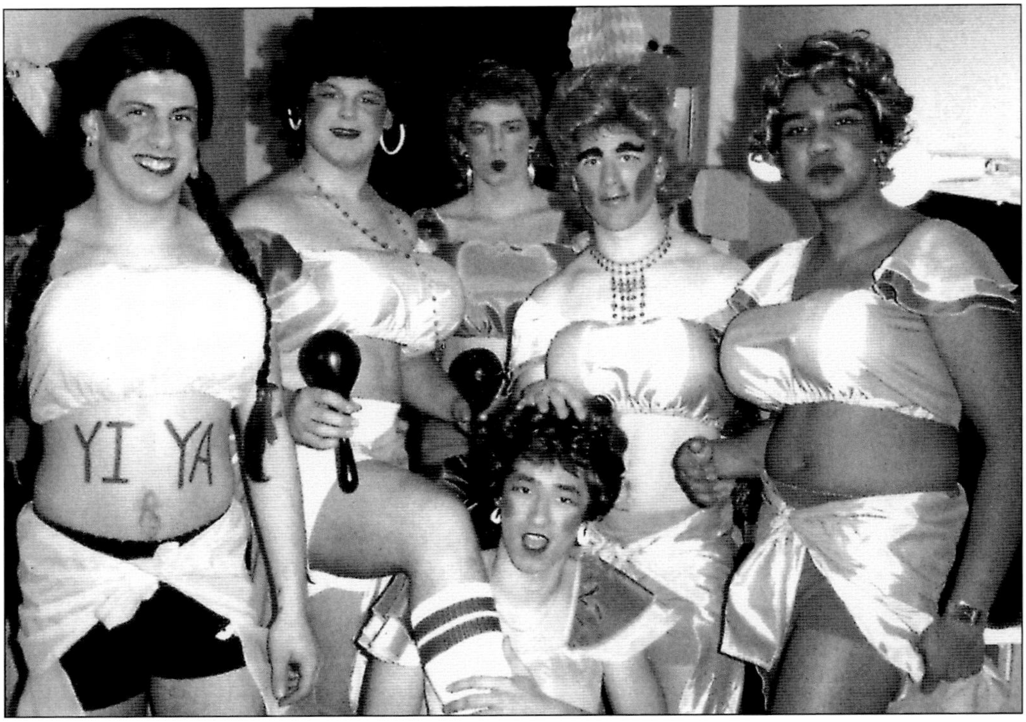

The Stage Beauties, 1987. Almost a tradition in itself is the annual appearance of the "stage beauties" at the Linsly Minstrel and Extravaganza. The origin of this extraordinary performance is lost in time but the traditional act, which involves male students in women's attire, persists today and continues to be a popular feature of the annual show.

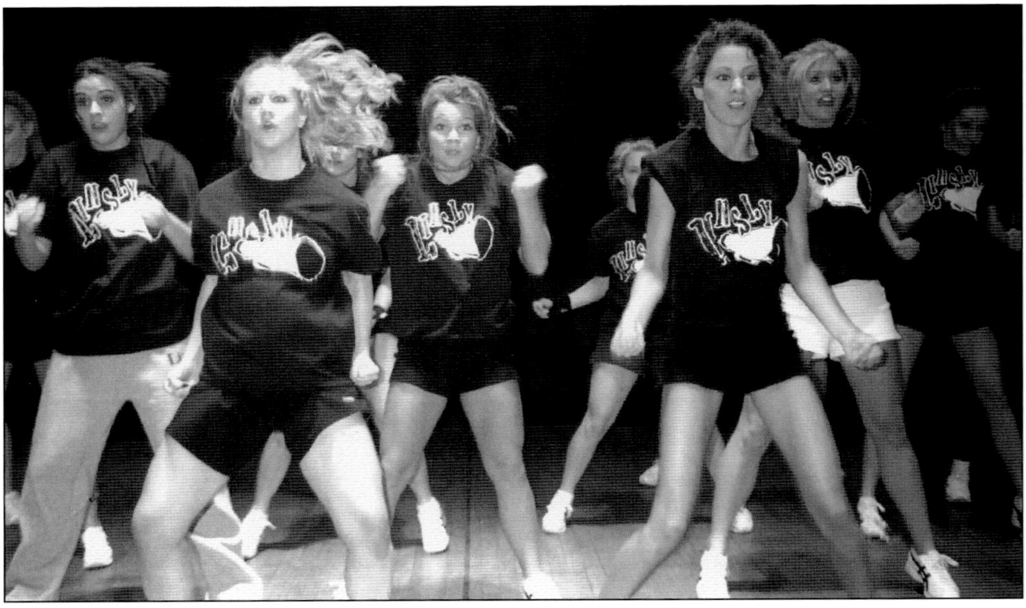

Extravaganza, 2003. Peter Donathon took over as director in 1974 and changed the format of the production and the name to the "Extravaganza." Before Linsly went coed in 1988, junior-high and high-school girls from Mount de Chantal, Wheeling Country Day School, and Triadelphia participated in the production. Frank Wilson became director in 1980.

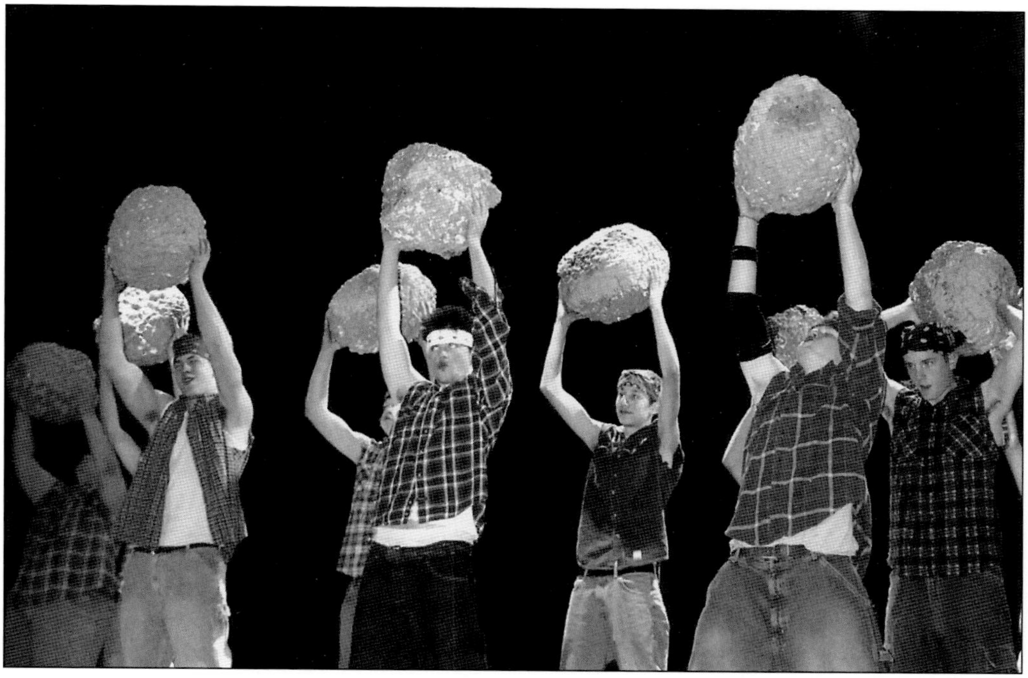

EXTRAVAGANZA, 2001. The Extravaganza continues today and is bigger and better than ever. Virtually every member of the student body and faculty becomes involved in some way in this annual production that has become one of Linsly's finest traditions

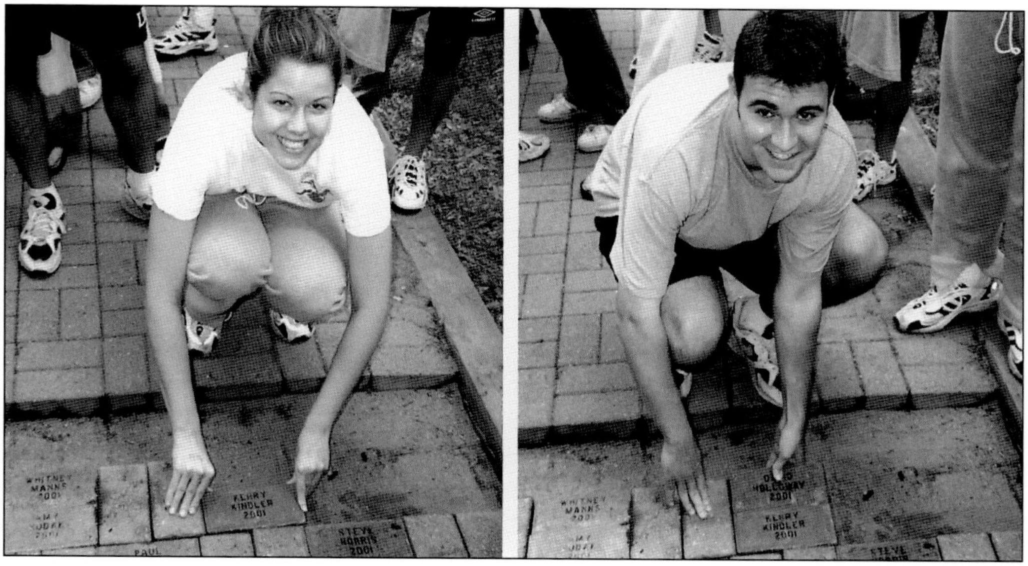

THE SENIOR WALK. A new tradition, known as the Senior Walk, was begun in the year 2000 at the suggestion of Headmaster DiOrio. A brick walkway was created on campus as each senior laid a brick inscribed with his or her name and date of graduation. Just as each graduate's name is inscribed on Linsly's campus, the Linsly experience, as well as the Linsly spirit, is inscribed on every graduate.

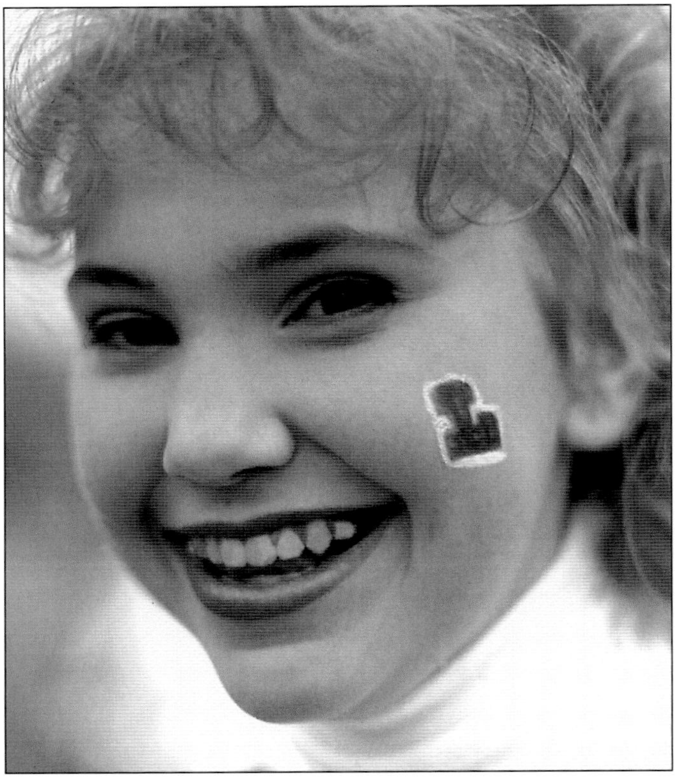

Pride. The least tangible and possibly the most important tradition is the "Linsly Spirit." It is hard to define but is the factor that ties together everything that Linsly is, has been, and will be in the future. It is this spirit that motivated John Birch to initiate programs that would make Linsly unique, and brought him back to serve twice more after he had left for other interests. It is this spirit that sustained Guy Holden when he fought to save Linsly from the great depression. It guided Basil Lockhart throughout his long tenure and campaign to enlarge the school both physically and academically while treating each cadet with the same interest he would reserve for his own children.

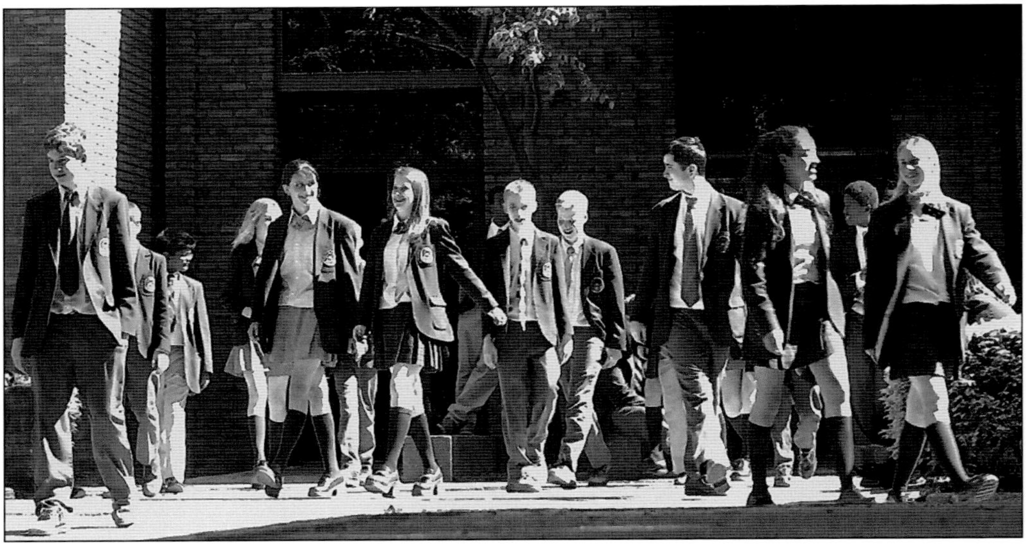

Modern Students, 2003. The Linsly Spirit has guided the members of the board through many difficult times and provided them with the courage to make hard decisions, when necessary, for the good of the institution. It is the Linsly Spirit that has infused hundreds of its sports teams, making them victorious, and caused Linsly students to become outstanding achievers in all that they set out to accomplish. This spirit can be found in the pride that Linsly alumni feel and their willingness to help their old school and fellow graduates if needed. Today the school's current theme is "Never, never, never quit!" One hundred and eighty-nine years ago Noah Linsly said, "Forward and no retreat!" The language is different but the thought is the same.

Eight

STUDENT LIFE PAST AND PRESENT

What is recorded in historical documents is usually the important events; therefore, unless someone has kept a diary of day-to-day minutia it is difficult to imagine what life was like in the past. Fortunately, since about 1840, the invention of photography, its growing popularity, and the development of easy-to-operate cameras and fast film gives us a wealth of information in the form of photographic images. Herein we can see the style of dress, the body language, and the facial expressions, which convey the feelings of the people in the photographs. This chapter is an attempt to present a photographic record of the activities of Linsly students from the past to the present. The number of activities is so diverse and the time period is so great (163 years) that it is not possible to show it all. What follows is just a small, but representative, sample of carefully selected images designed to give the reader an idea of life on Linsly's campus.

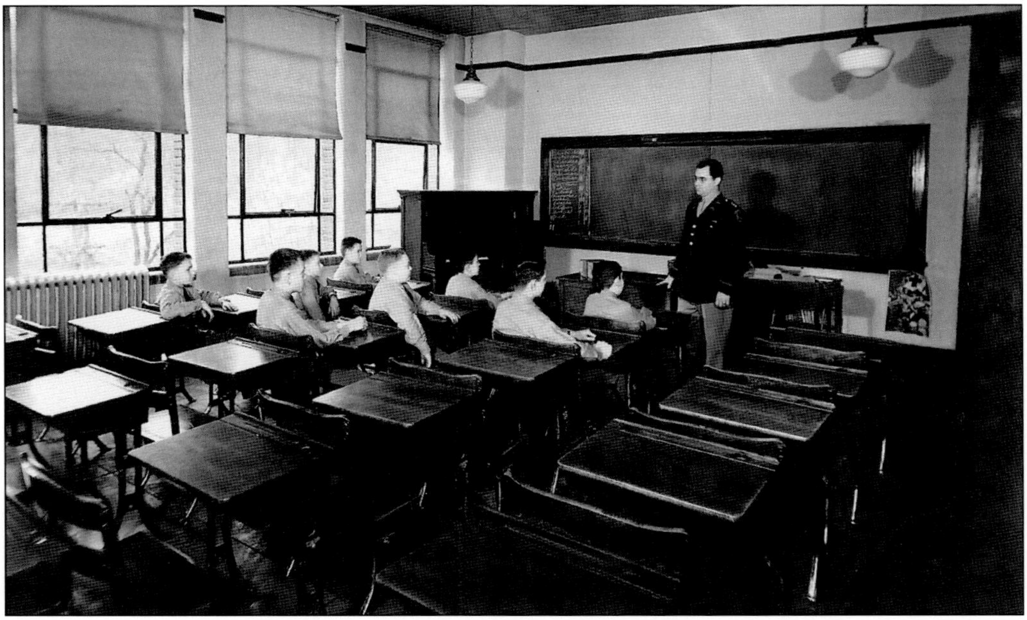

A TYPICAL CLASSROOM, OLD MAIN, 1943. This social science class was being instructed by Captain Haigwood. The small class size was typical. Notice the real slate chalkboards and the upright grand piano.

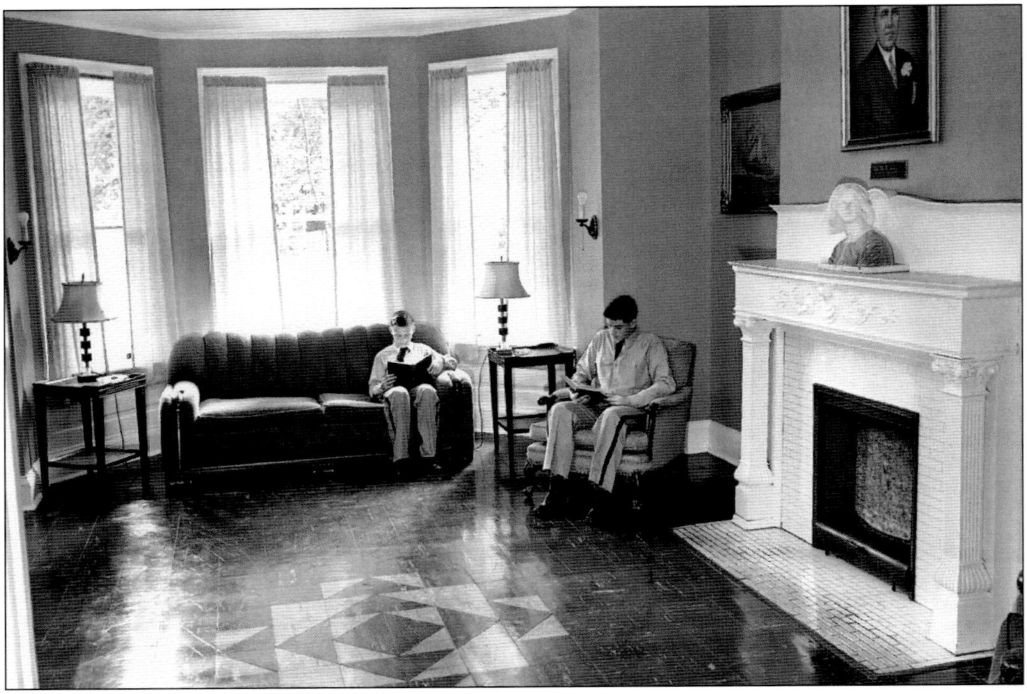

STUDENTS IN WEISS HALL LIVING ROOM, 1943. The dormitories were designed to have a home-like atmosphere with lots of areas to study and relax.

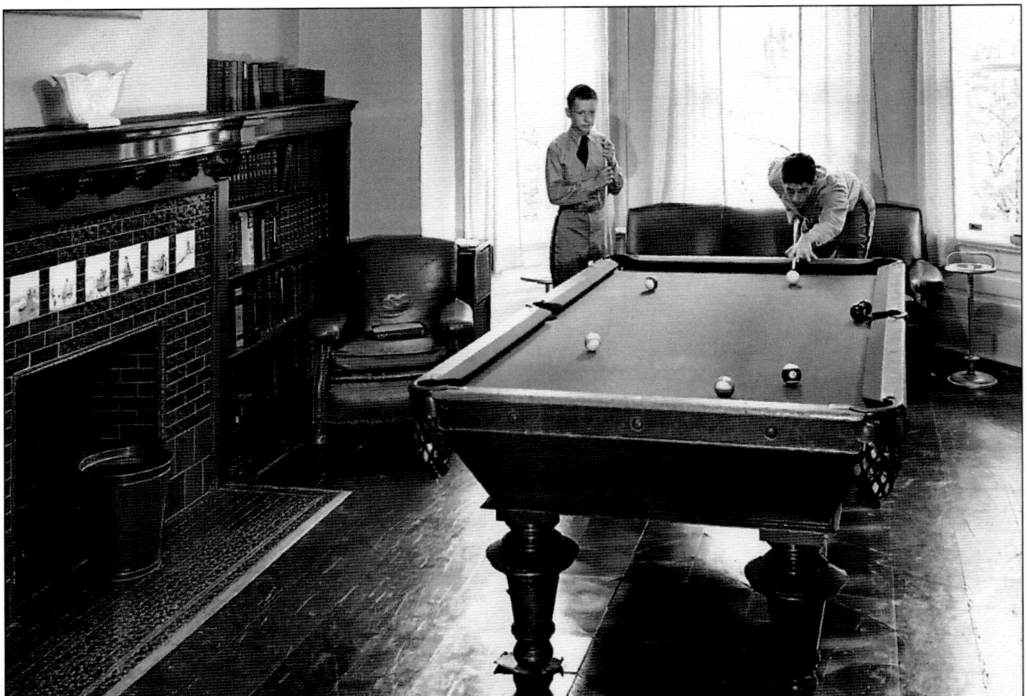

A GAME OF POOL, WEISS HALL, 1943. Recreational areas such as this billiards room were available. Of course, in 1943 there were no television stations locally, but radio was a source of entertainment and the recreational areas were equipped with radios and record players.

LOWER HALL, OLD MAIN, 1960. By the 1960s, Old Main was becoming crowded. The hallway was lined with lockers, and between classes the cadets were trying to visit their lockers, visit the restroom, and get to the next class on time. During class, the halls were empty except for a hall guard and perhaps a senior officer who was officer of the day (O.D.).

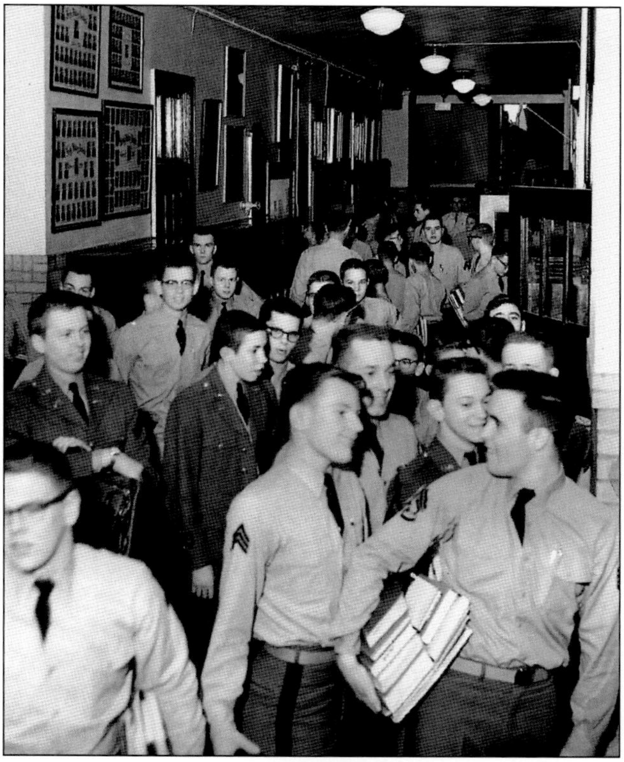

A CORNER OF THE LIBRARY, OLD MAIN, 1947. E.K. Merriner was the school librarian. He decorated the school library with trophy cases, interesting objects, plants, and photographs. Notice the hand-lettered sign reading, "Industry is a Virtue."

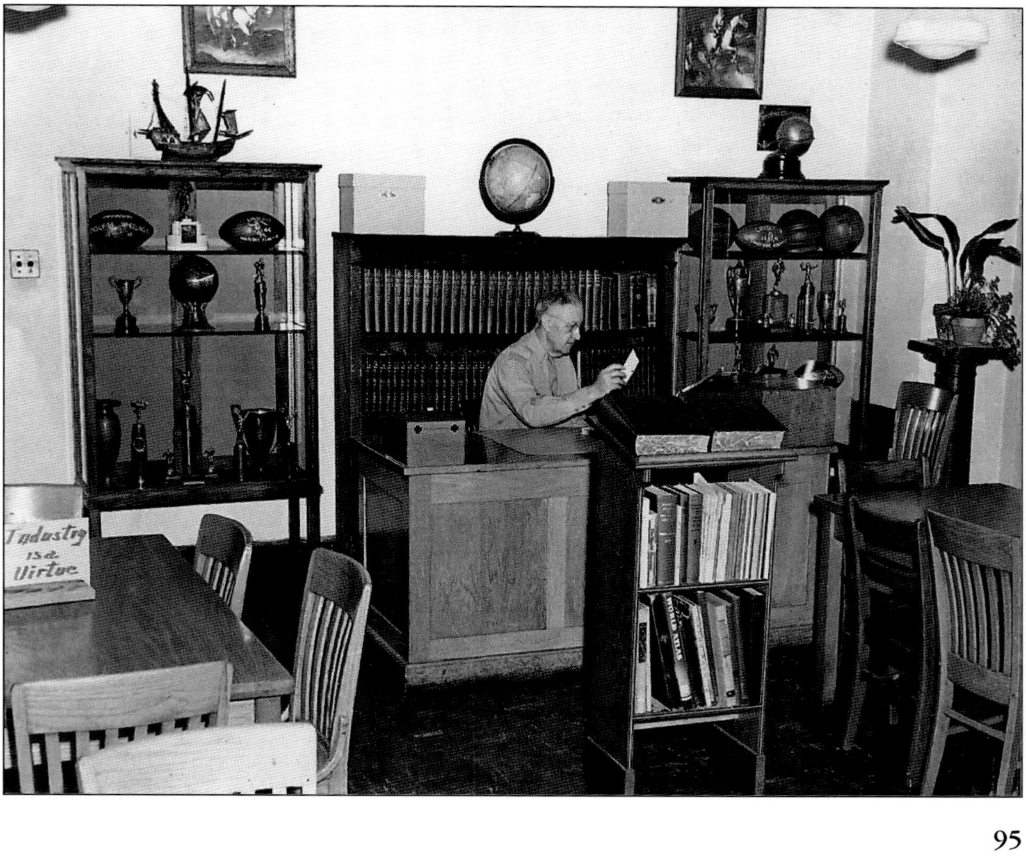

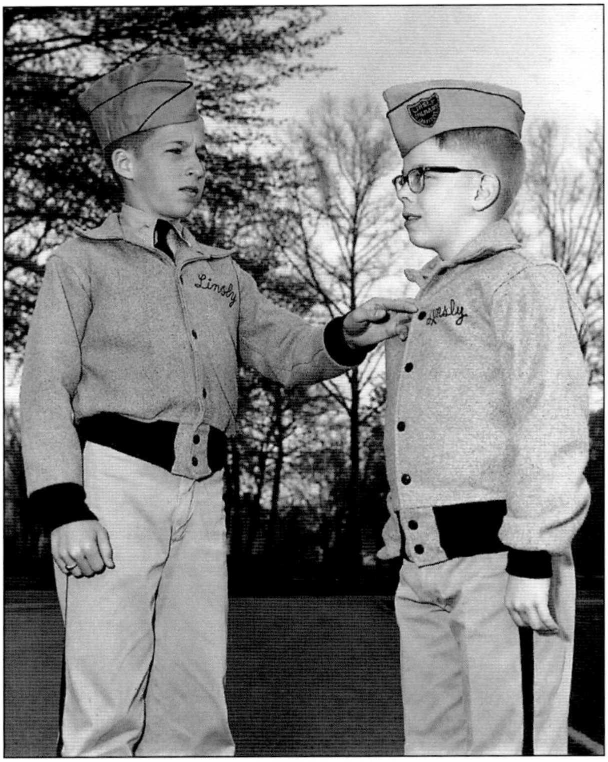

Grade School Students, c. 1960. The sixth-grade student on the left is providing a little instruction to the fifth-grade cadet on the right about the proper way to wear one's uniform. The boys are wearing what was known as the summer uniform.

Mrs. Goldie Becker and Her Assistants, 1957. From left to right are Edith Thompson, Anne Knabe, and Mrs. Goldie Becker. Every school day Mrs. Becker cooked and served a hot lunch to the entire student body. Her pies were delicious and much appreciated by the cadets. The seniors, who were the cadet officers, had the privilege of going to the head of the line.

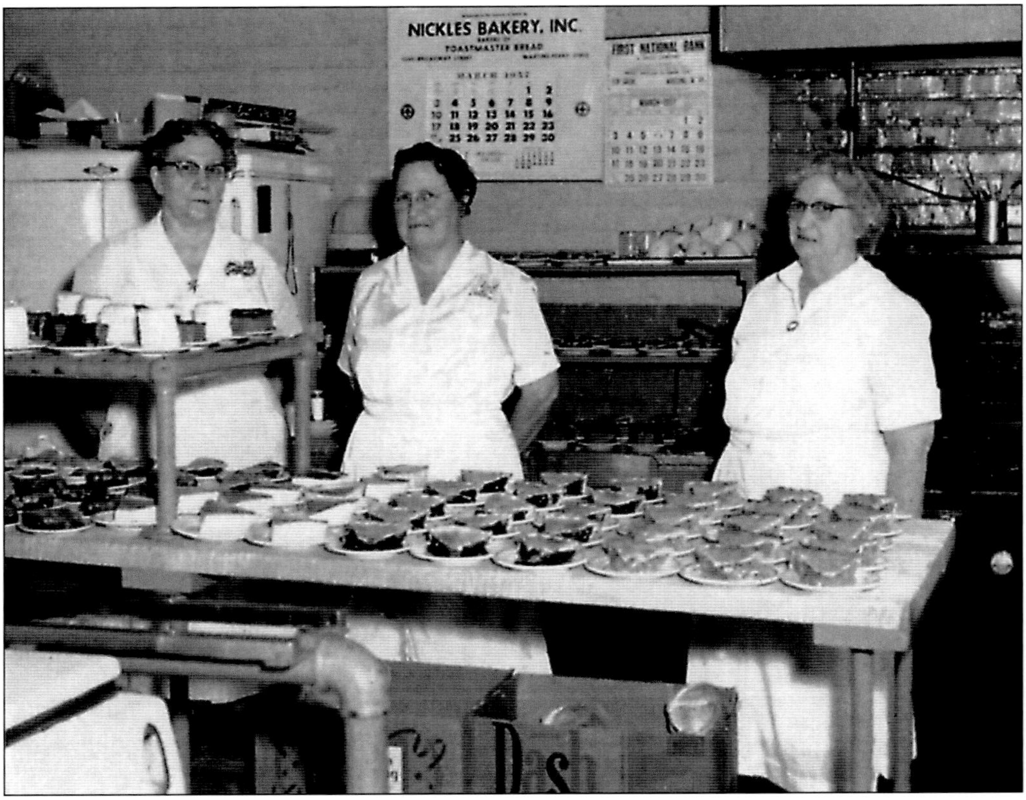

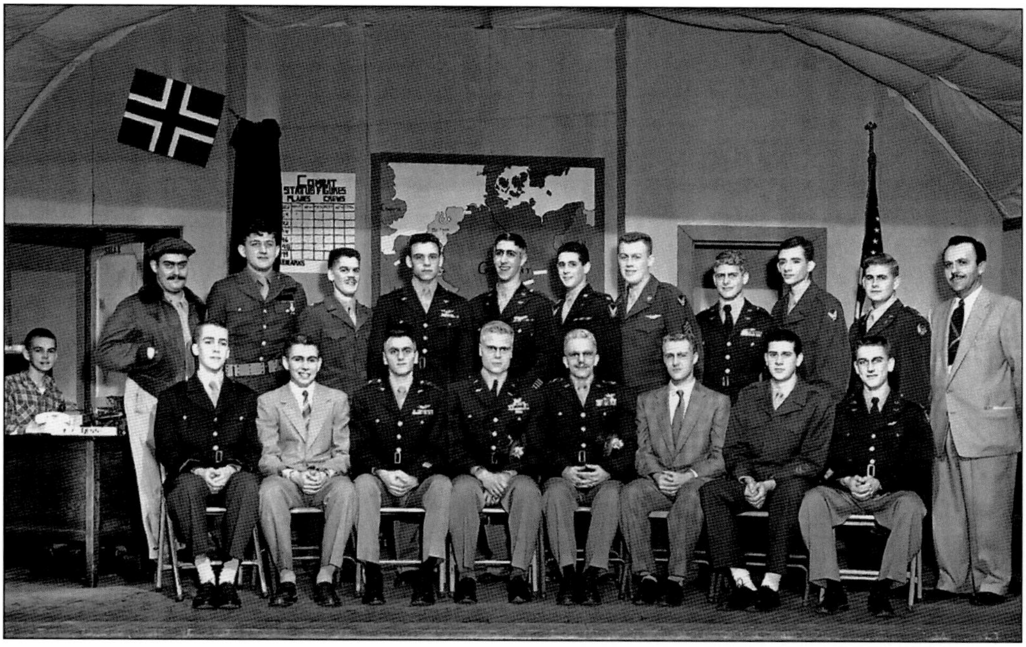

Senior Play, 1956. For many years Captain Peters (far right) organized a senior play. The players are shown in costume on the set of "Command Decision," which was held the the Behrens Gymnasium. Not shown are the members of the production crew and stage manager. Almost the entire senior class participated. Note: Only Captain Peters' moustache is real.

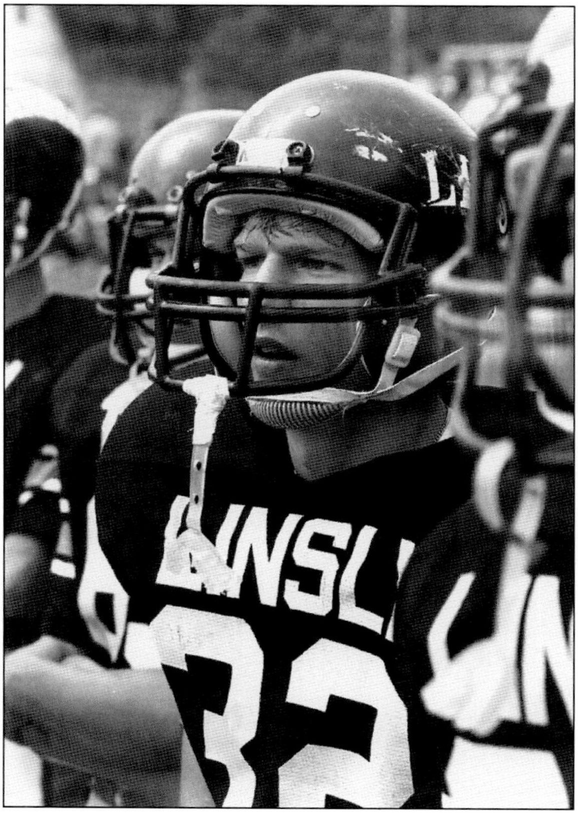

A Concerned Team Member, 1982. Even when players are on the sidelines they are involved in every second of the game.

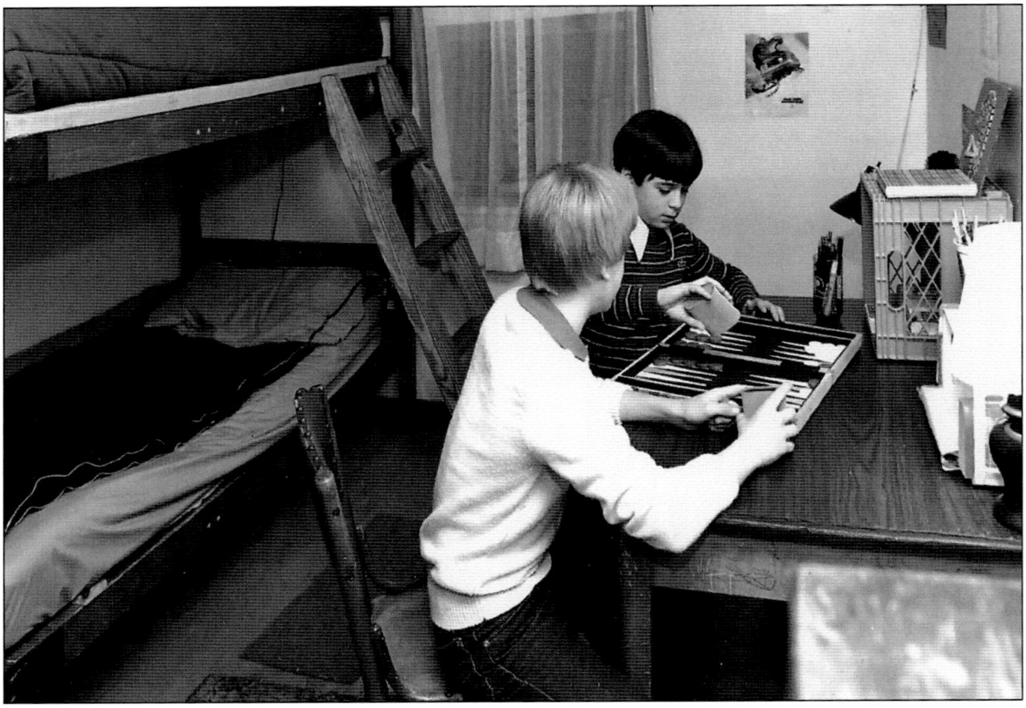

Backgammon Players, 1982. Board games are a common way to relax in the dorm after studies are completed.

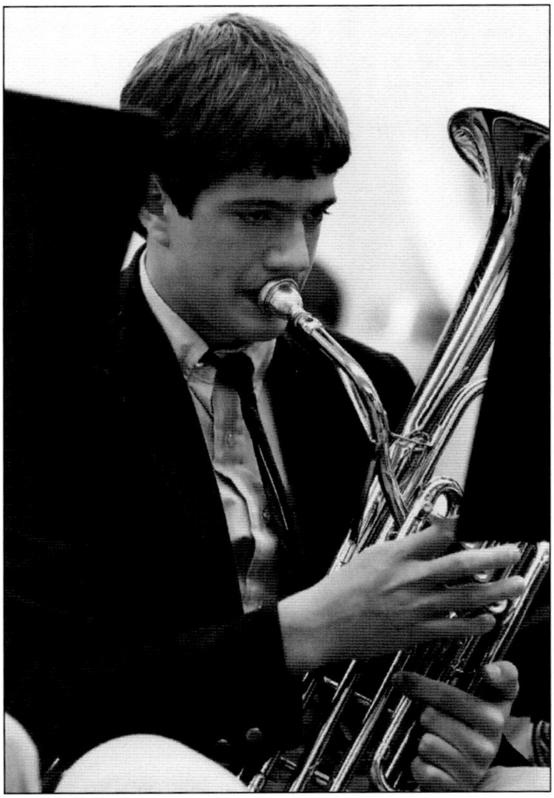

Concentration, 1982. This horn player is concentrating so intensely on getting all the notes right that he doesn't notice the photographer.

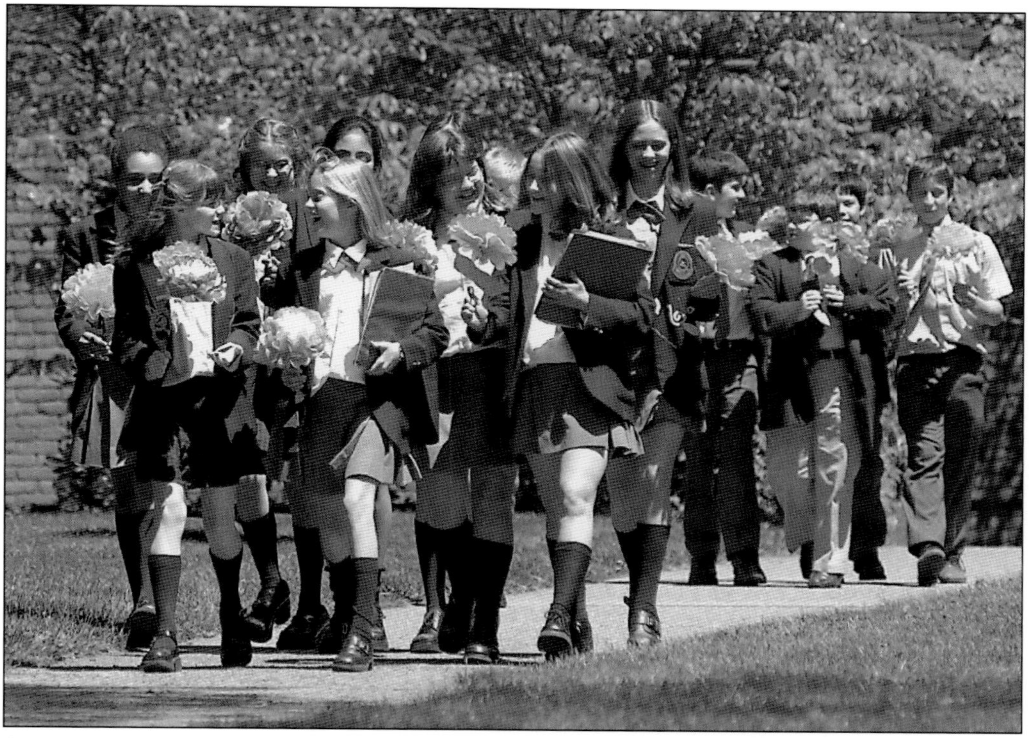

Students After an Art Class, 2002. Linsly's campus is especially beautiful in the spring and fall. The walk from one building to another between classes provides an opportunity to visit with friends and classmates. These students are carrying the paper flowers they created in art class.

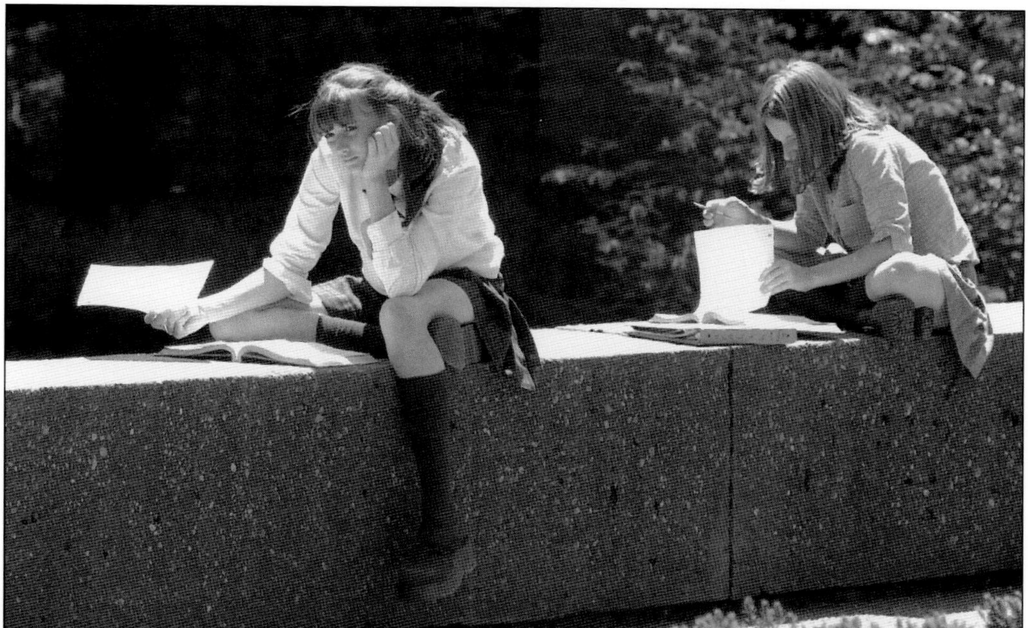

Outside Study, 2001. The wall above *The Aviator* is a favorite location for catching up on some homework during pleasant weather. There are many quiet niches around the wooded campus where students can go to study or just relax and talk with friends.

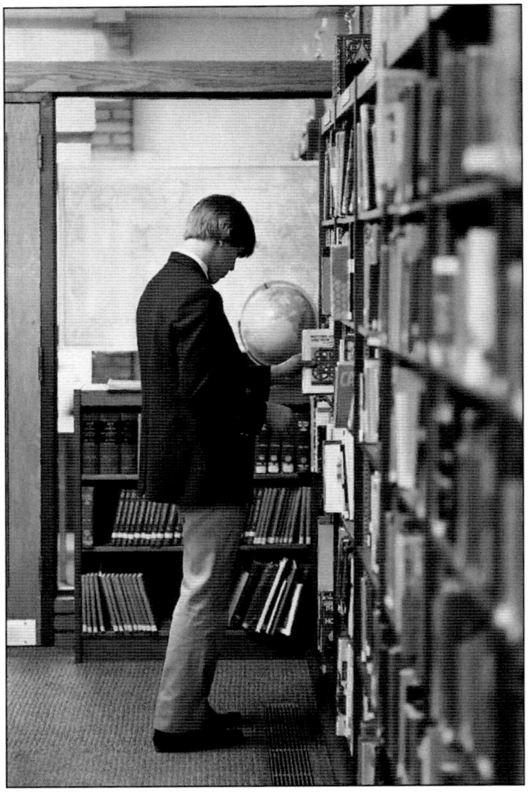

In the Library, 1982. Whether doing research for a paper or just browsing, the library is a quiet oasis where one can spend many profitable hours.

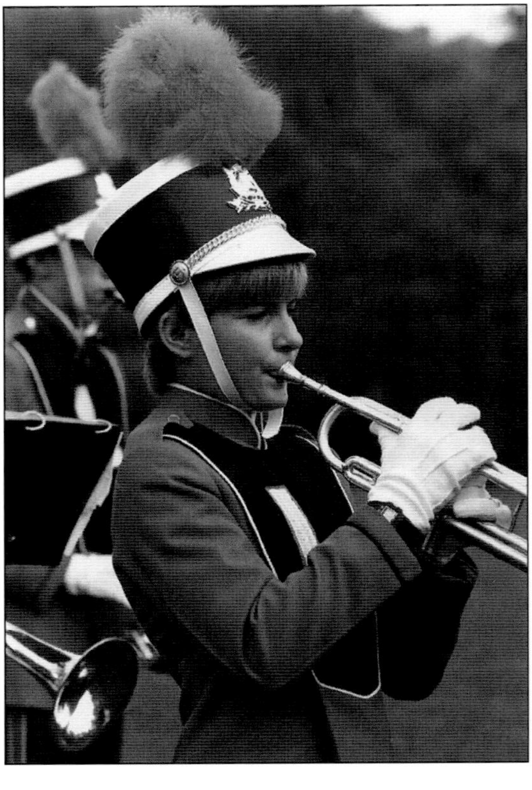

Marching Band Member, 1982. In a marching band one has to concentrate not only on the music but also on keeping in step and staying in line.

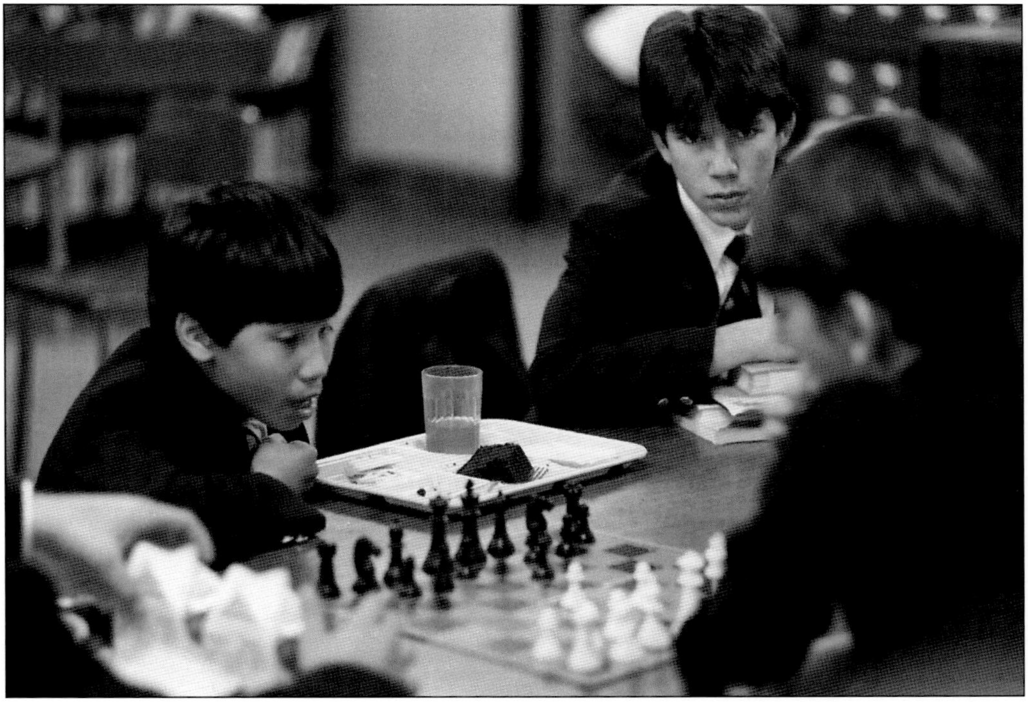

Lunch and Chess, 1982. These young chess players are so devoted that they are using part of their lunch period for a game. The boy on the left seems to be more interested in the next move than in his dessert.

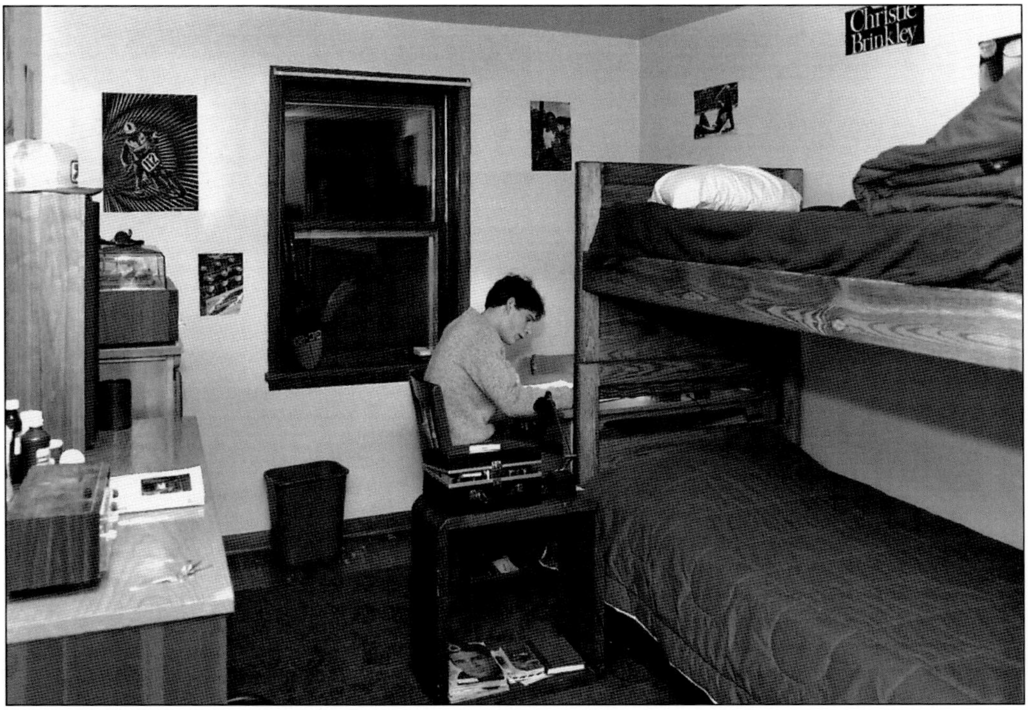

Study Time, 1982. A boarding student puts in some time at homework. Every dorm resident had his own study area.

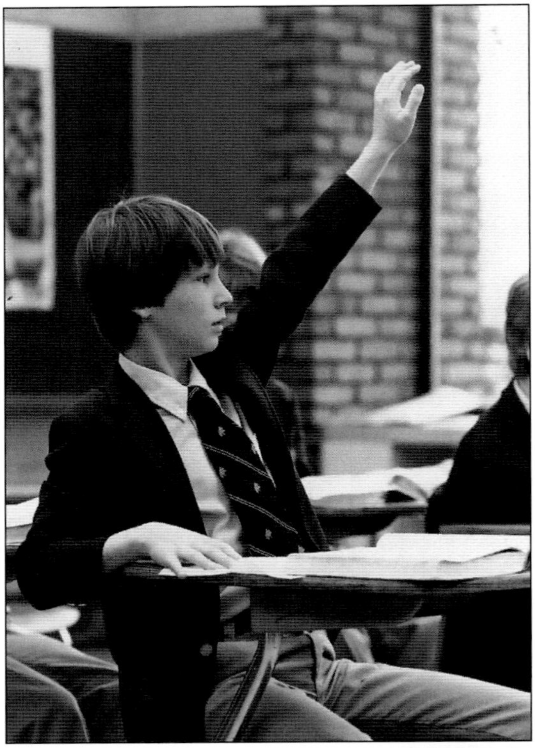

Yes! I Know the Answer, 1982. Linsly's small classes provide ample opportunity for students to interact with the instructor in the classroom.

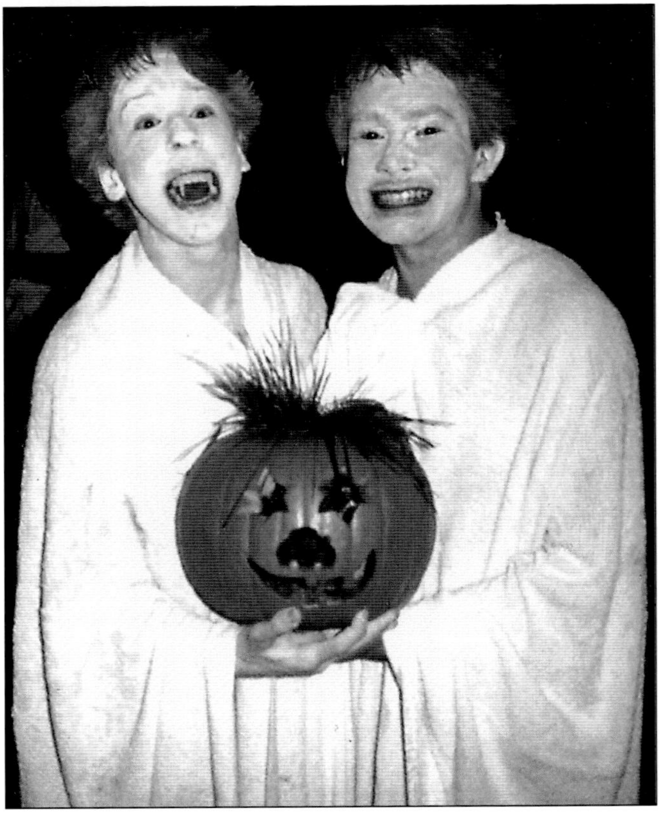

Ghosts! 1985. These dorm students have created appropriately scary costumes for a Halloween party.

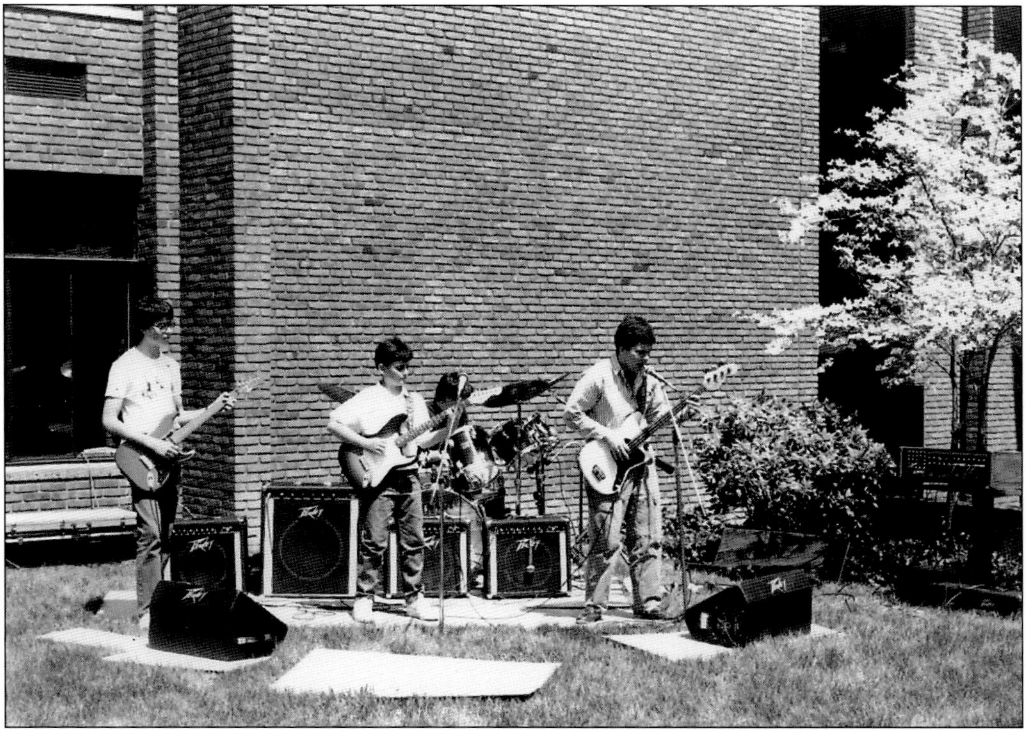

A Student Band, 1987. From left to right are Dennis Campbell, Brad Paisley, Bill Bedway, and Todd Thonen. This group played for Youth Appreciation Day in 1987.

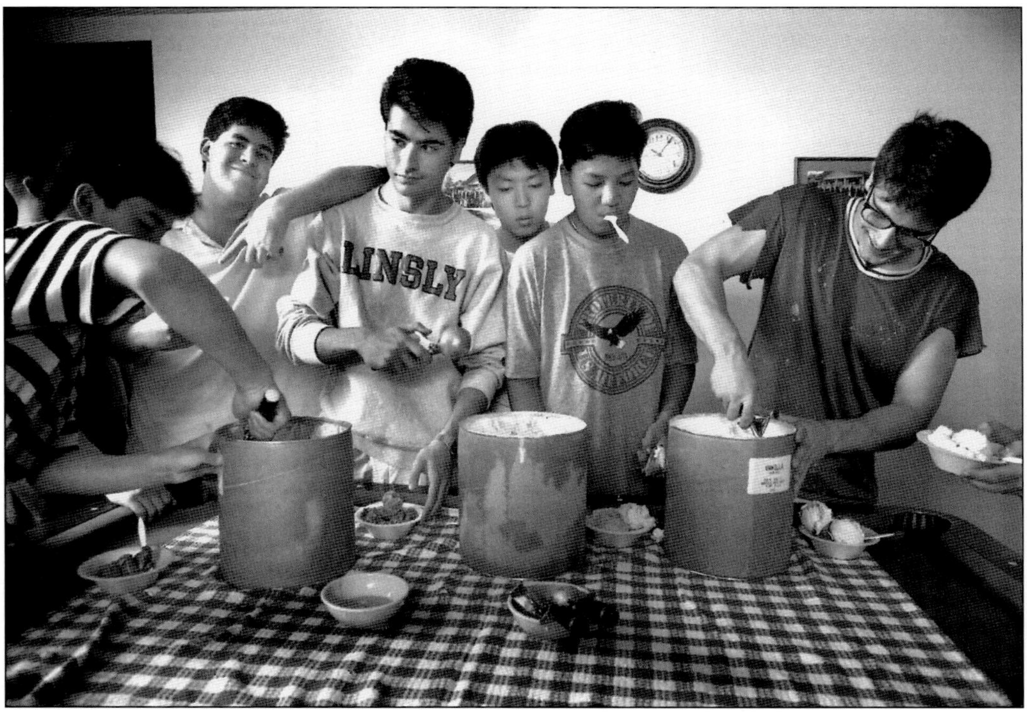

Ice Cream Party, 1988. Dormitory parties were common and often had a theme like this one.

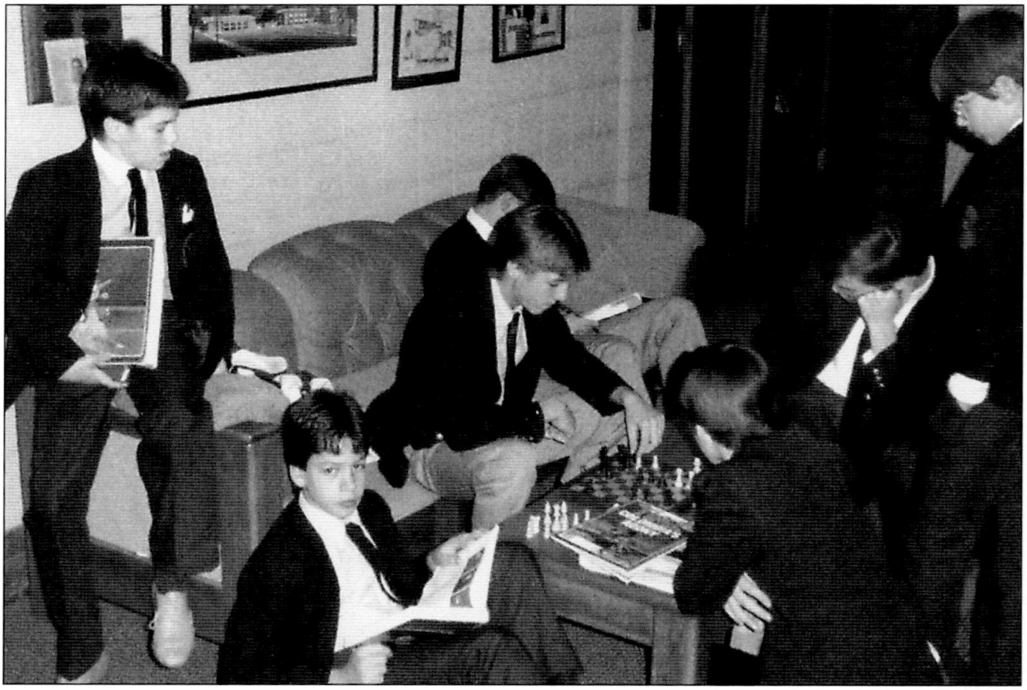

Dorm Scene, 1985. Dormitory residents relax in the living room area while waiting for dinner. Evening meals and breakfast were prepared and served by the staff in each dormitory.

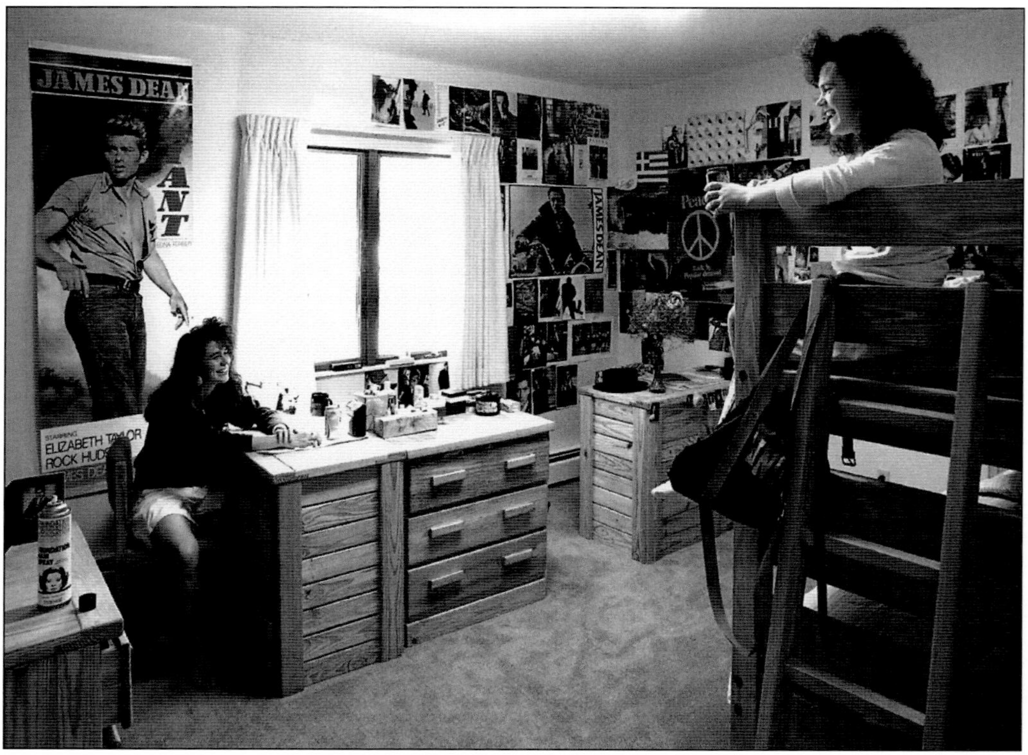

Girls' Dorm Room, 1989. Even if the young ladies were not present, the decor would be a clue as to whether this was a girls' or boys' room.

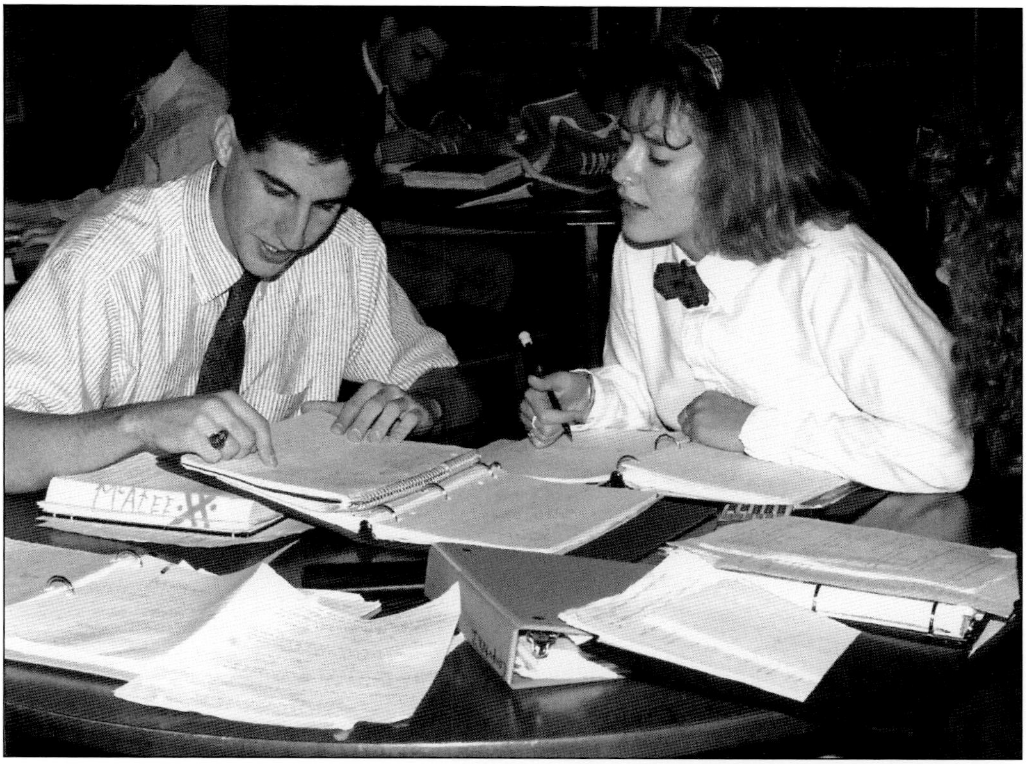

Coed Study, 1989. Studying with a friend is always more pleasant than working by yourself. Is the young man explaining something or asking a question?

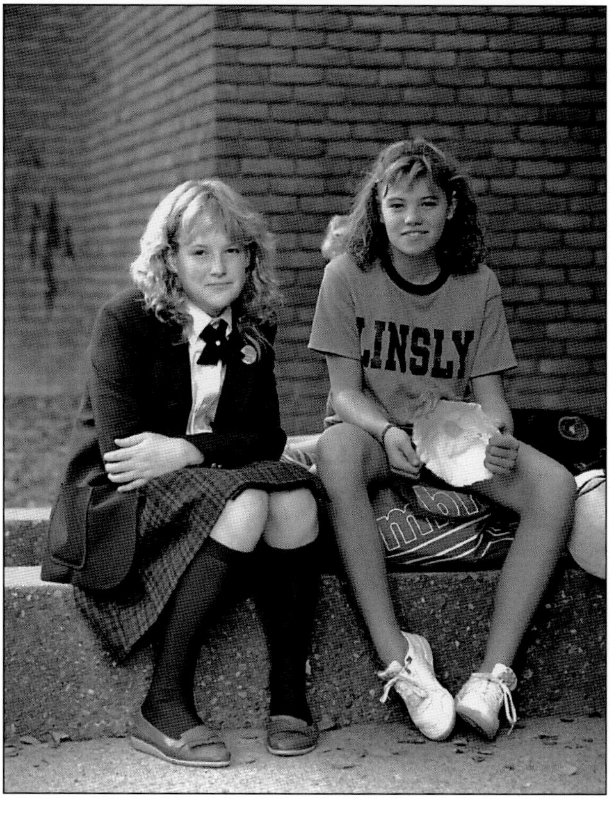

Two Friends, 1989. The difference between the uniform required for classes and the informal dress adopted after the day's classes can be seen here. Perhaps the young lady on the right is on her way to participate in a sport.

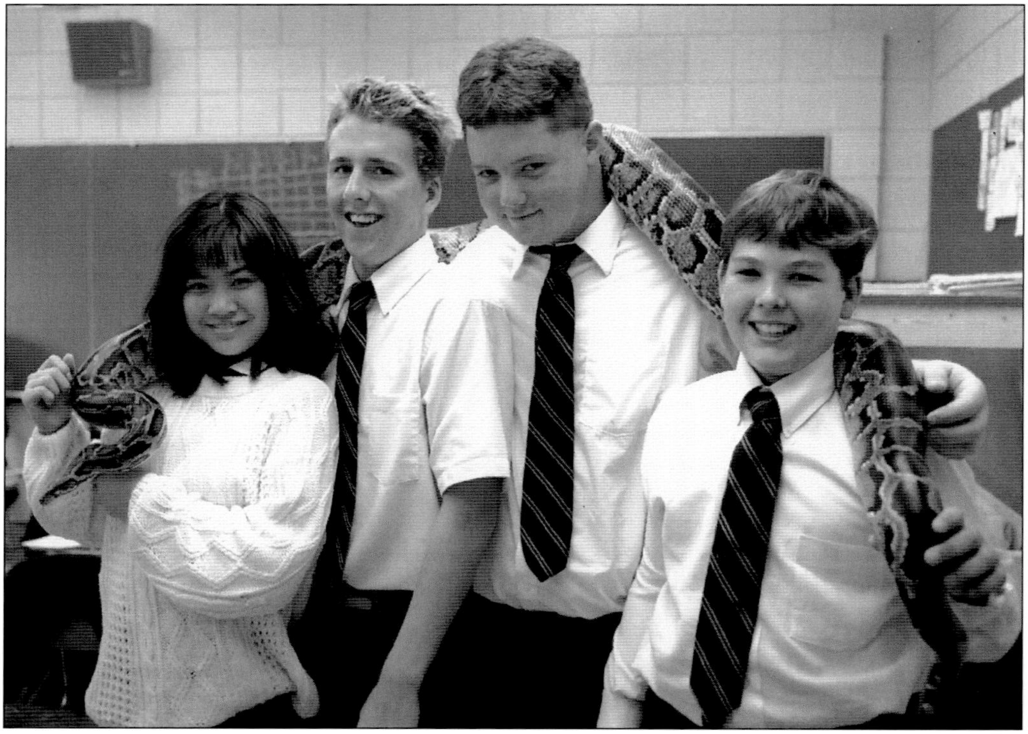

Four Friends and a Friendly Snake, 1989. When you need to handle a snake of this size, it's best to have some help from your friends. Who said girls don't like snakes, anyway?

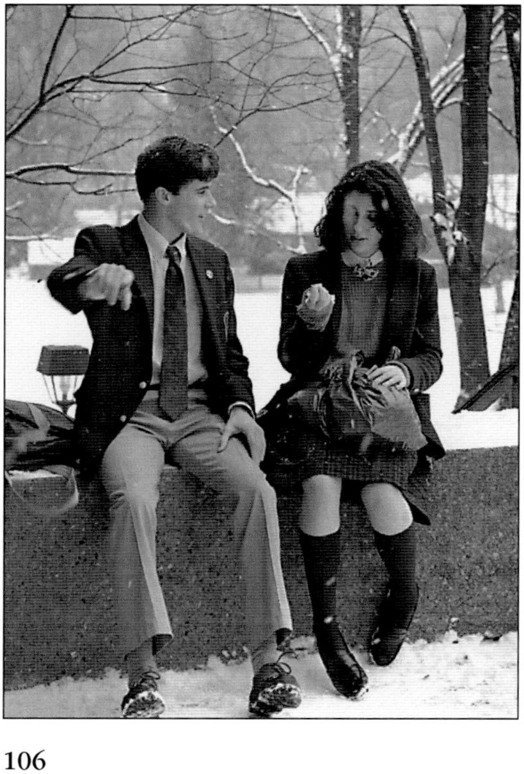

What Is This Stuff? 1989. Some of the boarding students from the southern states have never seen snow before. The girl seems to be fascinated by a handful of snow and the boy is probably explaining its characteristic properties and maybe what you can do with it.

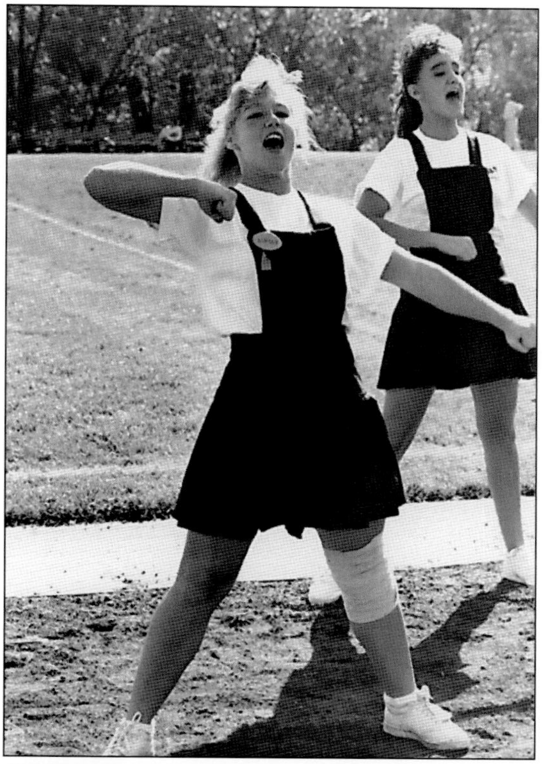

Cheerleaders, 1990. Linsly's cheerleaders are always up, always excited, and always fun. Their enthusiasm and dazzling routines are an essential part of every football and basketball game.

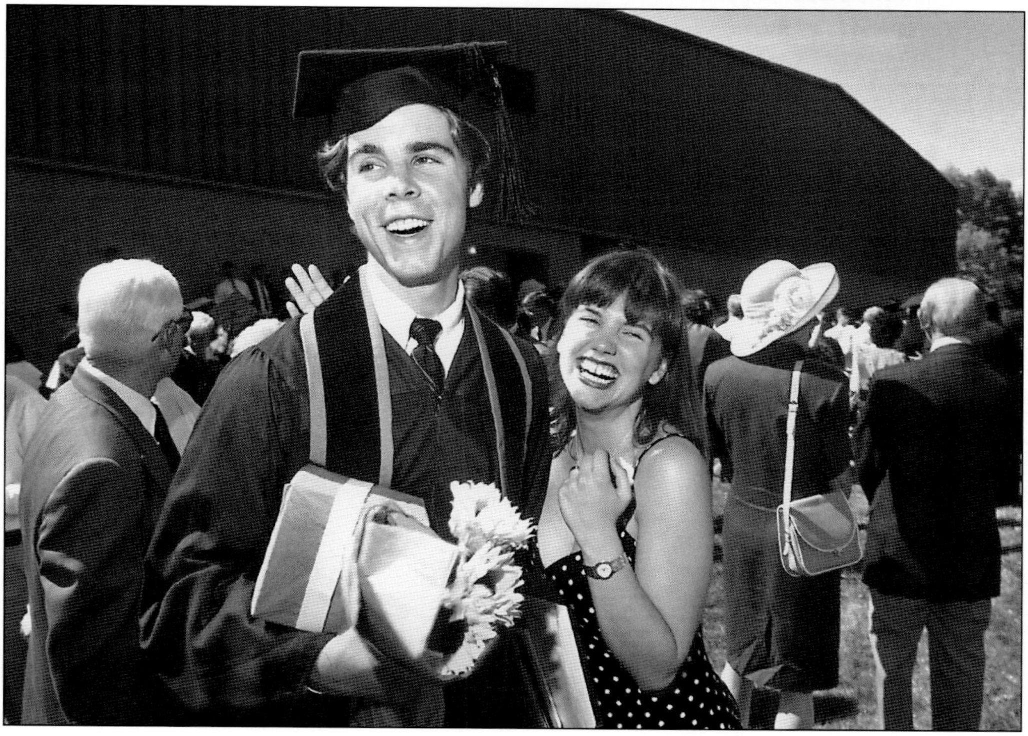

Graduation Day, 1992. Parents and relatives are happy, girlfriends are happy, but no one is happier that the graduates.

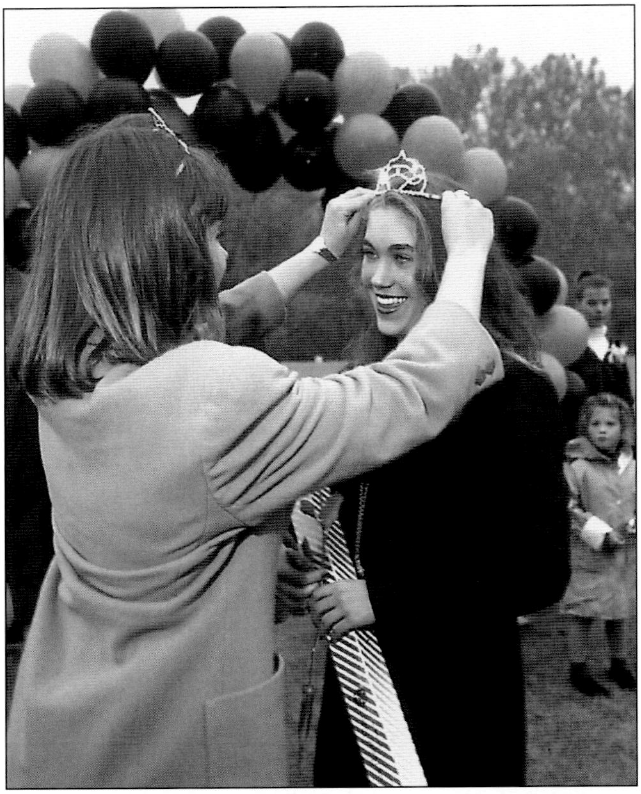

Crowning the Homecoming Queen, 1992. This is just one of the exciting homecoming rituals enjoyed by students, parents, family, friends, and old grads.

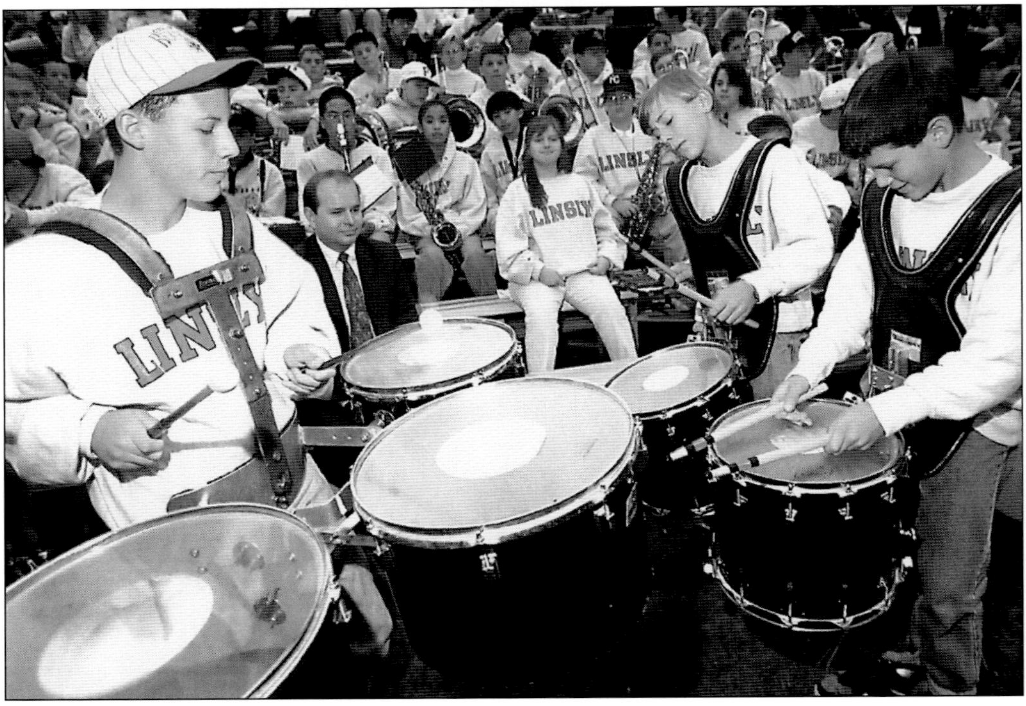

Linsly's Pep Band, 1992. By the 1990s, Linsly no longer had a marching band, but this pep band livened up football and basketball games. Featured in this photograph is the drum section.

AT THE PROM, 1990. The uniforms, the dance cards and the grand march that were all part of the military ball are gone, but the young ladies still wear beautiful prom gowns and the young men dress in tuxedos for this annual event. This couple seems to be relaxing between dances.

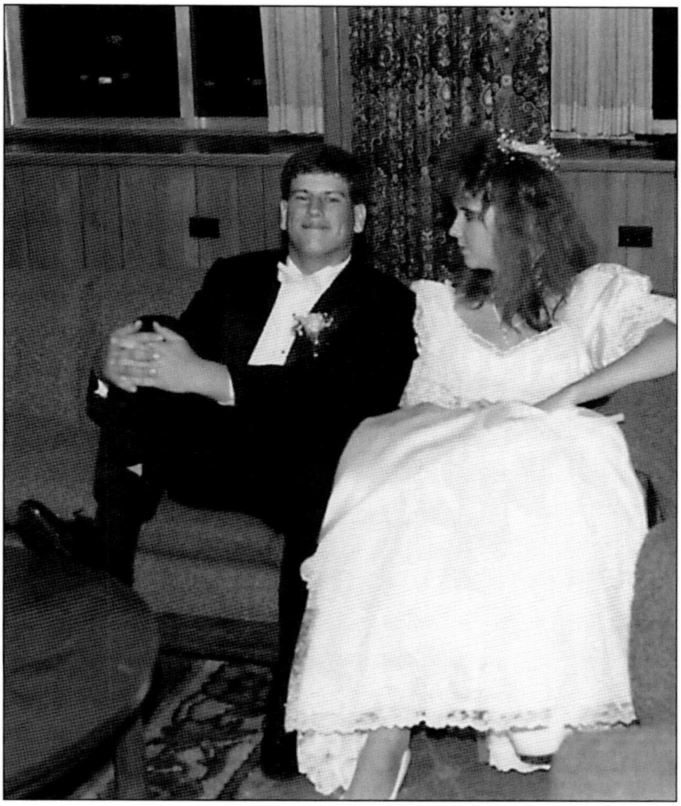

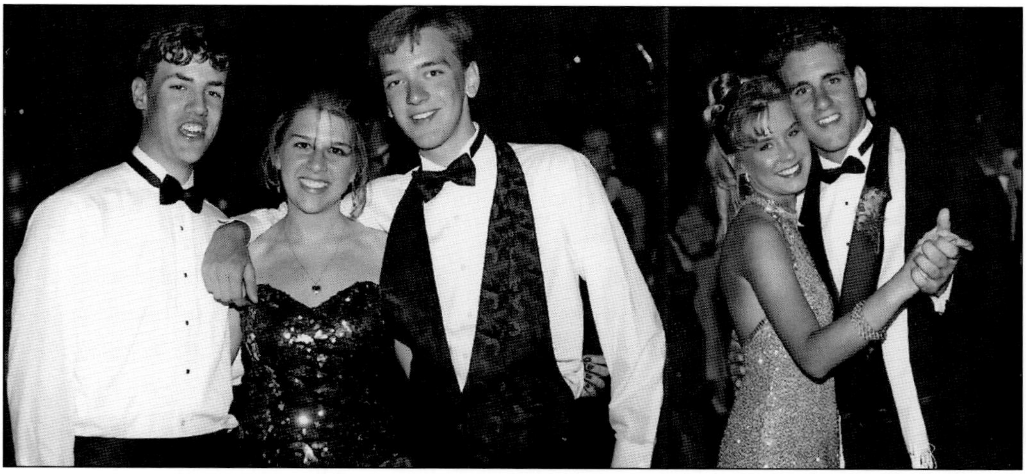

AT THE PROM, 1993. The young lady on the left appears to have two dates. The photo of the couple on the right is timeless and could be almost any year. The music, the style of dress and the dances change but having fun does not. Today's prom lasts longer than the military ball and is much less formalized. It usually ends with everyone going out for breakfast.

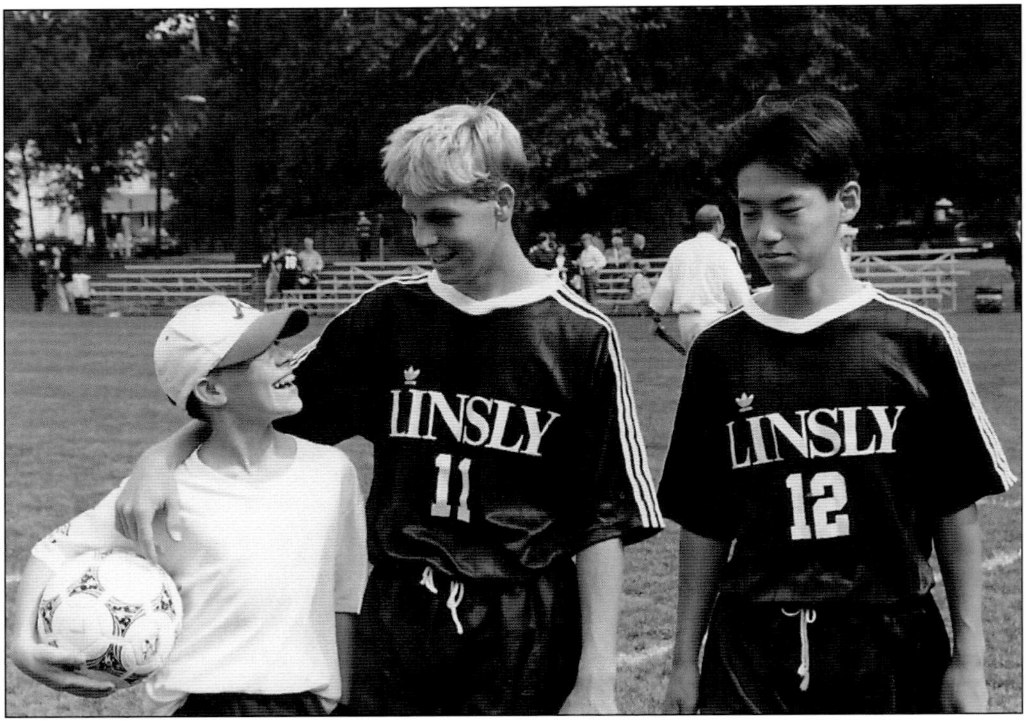

SOCCER BUDDIES, 1994. Throughout the entire history of The Linsly School the older students have helped and befriended the younger students.

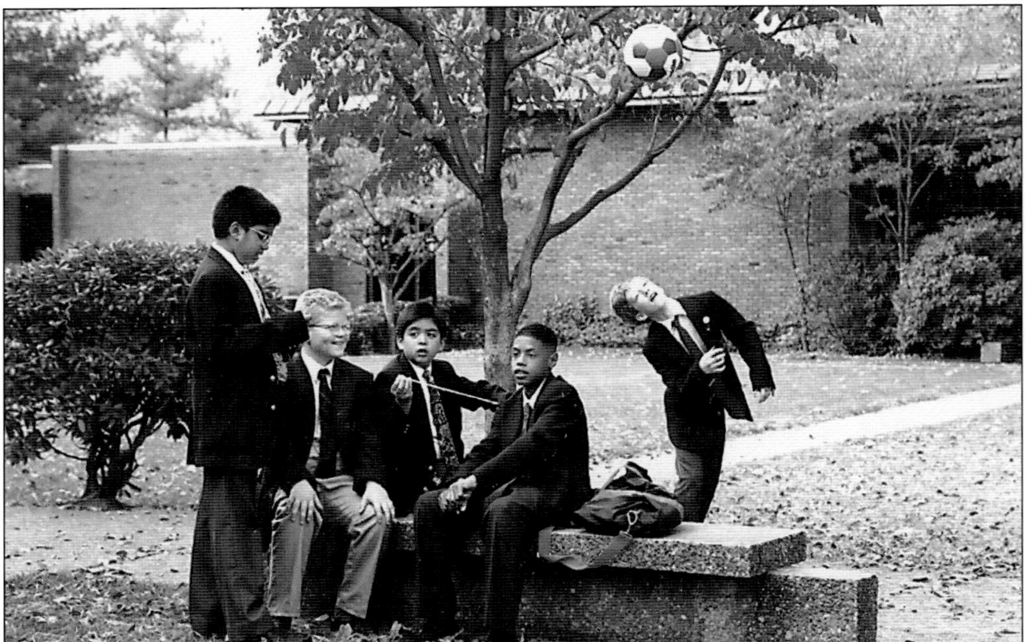

HANGING AROUND ON CAMPUS, 1994. Lower school students enjoy a break between classes on a beautiful fall day. Though located in the city of Wheeling, the wooded campus is isolated and beautiful during all seasons of the year, but especially in the fall and the spring.

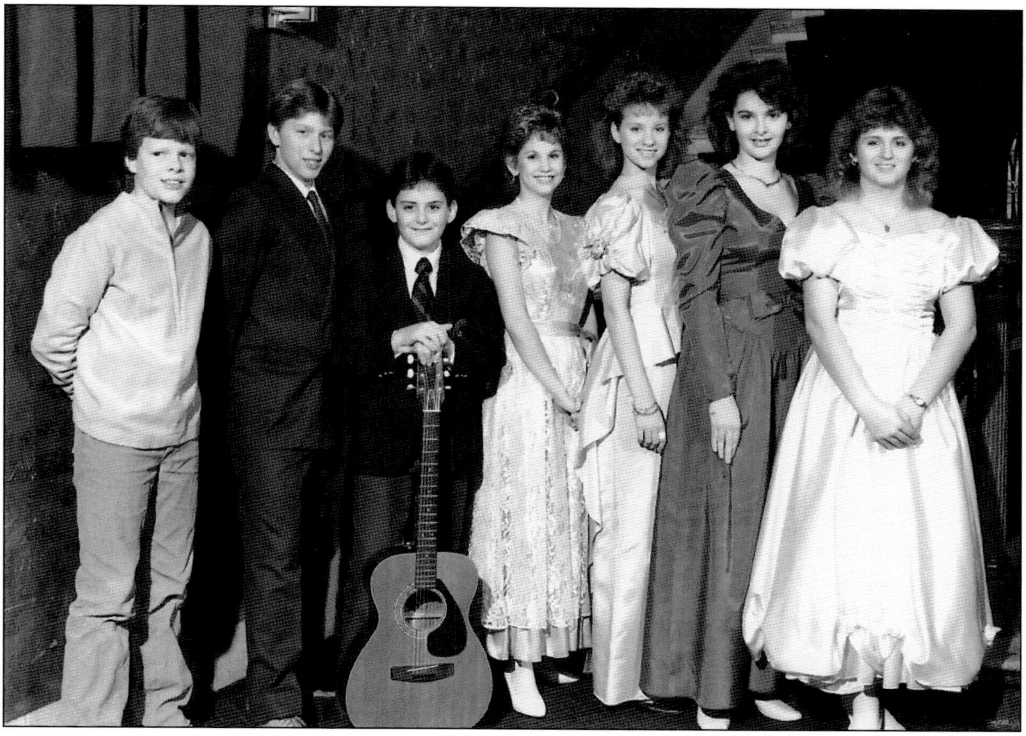

Extravaganza Group. The young man with the guitar went on to become country music singer/songwriter, Brad Paisley. The annual Linsly Extravaganza is held in the Capitol Music Hall in Wheeling, which is the home of the WWVA Jamboree. This theater seats 2000 people and is always packed on the evening of the show.

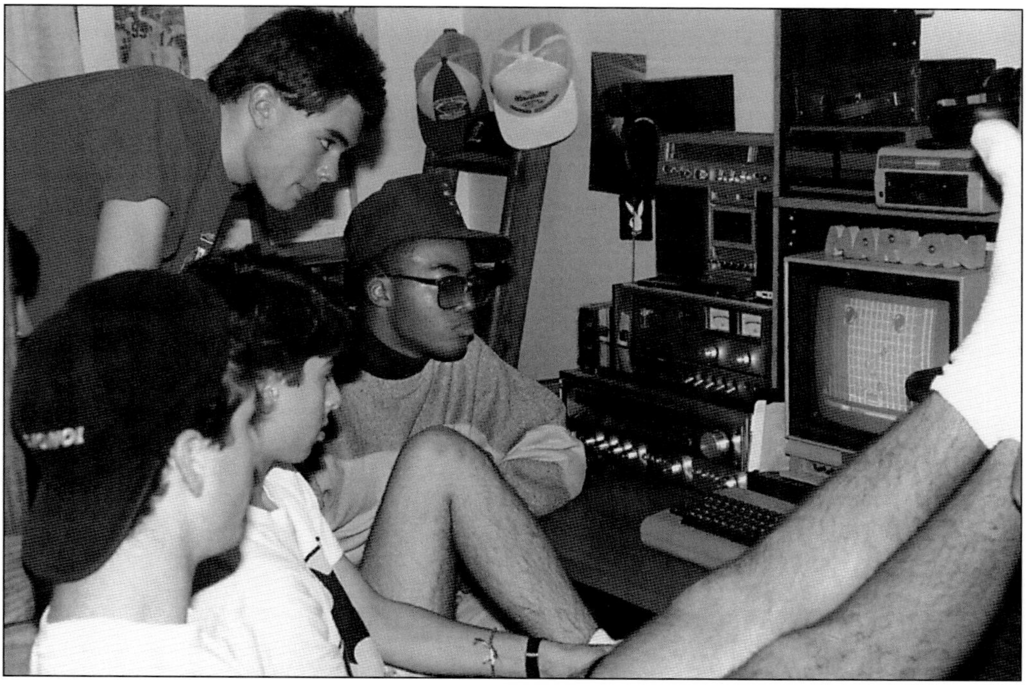

Computer Games. Electronics play an important part in today's amusements.

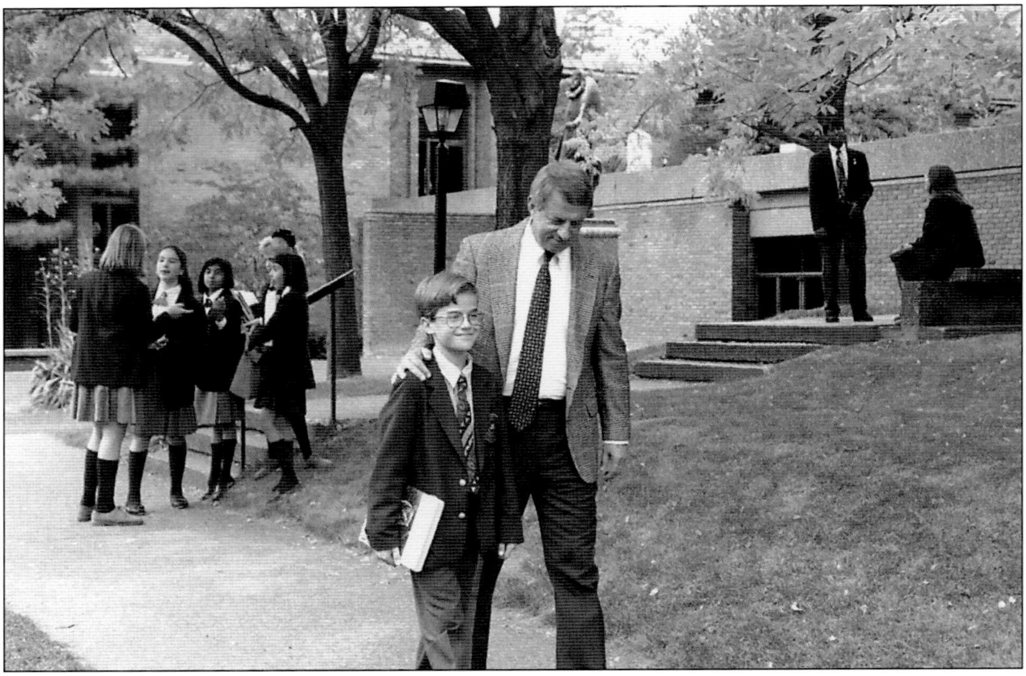

Headmaster DiOrio and Friend. Between classes students have time for a quick chat with their friends.

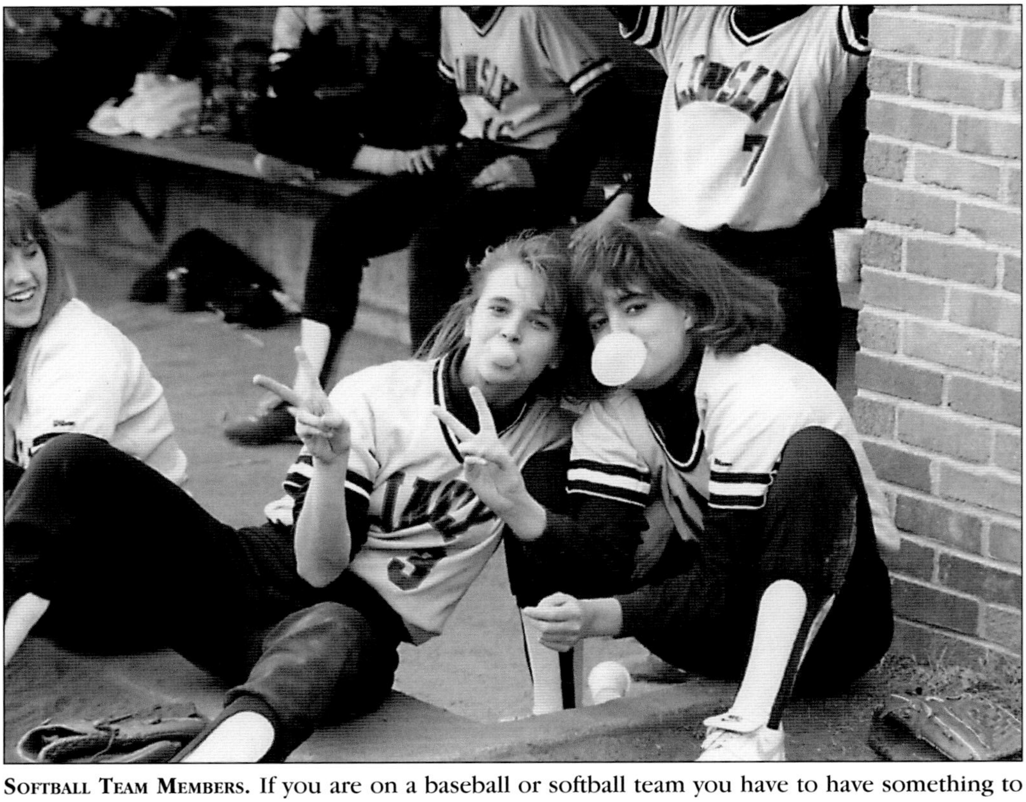

Softball Team Members. If you are on a baseball or softball team you have to have something to chew. The "V" it is presumed, is for "Victory."

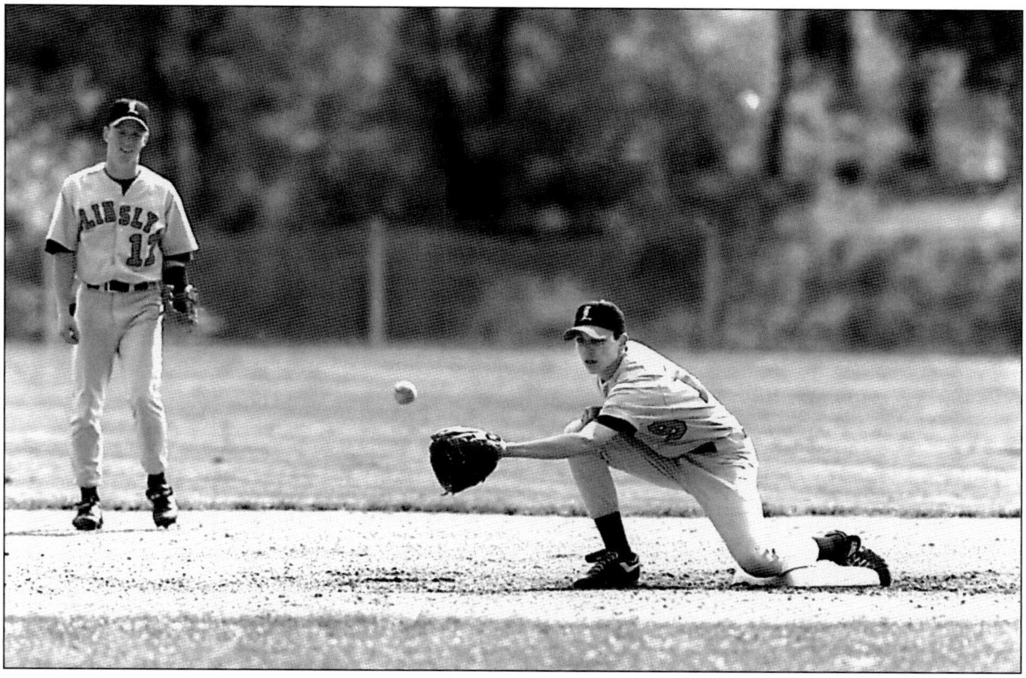

That's One Away! In 1975, a generous donation by William Holloway allowed the construction of an outstanding new facility for baseball and softball on Linsly's campus. No doubt this has contributed to the success of both the boys' and girls' teams.

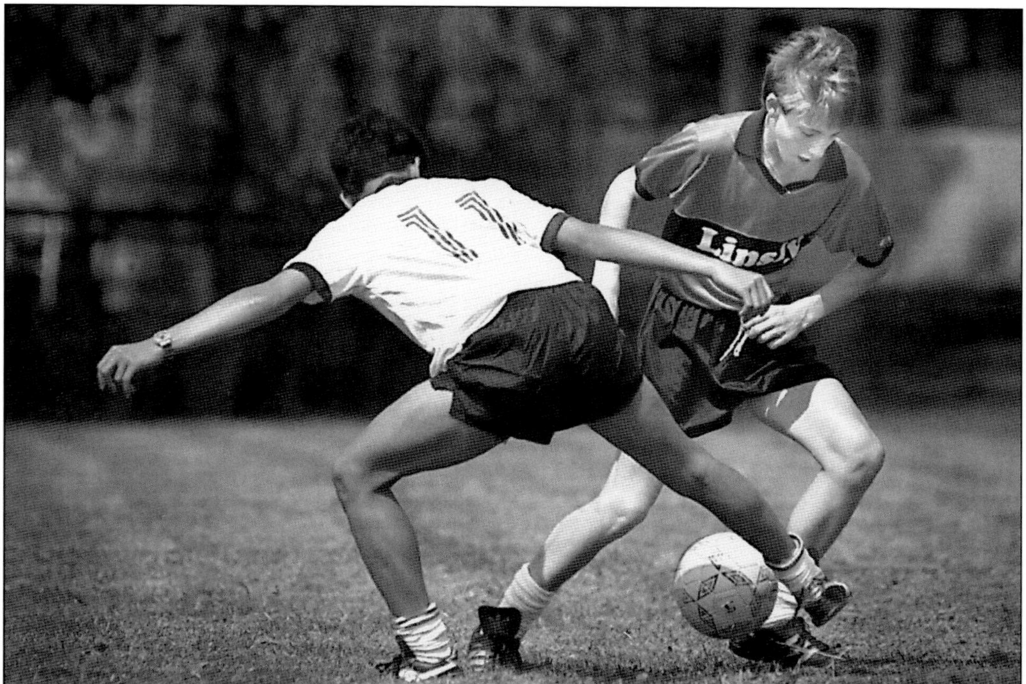

Mixing It Up on the Soccer Field. Soccer is becoming very popular at Linsly and in the surrounding area. Although Linsly already has two soccer fields, at least one new field is planned for the immediate future.

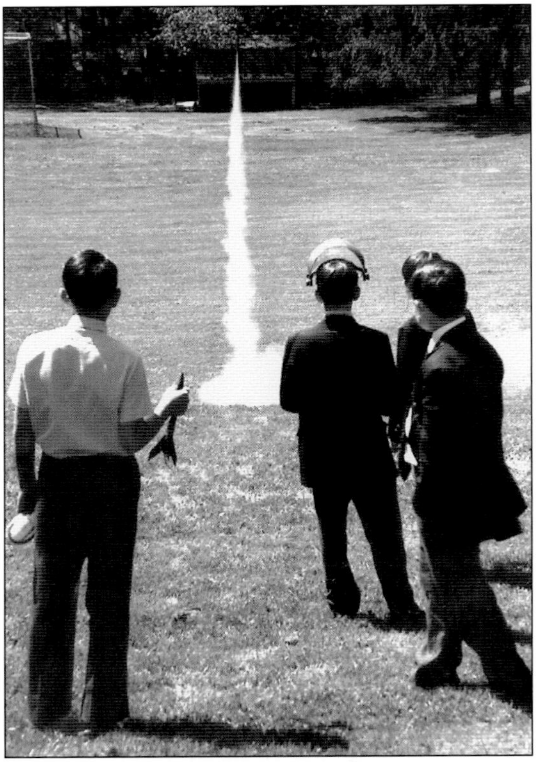

The Rocketeers. These science class students have constructed a large number of rockets, both large and small, and are testing them.

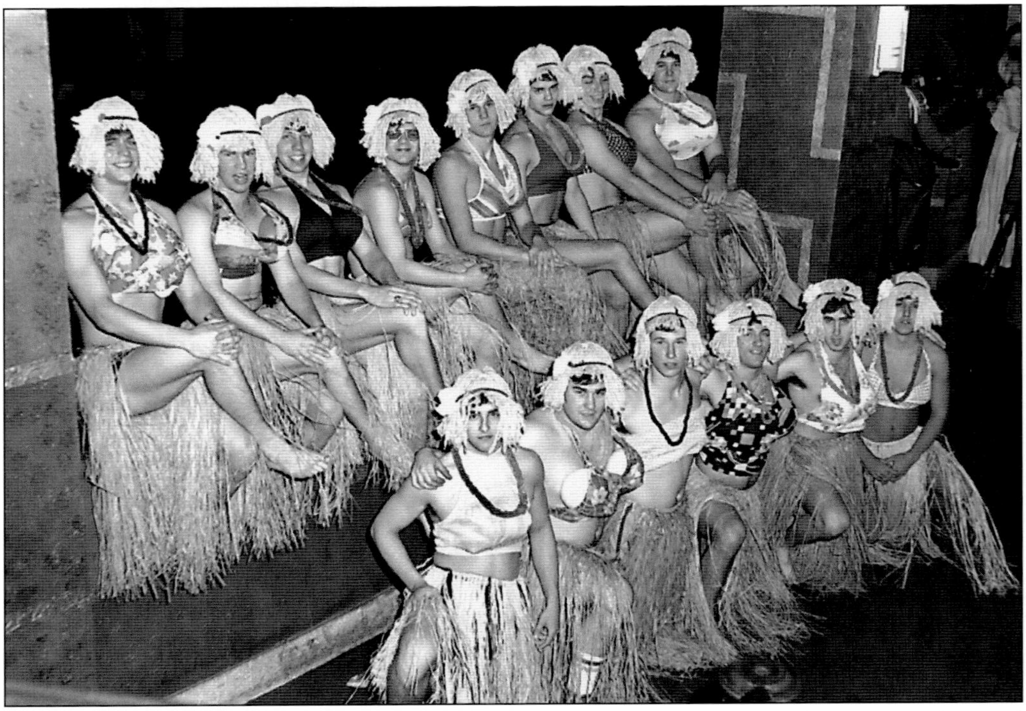

Stage Beauties from the Extravaganza, 1978. It was probably Douglas Haigwood who dreamed up the idea of the Stage Beauties, which, back in the 1950s, were made up almost exclusively by members of the varsity football team. In any case, this traditional act never fails to get a laugh.

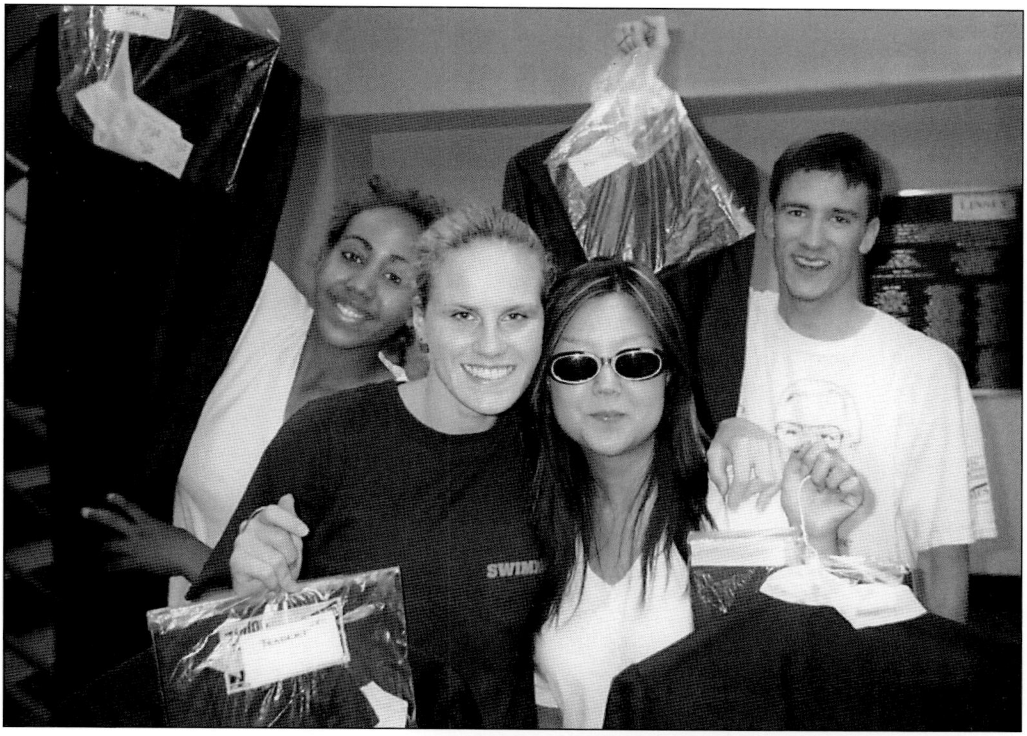

Getting Ready for Graduation, 2001. The students above know that it won't be long now. All they have to do is to put on their caps and gowns. The rest should be easy. But then there is that special moment when, with all eyes on you, you climb the stairs to the platform and receive your diploma. Graduation was held outside for many years, usually in front of Merriman Hall. Once the Field House was completed, graduation ceremonies were held there.

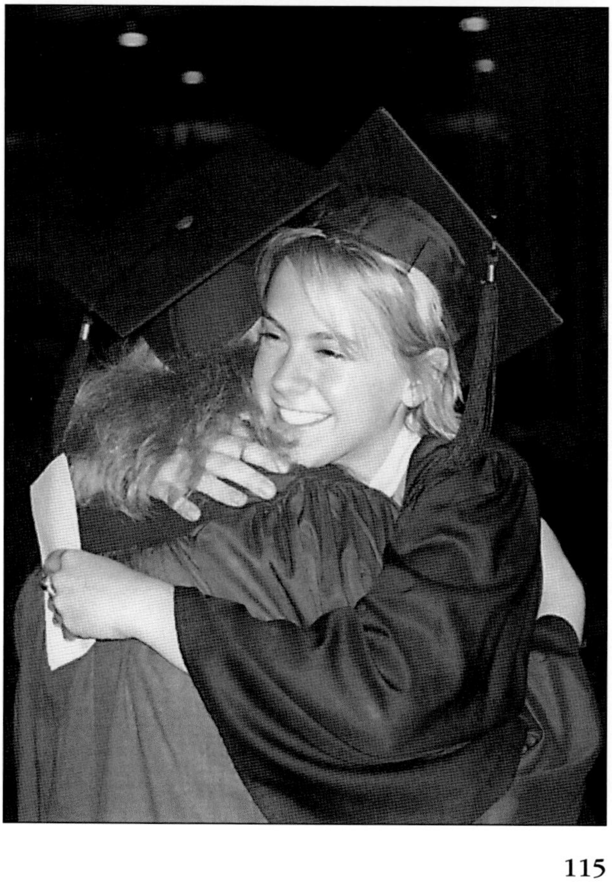

We Made It! 2001. Mixed in with the excitement of finally graduating and the words of congratulations and praise from family and friends is the sadness of separating from one's classmates. For graduates of Linsly it has been more than a school—it has been a home and a way of life.

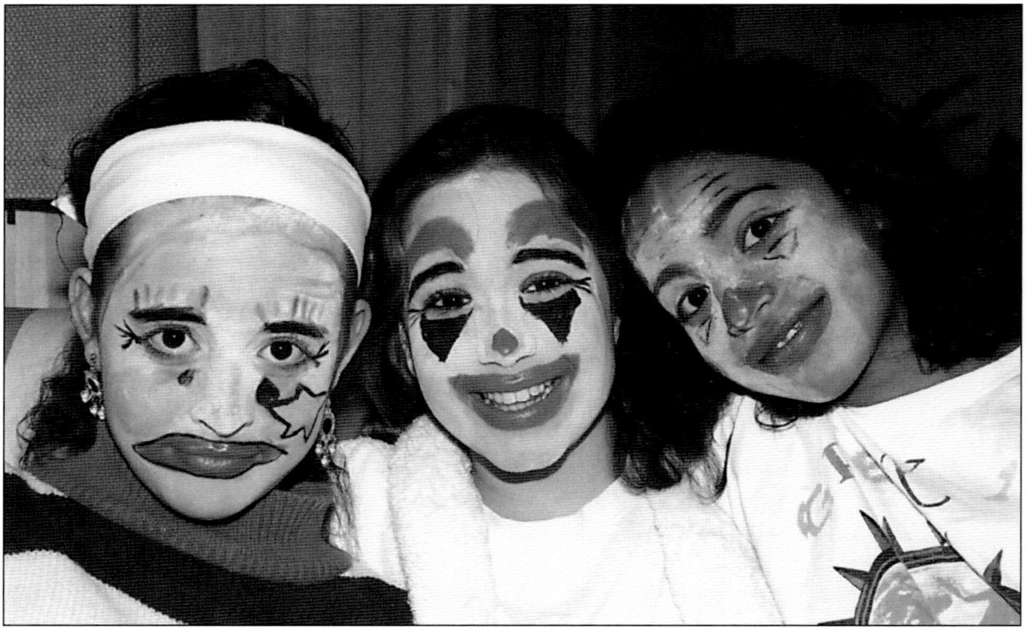

All Made Up for the Extravaganza. Above all, being part of the annual Extravaganza is just plain fun. There is something for everyone to do, making use of their talents whether on stage or behind the scenes. When the curtain comes down at the end of the performance, all of the participants know that they have been a part of a special event to which virtually every member of the Linsly family has contributed.

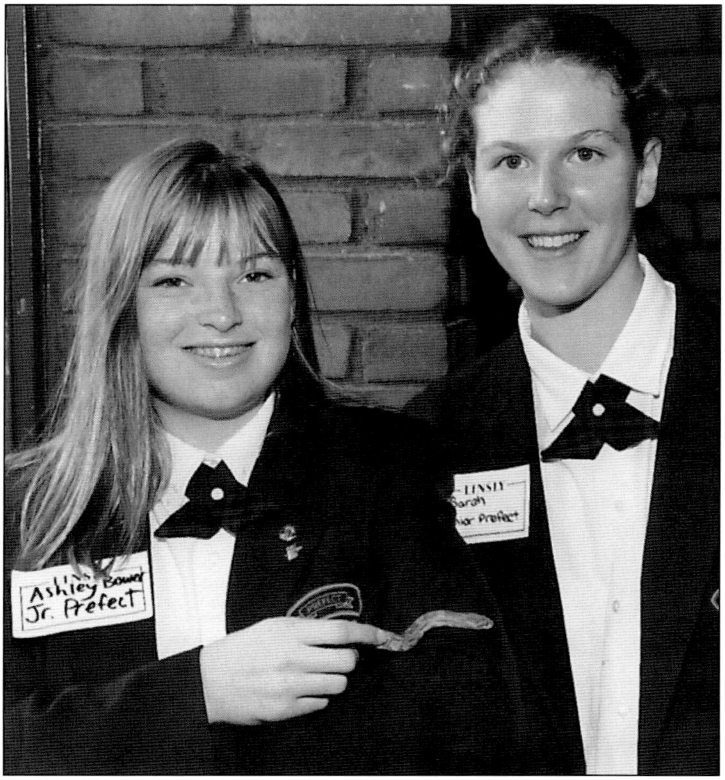

Two Prefects and Friend, 1994. The prefect system provides role models for the other students and an incentive to excel both academically and socially. Students compete for the honor of being chosen prefect. The position itself contributes to the growth of those selected and placed in a leadership position.

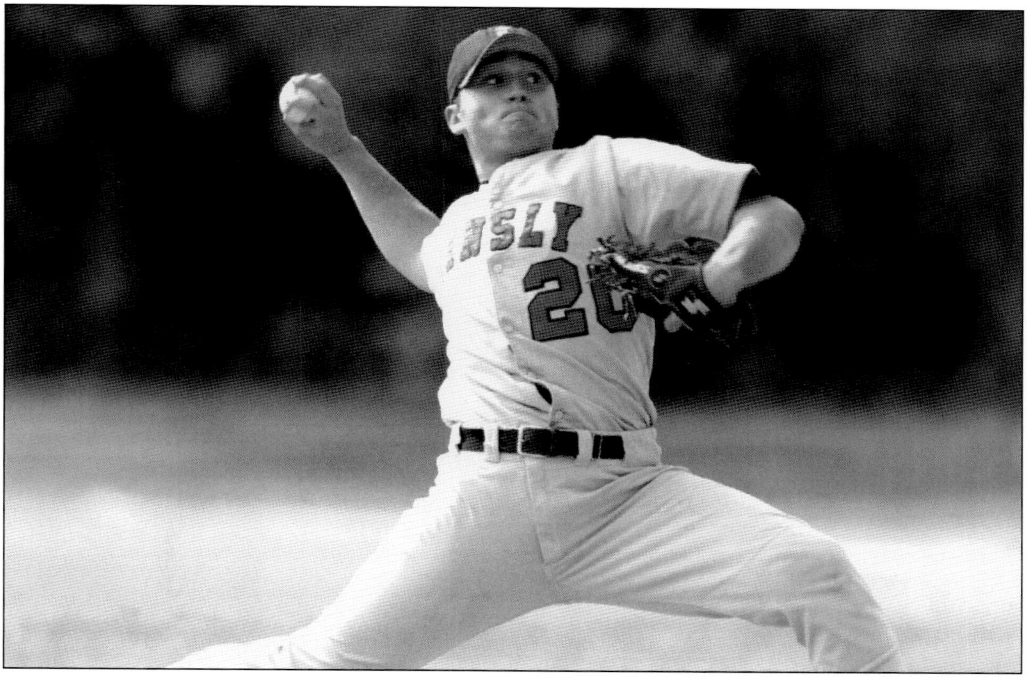

The Pitch. From the expression on his face to the tense muscle strain of his body one can read intense determination and the will to succeed by this Linsly baseball team member. The photo is a personification of the "no quit" policy.

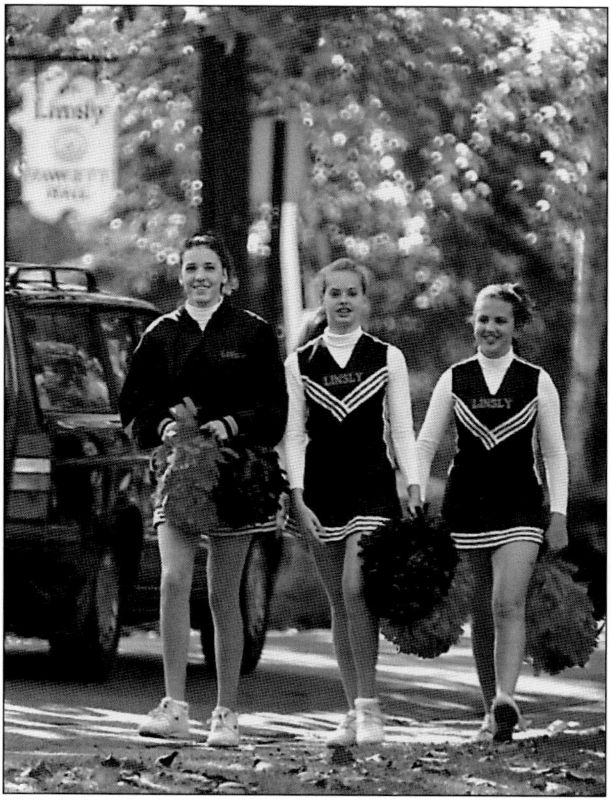

After the Game. It's a sunny fall afternoon and these Linsly cheerleaders are walking across campus after the football game at Lockhart Field. From the looks on their faces one might guess that Linsly won.

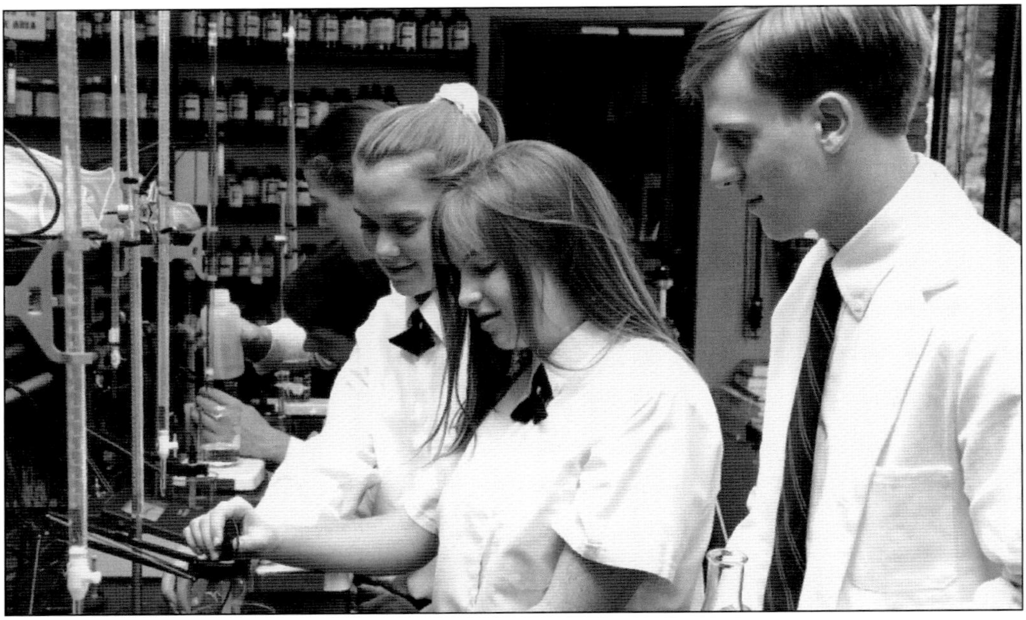

CHEMISTRY LAB, 1994. Linsly's science facilities are outstanding and on a par with college laboratories. Linsly has produced several female graduates who have become very successful in many areas of science. A good example is Ashley Mulroy, Linsly 2001, who won the grand prize at the West Liberty Regional Science Fair and the W.Va. State Science Fair and was honored as "grand laureate" at an international science competition in Stockholm, Sweden, which is considered by many as a virtual Nobel Prize for teenagers. Ashley's stepfather said of her, "She doesn't quit until she gets to the bottom of something."

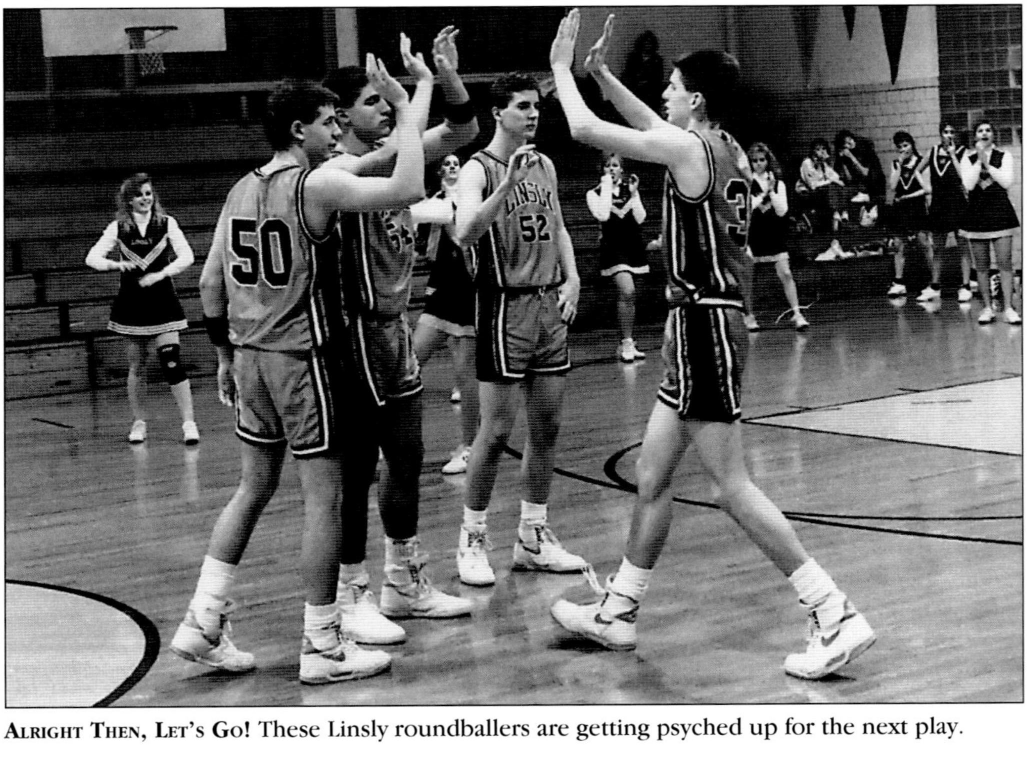

ALRIGHT THEN, LET'S GO! These Linsly roundballers are getting psyched up for the next play.

Getting Ready to Smash It, 1994. Linsly has had a tennis team almost as long as it has had a basketball team.

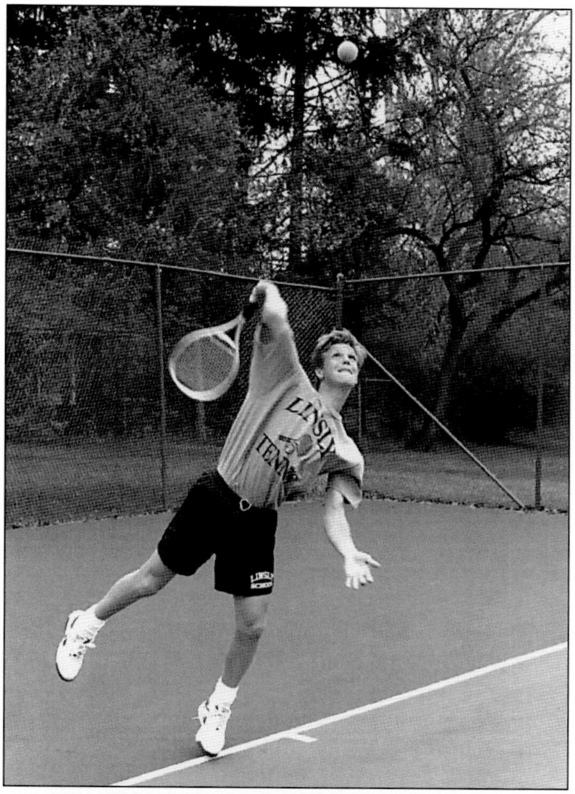

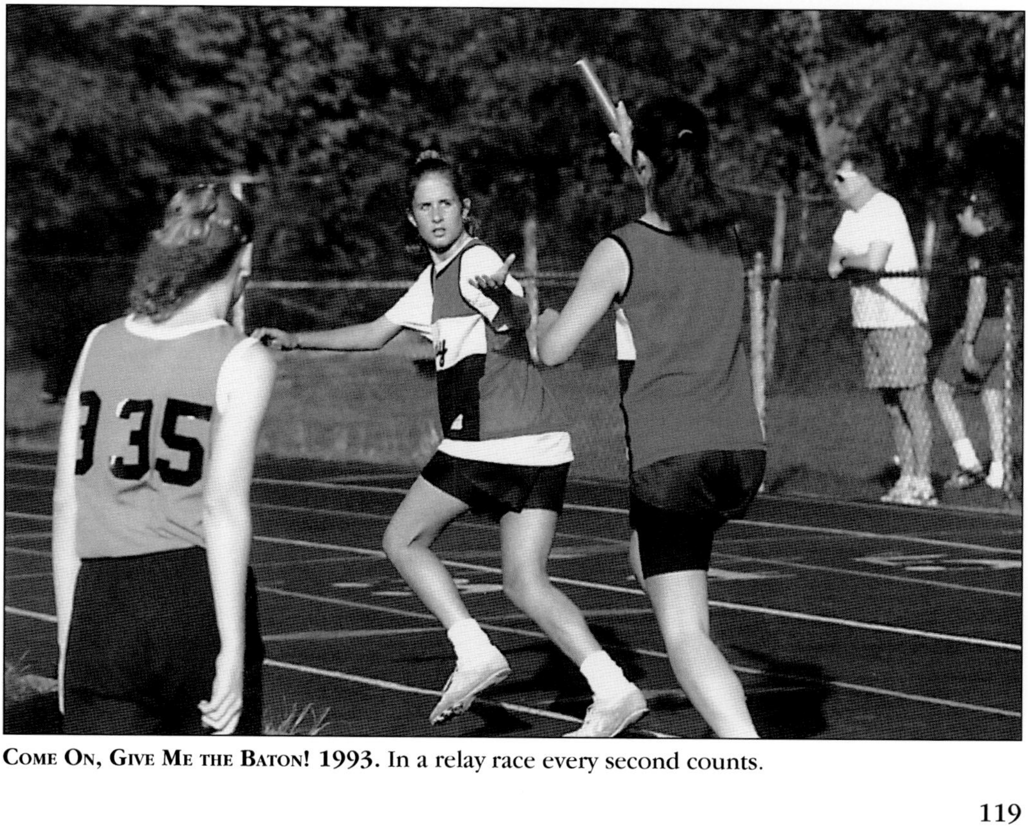

Come On, Give Me the Baton! 1993. In a relay race every second counts.

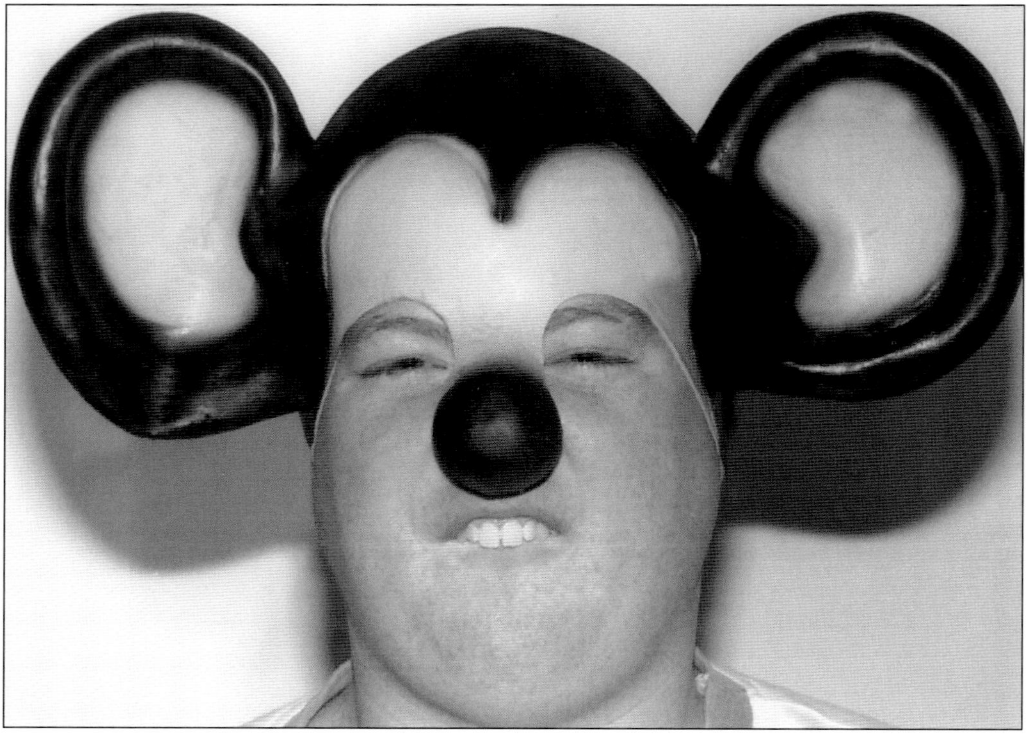

Here's Your Ears! A large rodent was seen mousing around at the Extravaganza.

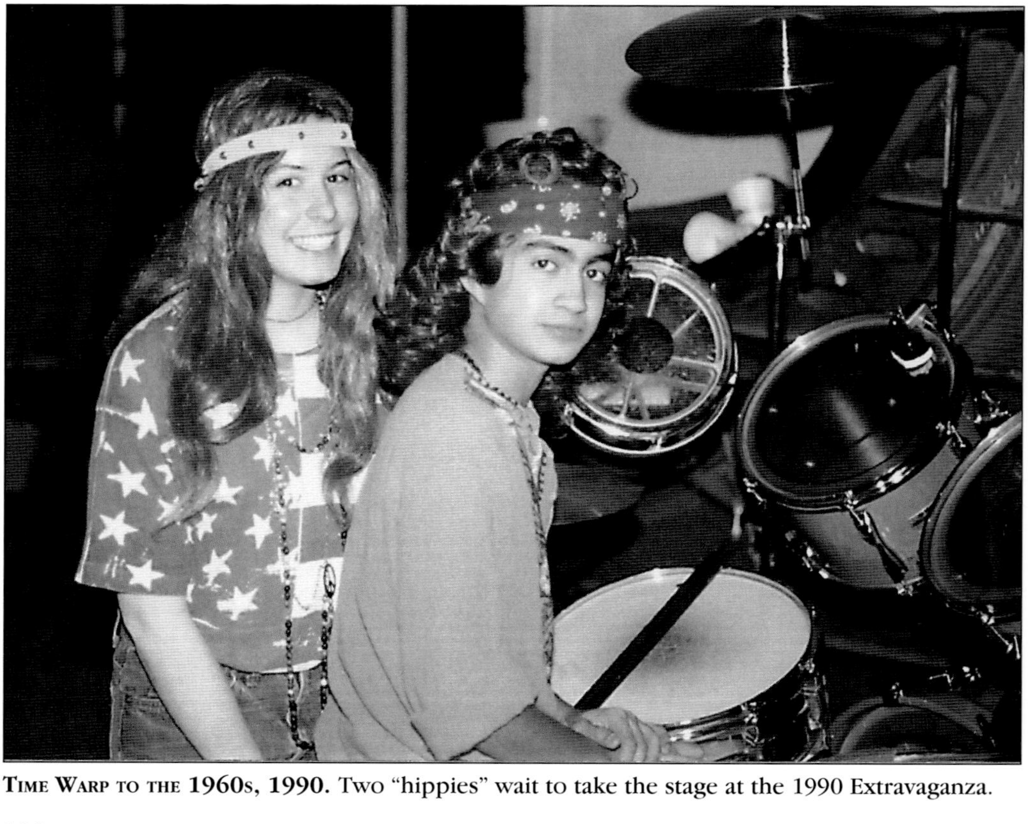

Time Warp to the 1960s, 1990. Two "hippies" wait to take the stage at the 1990 Extravaganza.

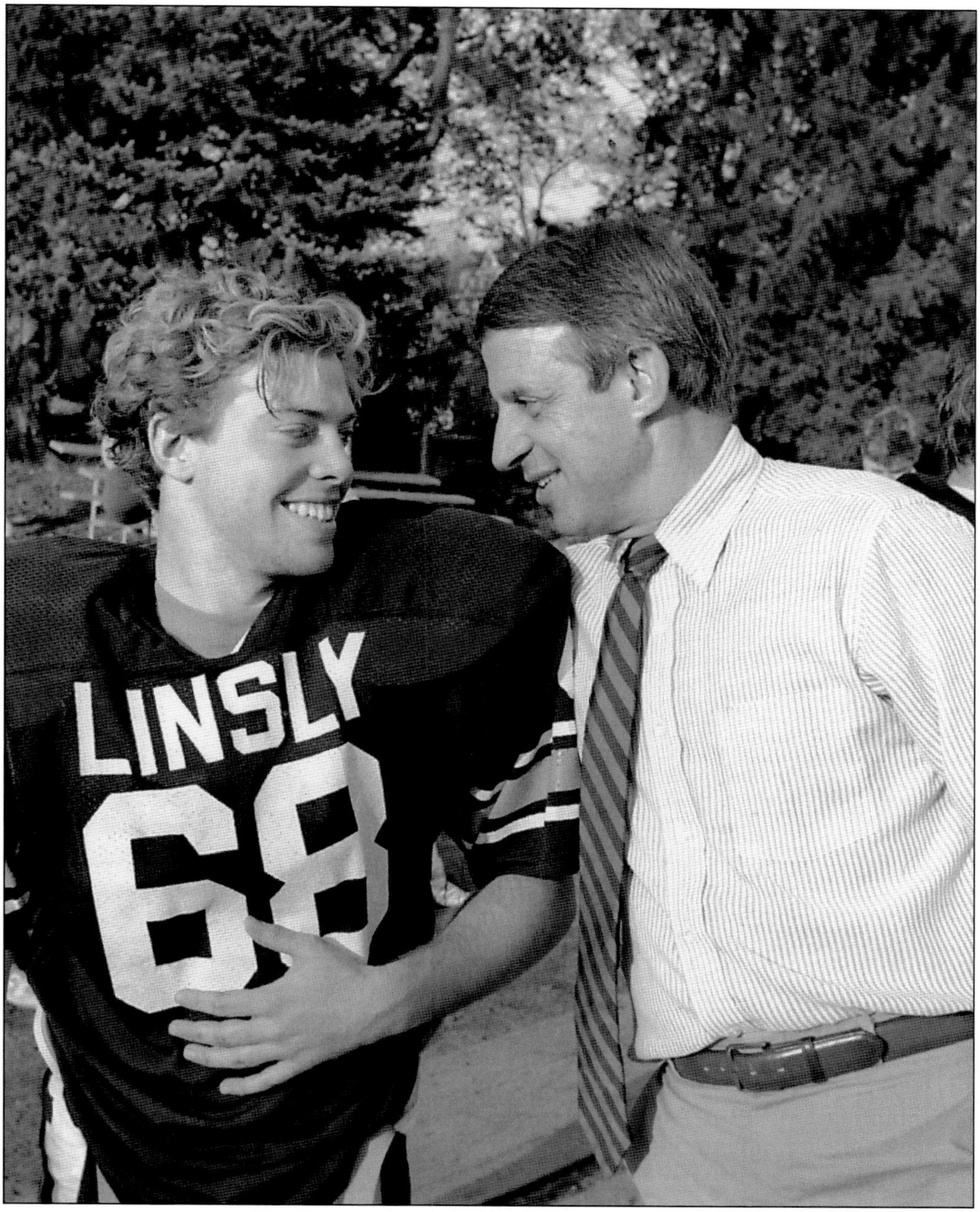

Reno DiOrio and Number 68. Headmaster DiOrio has a few words with the football players. Is he saying, "Never, never, never quit?"

CHRONOLOGY

1772	Noah Linsly is born.
1778	Noah Zane is born.
1814	Noah Linsly dies and makes a bequest to establish a Lancastrian Academy in Wheeling. The State of Virginia issues a charter on November 29 for the Lancastrian Academy (Founders' Day).
1815	The first meeting of the Linsly Board of Trustees is held.
1818	The Cumberland, Md., to Wheeling, Va. road (National Road) is completed.
1819	Construction begins on the first building.
1820	The first building is completed at Thirteenth and Fourth Street (Chapline Street). John F. Truax becomes the first teacher.
1821	George Washington's nephew, Lawrence, serves on the Linsly Board of Trustees. The first glass is made in Wheeling. The *Wheeling Gazette* is established. A fence is installed to provide separate play yards for the boys and the girls.
1825	General Lafayette visits Wheeling and is escorted down Main Street by Noah Zane and students from the Lancastrian Academy.
1833	Noah Zane dies in the Great Cholera Epidemic in Wheeling.
1837	West Liberty Academy, which is now West Liberty State College, is established.
1840	The famous Wheeling "stogie" makes its first appearance.
1841	Bethany College is established.
1847	First telegraph line completed to Wheeling.
1848	Wheeling Female Seminary (later known as Mt. de Chantal) is established.
1849	The Suspension Bridge in Wheeling is completed.
1851	Noah Linsly's body disinterred from the Thirteenth Street location and moved to Mt. Wood Cemetery. Natural gas lines are installed in Wheeling.
1853	The first railroad train (B&O) enters Wheeling on New Year's Day.
1856	A monument to Noah Linsly is erected in Mt. Wood Cemetery.
1858	Construction begins on the second building at Fifteenth and Eoff Street.
c. 1861	Linsly becomes an all-boys school at the beginning of the Civil War.
1863	West Virginia is admitted to the union as a state.
1863–1870	The State of West Virginia occupies the Linsly building as the State Capitol.
1870	The state capital is moved to Charleston.
1874	John M. Birch becomes headmaster until 1881 and again from 1889 to 1890 and from 1910 to 1911.

1875 The state capital is moved from Charleston to Wheeling.

1877 Principal John Birch revives the cadet battalion and originates the college preparatory program, the literary society, and the first school newspaper. The first street cars (horse-drawn) run. City of Wheeling builds a state capitol building. The first street cars run from Wheeling to Wheeling Park.

1879 The first telephone is used in Wheeling.

1882 Electric lighting is introduced by A.J. Sweeney and Son.

1885 The state capital is moved from Wheeling and permanently established at Charleston. John M. Birch is appointed consul to Nagasaki, Japan.

1888 The first electric trolley car operates in Wheeling.

1889 An armory is constructed to provide for indoor drill practice.

1891 Lt. William Braunensreuther, an officer of the United States Army, is detailed to Linsly as a professor of military science and tactics.

1892 Gymnastic equipment is installed in the armory.

1898 Golden Jubilee of Mount de Chantal is held.

1899 Equipment for the teaching of physics is purchased for the science laboratory. Linsly's football team achieves a record of 5-1-1, and they secure the city championship.

1907 A proposal to turn the property of Linsly over to the City of Wheeling to be used as a high school is unanimously defeated by the board of trustees.

1907–1910 The military program is temporarily suspended.

1910 A Linsly alumni organization is formed.

1913 C.H. Patterson becomes headmaster.

1914 During the centennial year the board begins considering a new location in the suburbs for the growing school.

1916 Guy E. Holden becomes headmaster until 1940. Linsly's football team plays Franklin College and wins. The score is 105 to 0. The team also beats Morris-Harvey College 13 to 7.

1921 Guy Holden proposes a merger of West Liberty Normal School and Linsly Institute. West Liberty supporters successfully argue against such a merger before the state legislature.

1924 After considering several locations—Wheeling Park, land belonging to Greenwood Cemetery, the county "poor" farm in Elm Grove, and a hill behind Warwood—property at Theda Place was purchased. The Fifteenth and Eoff Street building is sold.

1925 The cornerstone was laid in May, and Linsly's third building at Theda Place is completed in time for the opening of the 1925–26 school year. *The Aviator* monument, in memory of Lt. Louis Bennett Jr., was accepted and installed in June.

1926–1932 Linsly operates a junior college.

1932 Henry C. Brown joins the faculty until retirement in 1974 (42 years). The Linsly Institute of Technology opens, offering B.S. degrees in engineering.

1933 The first college degrees in Wheeling are conferred by the Linsly Institute of Technology.

1936 H. Douglas Haigwood joins the faculty, and remains until retirement in 1981 (45 years).

1939 The first Linsly Minstrel is held.

1940 Basil G. Lockhart becomes headmaster until 1972 (32 years).

1941	Linsly is accredited by the North Central Association, Merriman Hall is acquired, and the original footbridge is constructed. Since military training was under the jurisdiction of the United States Department of War at this time, Linsly becomes known as "Linsly Military Institute."
1942	Linsly acquires the official name, by charter, of "Linsly Institute" (changed from "The Lancastrian Academy"), giving the school the right to conduct primary, secondary, and college programs. The Linsly Institute of Technology is accredited by the West Virginia State Board of Education as a junior college.
1943	Weiss Hall is acquired. The Linsly Institute of Technology ceases operations.
1947	Behrens Memorial Gymnasium is completed and the swimming pool is completed in Old Main.
1948	The President's Home (first used by Col. Lockhart) is completed.
1953	The footbridge is rebuilt.
1955	An addition to Weiss Hall is completed.
1959	The original Weiss Hall is taken by the construction of Interstate 70 and a new Weiss Hall is completed.
1961	The Ivan Fawcett M.D. Memorial Infirmary is completed.
1962	The Lee Spillers Tennis Courts are dedicated.
1963	The footbridge is destroyed by ice and water in March and rebuilt during the summer.
1966	Groundbreaking is held for Banes Hall (Linsly's fourth building).
1967	Old Main is leased to Wheeling Steel. The footbridge is dismantled.
1968	Linsly's fourth building, Banes Hall, is completed and dedicated.
1972	Harry A. Chorpenning becomes headmaster and remains until 1976. Colonel Lockhart retires.
1973	Lockhart football field is dedicated.
1975	There is a rededication of *The Aviator* statue on its 50th anniversary. Holloway Field is dedicated.
1976	Due to a natural gas shortage, Mount de Chantal girls "invade" Linsly. Linsly students attend classes at Mt. de Chantal. Ron Salvador becomes interim headmaster and serves until 1977.
1977	Kenneth O. Kiesler becomes headmaster and serves until 1979.
1979	The school's military program is discontinued. Reno F. DiOrio becomes headmaster.
1983	A new men's dormitory is completed (East Hall). The school's name is changed to "The Linsly School."
1984	Linsly's swimming team wins its 36th consecutive OVAC championship.
1988	A new women's dormitory is completed (West Hall). Linsly becomes coeducational after 128 years as an all-male institution.
1992	A new field house and recreational center is completed. Kuchinka Hall (Hearnlee Place) is acquired and remodeled as an administration building and infirmary.
1996	Old Main and the drill field is sold to the Kroger Company with the provision that the property will be returned to Linsly after 50 years (2046).
1997	The Dallas Apartments is acquired.
1999	The Williams Fine Art Center is constructed.
2001	The Hess Center is completed.

Linsly Teachers, Principals, and Headmasters

Teachers

1st	John F. Truax	1820–1827
2nd	Daniel Deady	1827–1828
3rd	Alexander Magee	1828–1830
4th	Thomas I. Lees	1830–1846
5th	James McBurnie	1846–1847

Principals

6th	Rev. John W. Scott (principal and teacher)	1847–1852
	James C. Orr	1852–1859
	James Paull	1859–1862

Headmasters

Rev. R.V. Dodge	1862–1864
T.J. Jones	1864–1865
Prof. John M. Birch	1874–1881
	1889–1890
	1910–1911
Alex R. Whitehill	1881–1885
G.C. Orr	1885–1889
Lt. Braunreiter	1890–1893
Lt. W.C.P. Muir	1893–1895
Lt. L.S. VanDuzen	1895–1897
Lt. J.R. Blakeley	1897–1898
Lt. B.C. Den	1899–1906
Harry E. Odgers	1906–1910
William T. McClure	1911–1913
C.H. Patterson	1913–1916
Guy E. Holden	1916–1940
Basil G. Lockhart	1940–1972
Harry A. Chorpenning	1972–1976
Ron Salvador	1976–1977
Kenneth O. Kiesler	1977–1979
Reno F. DiOrio	1979–

BIBLIOGRAPHY

Ainsworth, Elizabeth Yeager and Robert G. *Wheeling—A Pictorial History*. Norfolk: Donning Company, 1977.

Ambler, Charles H. *A History of Education in West Virginia.* Huntington: Standard Printing & Publishing Company, 1951.

Boyd, Peter *History of Northern West Virginia Panhandle.*Topeka: Historical Publishing Co., 1927.

Callahan, James Norton *History of West Virginia.* Semi-Centennial Commission of W. Va.,1913.

Cramer, Gibson Lamb *History of Wheeling City & Ohio County, West Virginia and Representative Citizens*. Chicago: Biographical Publishing Co., 1902.

Hayes, E. L. *Illustrated Atlas of the Upper Ohio Valley from Pittsburgh, Pa. to Cincinnati, Ohio*. Philadelphia: Titus, Simmons and Titus, 1877.

Huff, Doug *Sports in West Virginia—A Pictorial History*. Virginia Beach: Donning Company Publishers,1979.

The Linsly School *Alumni Directory*. White Plains: Bernard C. Harris Publishing Co., Inc., 1967.

The Linsly School. *Archives.* Photographic and document files.

The Linsly School. *The Linsly Bulletin*. Student Newspapers.

The Linsly School. *The Cadet*. Student Newspapers.

The Linsly School. *The Linsly Echo.* Student Newspapers.

The Linsly School. *The Linsly Line.* Student Newspapers.

McKinley, David B. *Ready To Serve—The Life of Lt. Louis Bennett, Jr.* Privately published, 2002.

Minutes of Meetings of the Board of Trustees of Linsly Institute, 1814-1924.

Ross, Philip W. *"Forward and No Retreat" : The Linsly Story*. Privately published ,1994.

West Virginians Worthwhile in Caricature, West Virginia Cartoons Association Wheeling News Litho Company, 1914.

Wingerter, Charles A. *History of Greater Wheeling and Vicinity*. Vol. I & II, Chicago & New York: Lewis Publishing Company, 1912.

INDEX